EL ALAMEIN

This one is for Graham

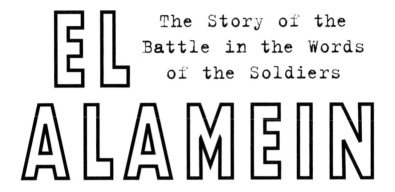

EL ALAMEIN

The Story of the Battle in the Words of the Soldiers

JOHN SADLER

AMBERLEY

First published 2010
Amberley Publishing Plc
Cirencester Road, Chalford,
Stroud, Gloucestershire, GL6 8PE
www.amberley-books.com

British Library Cataloguing in Publication Data.
A catalogue record for this book is available from the British
Library.

ISBN 978 1 84868 101 9

Typeset in 10pt on 13pt Adobe Caslon Pro.
Typesetting and Origination by Fonthill.
Printed in the UK.

Contents

	Glossary	7
	Introduction: 'Up the Blue'	9
1.	Prelude	21
2.	'Compass': June 1940 – March 1941	27
3.	A New Thermopylae: March 1941 – May 1941	37
4.	'Brevity' & 'Battleaxe': May 1941 – July 1941	49
5.	'Crusader': August 1941 – January 1942	59
6.	'Msus Stakes' & 'Gazala Gallop': January 1942 – June 1942	69
7.	Mersa Matruh & First El Alamein: June 1942 – August 1942	80
8.	Alam Halfa: August 1942 – September 1942	93
9.	Prelude: September 1942 – October 1942	105
10.	Break-in: 23 October 1942 – 24 October 1942	152
11.	'Crumbling': 25 October 1942 – 28 October 1942	167
12.	'Supercharge': 29 October 1942 – 3 November 1942	181
13.	Break-out: 4 November 1942 – 23 January 1943	196
14.	'Torch' to Tunis: November 1942 – May 1943	207
	Appendix 1: Desert Tactics	212
	Appendix 2(a): Orders of Battle	224
	Appendix 2(b): Extract from a Tactical Appreciation 27 July 1942	229
	Appendix 3: The Ultra War	231
	Appendix 4: The Battlefield Today	236
	Notes	237
	Acknowledgements	252
	Chronology	253
	Dramatis Personae	257
	Bibliography	265
	List of Illustrations	268
	Index	283

This is not the end. It is not even the beginning of the end. But it is, perhaps, the end of the beginning.

Winston S. Churchill

I wanted to beg you to stay, instead I smoothed my apron and watched you walk away.
I wanted to fall down on my knees and cry and scream and plead and plead and plead,
Instead I boiled water, made tea while you fastened braces, polished boots, shone buttons.

'I'm more likely to die down that bloody pit' you said, we both knew it wasn't true.
'This is our way out, our chance to get away, from the grime and the dirt and the same places/faces day after day.'

You always thought you were better than our little town, where we grew up side by side.
Always the tallest, strongest, fastest and bravest lad at school. Born for better things.

I knew you all my life, loved you since we were fifteen, and now I had to say goodbye.
'its not for long love' you said 'we will all be home by Christmas love' you kissed me, held my gaze with those blue, blue eyes and turned and walked away.

I held that image in my mind till this day, you striding down the street, proud to be in khaki, prouder still of the red cap covering your sandy blond hair.
Played it over and over in my mind over the years, wondered if I could have changed things in anyway.

Sixty-five years to the day I watched you stroll down our street round the corner, gone.
I'm old now Johnny, and now at last, I hope, soon, to see you again.

Waiting by Samantha Kelly

Glossary

AA – Anti-aircraft
AFV – Armoured Fighting Vehicle
AP – Armour-piercing
A&SH – Argyll and Sutherland Highlanders
AA – Anti-aircraft
AT – Anti-tank
ATS – Auxiliary Territorial Services
BAOR – British Army of the Rhine
Bde – Brigade
BEF – British Expeditionary Force
Bivvy – Bivouac
BN – Battalion
CIGS – Chief of the Imperial General Staff
C in C – Commander in Chief
CLY – County of London Yeomanry
CO – Commanding Officer
Coy – Company
CP – Command Post
CRA – Commander, Royal Artillery
CSM – Company Sergeant-Major
CWGC – Commonwealth War Graves Commission
DAF – Desert Air Force (RAF)
DAK – *Deutsches Afrika Corps*
DCM – Distinguished Conduct Medal
De-lousing – Minefield Clearance
Div – Division
DLI – Durham Light Infantry
DSO – Distinguished Service Order
ENSA – Entertainments, National Service Association

EP1 – Egyptian Pattern mark one mine
FANY – First Aid Nursing Yeomanry
FAP – Forward Aid Post
FOO – Forward Observation Officer
FUP – Form-up Position
GOC – General Officer Commanding
GSO1 – General Staff Officer 1st Class
GSO2 – General Staff Officer 2nd Class
HE – High Explosive
IO – Intelligence Officer
I-Tank – Infantry Tank
KD – Khaki Drill
KRRC – King's Royal Rifle Corps
LOB – Left out of Battle
LRDG – Long Range Desert Group
MC – Military Cross
MG – Machine Gun
MP – Military Police
NAAFI/EFI – Navy, Army and Air Force Institutes/Expeditionary Forces Institute
O Group – Orders Group
OH – Official History
OKH – *Oberkommand des Heeres*
OKW – *Oberkommand der Wehrmacht*
OP – Observation Post
PBI – Poor Bloody Infantry
POL – Petrol, Oil and Lubricants
QM – Quartermaster
RA – Royal Artillery
RAC – Royal Armoured Corps
RAF – Royal Air Force
RAP – Regimental Aid Post

RAC – Royal Armoured Corps

RAOC – Royal Army Ordnance Corps

RASC – Royal Army Service Corps

RE – Royal Engineers

Regt – Regiment

REME – Royal Engineers Mechanical Engineers

RHA – Royal Horse Artillery

RN – Royal Navy

RND – Royal Naval Division

RSM – Regimental Sergeant-Major

RTU'd – Returned to Unit

RTR – Royal Tank Regiment

SAS – Special Air Service

Scarper – Disorganised and precipitate retreat, verging on rout

SIW – Self-inflicted Wound

SOE – Special Operations Executive

SP – Self-propelled; refers to artillery

TA – Territorial Army

TAC HQ – Tactical Headquarters

TAVR – Territorial Army Volunteer Reserve

WD – War Department

WO – Warrant Officer

W/T – Wireless Telegraphy

USAAF – United States Army Air Force

USAMEAF – United States Army Middle East Air Force

VC – Victoria Cross

Introduction: 'Up the Blue'

A few yards from where I was standing there was a depression in which there were several bodies hastily covered with sand, here and there a leg or arm protruding and part of a machine-gun barrel also sticking up. I was idly watching these as the last of the vehicles passed, and was waiting to be picked up. My opposite number was on the British side of the minefields some distance away, also waiting. It had been very hot, around 100 degrees I should think, but now the sun was beginning to set and it was getting colder. I put on my greatcoat, although I had been wearing shorts and khaki shirt all day, when I noticed the arm that was sticking out of the sand with its fingers outstretched. As I looked I saw the fingers slowly close to a clenched position. I felt my hair bristle as I was certain the poor fellow must be dead underneath the sand, for the hand was already turning black. I felt very relieved when I suddenly remembered the sharp difference in temperature that was causing this contraction. However, I was glad when our relief truck arrived and picked me up.

A. W. Evans, Provost Company, 50th Division

The great swathe of the Sahara Desert covers a vast expanse. It has an enduring aura of romance and exoticism, experienced by very few of those who fought in the Desert War. Armies have fought in desert conditions both before and after but never on such a scale and of such duration. Desert ('the Blue') threw up a whole catalogue of factors to hinder military activity and increase the misery of individual combatants. For these, British and Dominion, the Germans, Italians, French, Greeks and others, it seemed they had arrived in the very cauldron of a particular version of hell.

> ... my three strongest recollections are: the heat, sweat pouring and oozing from me, until I ached and itched with it ... the strange lack of fear ... the seemingly endless hours of utter boredom, observing a low ridge about 2,000 yards away with nothing moving, nothing happening, except the sun beating mercilessly down and one's eyes straining (as I remember our gunner putting it) 'at miles and miles of f*** all.[1]

The Western Desert

'Sahara' derives from the word Tenere in the Tamajaq Tuareg. It is the world's second largest desert [2] and covers an area of some 9 million square kilometres, almost as big as the United States. On the west, the Sahara is bounded by the Atlantic, then by the Atlas and Mediterranean to the north, by Egypt and the Red Sea eastwards, Sudan in the south. It may have been in its present form, some of the barest, most arid and inhospitable terrain on earth for as long as three million years. The great sweep of desert is divided into several regions. The story of the Desert War from 1940 to the end of 1942 unfolds primarily in the Libyan Desert, a natural amphitheatre in which large armies wheeled and charged, stood at bay, gave and took ground. Men poured out their lifeblood over featureless, rock strewn ridges barely showing above the scorched desert floor. Tanks, like dusty men o' war cruised and fought, largely untroubled by the human landscape that defined other battlefields.

Along the Mediterranean coast, runs a narrow littoral of pleasant and cultivated land, the fertile coastal strip, along which most of the main settlements are located. This agreeable plain is bounded inland by a line of limestone cliffs, steep and bare, dragged through with narrow defiles or wadis. These create a formidable barrier, impassable to most wheeled vehicles. Atop the cliffs and running southwards in a gentle decline, is a bare plateau, scorched by the hot sun and scoured by millennia of harsh winds. The surface is comprised of rock and layered grit, like the topping on a primeval cake, varying in density from metres to centimetres. Where the base rock is denser, low hills have been left, insignificant humps or irregular ridges, possession of which was to be vital to the armies and demand a vast sacrifice in blood and materiel.

Where the limestone is more friable, depressions of varying size create undulations. These can form either obstacles or handy defences. Of all these pits in the desert floor the largest is the vast Quattara which lies to the south of the plateau, forming an impassable inland sea several hundred metres below the escarpment, bounded by steep cliffs with salt-marsh below. As one moves southwards towards this great depression the unyielding surface of the plateau gives way to a rolling, almost dizzying series of dunes. This, perhaps, is nearest to the classic image of the desert landscape so beloved of filmmakers. Theses dunes arise some fifty miles inland and the ground considerably restricts movement of large forces. Thus the armies were penned into the area between the coast and the dunes, a relatively narrow battlefield in so wide a landscape. This was never more than seventy miles in width but stretched for 1,000 miles and more east and west, creating a very thin oblong.

Though unremittingly harsh the desert was not devoid of either flora, fauna or, for that matter, inhabitants: '... there was virtually no animal or insect life. Just the occasional jerboa – the desert rat (a nice friendly little fellow) – the scorpion and an occasional gazelle. The Arabs and their camels kept well out of the way.[3] Of man made roads running east to west there was only one, the Via Balbia from Tripoli through Sirte, El Agheila, Benghazi, Derna, Gazala, Tobruk, Bardia, to Sollum. Westwards lay Sidi Barrani, Mersa Matruh, Fuka, the rail halt of El Alamein and finally the great jewel of Alexandria and the fertile sweep of the Nile. Of these coastal settlements only Tripoli, Benghazi and Tobruk had significant harbours. For transit north – south there were only local trackways ('trigh'). These were not hard-surfaced but beaten paths linking oases, hammered out by centuries of human and camel traffic. [4] Clearly, these had never been intended for wheeled vehicles and the passage of motorised convoys punished the surface, leaving a chaos of endless ruts. To avoid these, drivers tended to edge their vehicles to the side, thus beating an ever widening path. When the winter rains deluged the trigh, surfaces turned into a glutinous and unnavigable soup. Where these routes crossed, the location naturally assumed a clear local significant often marked by a saintly burial, (denoted by the prefix 'Sidi').

Such places became natural foci for area defence or supply stations. Without wishing to push the naval analogy too far, fighting in the largely featureless desert placed a premium on navigation, demanding an exact use of the compass.

> So five miles beyond Sidi Barrani we branched off into the open desert and bumped along over boulders and scrub as far as 'Fred Karno's Circus'. This was the name given to the gap in the wire on the Libyan-Egyptian frontier, at the southern end of the Halfaya escarpment. By this time we were beginning to realise just what driving in the desert meant. The sun was merciless, even at this time of year and our loads were floating about the lorry, bursting open tin after tin of priceless petrol. [5]

In addition to the magnetic compass, often upset by the steel in vehicles, the sun compass 6 was also relied upon. 'It was our first effort at movement, using only compass and sun compass. Fortunately, we had some guide in a row of telegraph poles that stretched away towards the forward area along the desert tracks.' [7]

In this, the work previously undertaken by pre-war cartographers was particularly useful. Mapping the desert had an appreciable provenance, beginning with Herodotus. Classical and medieval travellers were followed by British explorers such as Mungo Park and Major Laing who first crossed north – south to Timbuktu in 1826. During the inter wars years much work had been done by an eclectic group including two Englishmen who were both to serve in LRDG, Bagnold[8] and Clayton.[9] One of the more colourful of this colourful bunch was the Hungarian Lazlo Almasy.[10] Due to their combined efforts the empty canvas of the desert was marked by the network of ancient trails, with every feature in an otherwise bare landscape plotted and surveyed. The white bones of escarpments, sunken depressions, oases, salt marshes, dry wadis that could spring to brilliant life after rains.

During the summer months, from May to October, the climate is scorching hot, a blisteringly and relentless sun, furnace bright and searing dry. Only in the evenings before the dark cold of night, before the sun sinks, is the broiling fire of day mellowed into evening cool. Winters are drear and damp with frequent heavy downpours. Torrents flow down the scree-riven wadis but water is soon soaked up by the parched and greedy desert. Mainly in spring the enervating wind shifts direction and can whip the sands into the abrasive fury of the *Khamseen*. The land is harsh and gives nothing, shows no mercy to the unwary and punishes all who toil there. Yet there is great beauty and the desert can exert a powerful, almost obsessive pull. Dawn and sunset can be infinitely memorable and the stars glow with a clear cold light that conjures biblical images. Soldiers were thrown back on their recall of heroic conflicts as depicted in the *Iliad*. 'Wilfred Owen said that the poetry is in the pity; but that was in another war. This later war was one of great distances and rapid movement and for me the poetry came when least expected, in the interstices of a generally agitated existence, in the rush of sudden contrasts, and the recognition that, whatever else changes, one's own mortality does not.'[11]

Historical Background

'The Western Desert is a place fit only for War.' [*Desert Victory*, 1943]

Despite its apparent emptiness, the Sahara has a rich and ancient history. By 6,000 BC the Egyptians were evolving a pastoral society that would develop into and flourish as one of the greatest of classical and pre-classical civilisations, leaving its magnificent, enigmatic memorials along the course of the Nile. A southerly, developed agrarian civilisation existed in Sudan, ancient Nubia. The Phoenicians, a Levantine people, built an extensive trading network along the Mediterranean coast of North Africa. They mingled with the sparse peoples of Libya and the Berbers may be their descendants. Hanno the Navigator, in the sixth century BC, sowed further colonies in the Western Sahara and the power of Carthage competed with that of its emerging rival, Rome. The clash led to the bloody and destructive Punic Wars which saw proud Carthage reduced to dust. In the very heart of the Sahara an advanced and industrious people, the Garamantes, created a flourishing, urbanised culture, subduing and enslaving weaker neighbours. They husbanded precious reserves of water through ambitious and extensive digging of tunnels. Eventually the sparse supply was exhausted and their civilisation decayed, traces vanishing under the shifting sands, till revealed by the spade.

Following the fall of Rome, the Islamic conquest spurred a burgeoning prosperity of the coastal emirates. Salt was exported from the heart of the Sahara and the necklace of oases developed into trading and staging centres. Slaves were an equally important cargo. Though the subsequent opening of sea routes by European explorers of the Renaissance damaged these monopolies, the Ottoman hegemony over what is now Algeria, Tunisia, Libya and Egypt persisted till the expansion of European empires. In the nineteenth century the Sultan's jewels were progressively snatched by Victorian era Imperialists. France took Algeria in 1830, later added Tunisia in 1881 and then, in 1912, Morocco. The Egyptians expanded southwards conquering much of what is now Sudan in the 1820s and founding the city of Khartoum. After 1882 Egypt became an Anglo-French Protectorate though Sudan was temporarily lost to the Mahdists after the death of Gordon and not recovered till the decisive clash at Omdurman in 1898. In 1874 Spain had annexed Western (Spanish) Sahara and the Italians, late arrivals in this colonial scramble, conquered Libya in 1912.

Britain's interest in Egypt stemmed primarily from her need to safeguard the vital passage of the Suez Canal. This concern had led Britain to perceive a need for intervention in 1882, when nationalist sentiment in the Egyptian army simmered. After the army was suitably chastised at the Battle of Tel-el-Kebir (1882), Britain became the dominant force. Resentment lingered and, over time increased, with a host of divergent political groups from fledgling communists to the Muslim Brotherhood all sharing anti-British sentiment.

Egypt was vital to Britain's strategic interest during the Great War, even though the land was still nominally an Ottoman possession. A popular uprising broke out in 1919 and, in November 1924, the British representative to Sudan, Sir Lee Stack, was murdered. King Fuad, a British puppet installed in 1922, died in 1936 and his youthful successor, Farouk, was minded to enter into an Anglo-Egyptian Treaty. It was agreed that the British would withdraw from Egypt, save for a garrison of 10,000 who would remain for a certain period to defend the Canal. Fear of Italian aggression following Mussolini's invasion of Abyssinia was an influential factor. When war broke out again in 1939 Egypt once again assumed a key strategic role. Many in the opposition would not have been unhappy to see the Axis powers victorious.

If the British intervention in Egypt was largely driven by expediency and overriding commercial imperative, the Italian invasion of the twin Ottoman provinces of Tripolitania and Cyrenaica was a simple exercise in imperialism. Italy, as a newly unified state, was a relative latecomer to the race for territories. Her early efforts in Abyssinia ended in defeat and humiliation at Adowa. Though the Italians claimed, disingenuously, to act as liberators, the peoples of what had been classical Libya soon found their new masters far from benign. From the beginning the Senussi tribe resisted the invader but the Ottomans nonetheless ceded control by the terms of the 1912 Treaty of Lausanne.

Though King Idris of the Senussi was forced into exile, resistance, under Omar Mukhtar,[12] continued in a bitter war throughout the 1920s. General Badoglio and his successor Marshal Graziani did not consider themselves fettered by the niceties of international law. Killings, mass-deportations and the establishment of concentration camps followed. Perhaps as many as 80,000 Libyans died. Parallel to this ruthless repression something like 150,000 native Italians settled in Libya, mainly around Tripoli and the coastal towns. They prospered and undertook significant improvements to the local infrastructure. In 1937 Mussolini came on a state visit to celebrate the opening of the new arterial highway the Via Balbia. This subsequently proved very useful to the British in the Desert war.

War in the Desert

Q: Were they good days for you?
A: Oh yes. Happy days with my men … I have always longed to meet them again. Where are all the Geordie men I loved and commanded now?[13]

You can stew it, you can fry it
But no matter how you try it
Fundamentally it remains the same,
You can hash it, you can slash it,
With potatoes you can mash it,
But when all is done you've only changed the name.

A Cook's thoughts on Bully

Herodotus chronicles the dire warning offered by the unfortunate experience of King Cambyses II of Persia (d. 522 BC). The despot dispatched an army, said to be 50,000 strong, to punish the Oracle of Amun at Siwa Oasis. This entire force vanished in a sandstorm of suitably biblical proportions and was never seen again. Over centuries the legend flourished and many explorers since, (including Count Lazlo Almasy), have sought to solve the riddle of this lost army.

That the infantry who fought in the Desert campaigns should resent their comrades in tanks is understandable. An armoured vehicle could be used to transport a whole range of sought after commodities and offered the crew an easy route back to base camp or the fleshpots of Egypt. In addition to the normal perils of being under enemy fire and the hidden hazard of mines, there were flies in abundance, numerous forms of disease plus the odd poisonous snake or scorpion. The terrain was barren, scorched, featureless, waterless and invincibly hostile to man. It must at times have seemed almost unbelievable that such titanic efforts were exerted by both sides to win these arid, seemingly endless acres. '… In the desert, men asked "Why?" again and again. There had to be some good and justifiable reason for fighting in such inhospitable climes. No men fought merely for the sake of fighting.'[14] For the most part infantry inhabited trenches, much as their fathers had done on the Western Front, though these were less permanent affairs. To dig down into sand was not difficult but, where the surface had been whittled away by wind and the limestone exposed, powered tools were necessary to gouge out shallow trenches and fox-holes, supported by a rough parapet of stones, 'sangars'.[15]

Battles were large and terrifying though relatively rare. Smaller actions at platoon or company level were far more common and there was a constant need for patrolling, either light reconnaissance or the beefier and bristling fighting patrol:

> Recce patrols were messy affairs if we had to go through the pockets of some poor devil who had been killed and had been left lying out in the sand for a couple of days. People talk about rigor mortis, but after a day or two the limbs were flexible again and indeed, after a week or so, a quick pull on an arm or leg would detach it from the torso. Two day old corpses were already fly blown and stinking. There was no dignity in death, only masses of flies and maggots, black swollen flesh and the body seeming to move, either because of the gases within it or else the thousands of maggots at work. We had to take documents, identity discs, shoulder straps, anything of intelligence value. Pushing or pulling these frightening dead men to reach their pockets was sickening. Of course, we couldn't wash our hands – one rubbed them in sand – sometimes we rubbed them practically raw if it had been a particularly disgusting day.[16]

'Desert Rose' sounds like an attractive form of flora. To the Allied army however it denoted an altogether more basic convenience – the field latrine. For temporary arrangements the hollow shell of a petrol container was buried with another laid on top at a suitable angle to form a urinal. Where more creature comforts were needed a deep trench was sunk with a hessian sheet on timber frame arranged above. Chlorine was applied liberally.[17] Cleanliness and hygiene were essential in the desert climate where dysentery and other horrors stalked. Personal cleanliness and liberal application of AL63[18] were equally emphasised. Opportunities for washing one's person or attire were often limited, the soldier coated in a caked carapace of stale, dried sweat and dust. Cuts and scrapes could swiftly become infected and morph into most unpleasant weeping ulcers.

> Once ashore our first work was to build ourselves a camp. Within a few hours a tented camp had sprung up on the edge of the desert. We lived in this for three weeks and suffered the worst outbreak of 'spit and polish' that we had ever received … But the value of this apparently excessive discipline was soon realised when we reached the battle area. We then found that the British troops were expected, by all other nationalities, to be the finest disciplined troops in the world.[19]

For the majority of the young men who served in these campaigns any form of overseas travel, indeed any travel at all was a novelty. To such innocents the Levant appeared a distant and exotic place: 'Waiting for a taxi, he breathed the spicy, flaccid atmosphere of the city and felt the strangeness of things about him. The street lamps were painted blue. Figures in white robes, like night shirts, flickered through the blue gloom, slippers flapping from heels. The women, bundled in black, were scarcely visible.'[20] Few could deny that their apprehensions were overlaid by a sense of adventure: 'We sailed along the Red Sea for a century, it seemed. The heat was insufferable. Sleep was an impossibility. Tempers were frayed and fights developed freely … Curiosity replaced apathy. Stage by stage, and those men who had been to Egypt before found themselves in popular demand and frequent visitors to the canteen.'[21] At first their destination appeared almost delightful:

> As we clambered ashore we stamped and rubbed our feet delightedly … We ran the sand slowly through our fingers; it was warm and real and comforting. I could never have believed then that I would hate this self-same sand so bitterly; the crumbled, remorseless rock that sucked at the lifeblood of us who tried to master her vastness in the following months.[22]

They would find that the epithet, 'Desert Rat' was not accorded to novices as of right; it had to be earned, the recognition of an apprenticeship in desert warfare and survival. '… The name given to themselves by the soldiers of the Eighth Army … it became an expression of pride among the men. It soon became the entitlement only of experienced desert fighters and could not be claimed by any newcomer to the desert.'[23] Driver Crawford and his comrades had cause to be grateful to two old sweats who rescued them from their own faulty navigation:

> These were two of the original Eighth Army who knew all the tricks of the Desert. They taught us in a few moments how to make a petrol fire from sand, water and petrol in a disused tin. They showed us how to make porridge from biscuits and an appetising meal from bully beef. Finally they taught us how to sleep comfortably on the floor of the desert; and, incidentally, made us feel the simpletons we really were.[24]

In such surrounding the comradeship of war was inevitably heightened. Men might express fine sentiments and extol the nobility of sacrifice but such poetic expressions soon wilted in the face of reality. Endless hours of tedium, dirty, sweaty, beset by a constant and ravenous horde of lies, troubled by looseness of the bowels and all the other complaints that add endless misery to a soldier's life, were enlivened only by odd moments of sheer terror. The code of behaviour which evolved was dictated by pure pragmatism:

> Your chief concern is not to endanger your comrade.
> Because of the risk that you may bring him, you do not light fires after sunset.
> You do not use his slit trench at any time.
> Neither do you park your vehicle near the hole in the ground in which he lives.
> You do not borrow from him, and particularly you do not borrow those precious fluids, water and petrol.
> You do not give him compass bearings which you have not tested and of which you are not sure.
> You do not leave any mess behind that will breed flies.
> You do not ask him to convey your messages, your gear or yourself unless it is his job to do so.
> You do not drink deeply of any man's bottles, for they may not be replenished. You make sure that he has many before you take his cigarettes.
> You do not ask information beyond your job, for idle talk kills men.
> You do not grouse unduly, except concerning the folly of your own commanders. This is allowable. You criticise no other man's commanders.
> Of those things which you do, the first is to be hospitable and the second is to be courteous … there is time to be helpful to those who share your adventure. A cup of tea, therefore, is proffered to all comers …
> This code is the sum of fellowship in the desert. It knows no rank or any exception.[25]

Discipline was essential though the fire of combat tempered the parade ground bellowing of peacetime and the drill sergeant into a more businesslike focus:

> Discipline such as we had formerly known disappeared. In its place came a companionship. Officers no longer issued orders in the old manner. They were more friendly and more with the men. They realised that this was a team. We, for our part, never took advantage of this new association. While orders were given, except in emergency, more in the nature of requests, they were obeyed even more punctiliously than under peacetime conditions. It was a case of every man pulling together, willingly. From what we had seen of the German Army, no such relationship existed, and it was not long before we discovered this was our strength.[26]

Krieg ohne Hass[27] – was a description attributed to Rommel himself and insofar as war can ever truly be said to represent chivalry then it was here. The British had a high regard for the Desert Fox, both as a fighting soldier of the highest calibre and a man of impeccable honour. Some years after the war Lieutenant-General von Ravenstein[28] observed:

If the warriors of the Africa Campaign meet today anywhere in the world, be they Englishmen or Scots, Germans or Italians, Indians, New Zealanders or South Africans, they greet each other as staunch old comrades. It is an invisible but strong link which binds them all. The fight in Africa was fierce, but fair. They respected each other and still do so today. They were brave and chivalrous soldiers.[29]

Humour, as ever, was the soldier's balm. 'A typical example of the sort of thing that amused us was the story that Hitler had secretly contacted Churchill with the offer to remove Rommel from his command in return for Churchill retaining all his generals in theirs.'[30] Though the soldiers in the line observed a strict blackout procedure the sky to the east was lit up with the rich glow of the Delta cities. The brightness and gaiety of easy living these represented could not have contrasted more tellingly with the drab but dangerous austerity of the front. The contrast between the rigours of the line and the luxury of Cairo, 'Unreal City' could not have been greater:

> To an outsider like Alan Moorehead[31] coming upon Cairo early in the summer of 1940, a world of Edwardian privilege seemed to define the city's ambience. 'We had French wines, grapes, melons, steaks, cigarettes, beer, whisky and an abundance of all things that seemed to belong to rich, idle peace. Officers were taking modern flats in Gezira's big buildings looking out over the golf course and the Nile. Polo continued with the same extraordinary frenzy in the roasting afternoon heat. No one worked from one till five-thirty or six, and even then work trickled through the comfortable officers borne along in a tide of gossip and Turkish coffee and pungent cigarettes.[32]

Though Cairo might be a cushy billet, some at least were very much aware of what awaited them while preparing to deploy 'up the Blue' or on leave. The Countess of Ranfurly[33] was one:

> It is always the same. These young men come on leave or courses to Cairo or Palestine, or for a while they are on the staff. They take you out to dinner and talk of their families and what they are going to do after the war; they laugh and wisecrack and spend all their money in the short time they can be sure they are alive. Then they go down to the desert leaving their letters, photographs and presents to be posted home. So often they never come back.[34]

If the beauties of the desert could move this generation of war poets then even the simple army convenience could raise an ode:

> Of all the Desert flowers known.
> For you no seed is ever sown
> Yet you are the one that has most fame,
> O Desert Rose – for that's your name.

There's thousands of you scattered around,
O Desert Rose, some square, some round,
Though different in variety,
At night you're all damned hard to see.

Although you're watered very well
You have a most unfragrant smell;
And just in case you do not know,
O Desert Rose, you'll never grow.

For you are not a Desert Flower,
Growing wilder every hour;
You're just a bloomin' petrol tin,
Used for doing most things in.

To a Desert Flower (Crusader, issue no. 57, 31 May 1943)

Battleground

We got out of our trucks and turned off to the left at a crossroads. Presently, we drew up at the empty sidings. There was a sort of goods yard and a compound surrounded by barbed wire on a line of crazy poles. Behind the station buildings stood a row of shattered shacks with their doors hanging open. The whole place was littered with empty barrels and broken crates, and everywhere the brickwork was chipped and pockmarked by machine gun bullets. Where the road crosses the metals stood a signal, its arm inappropriately set at 'safety'. The entire neighbourhood seemed to be completely deserted and, as I mounted the platform, I read on the front of the building the name of the place, 'ALAMEIN'.[35]

Prior to the Desert War, few people had heard of this insignificant halt some fifty miles west of Alexandria. Indeed, there was little to see. Between the station and the sparkling waters of the Mediterranean a ridge, called Tel el Alamein ('hill of twin cairns'), rose and gave its name to the station on the landward side below. This rather shabby halt had the advantage of being close to the sea and it was possible to access the beach. This provided a welcome and refreshing experience for weary and dusty soldiery undertaking the train journey eastwards to Mersa Matruh. At about the time the 'Auk' assumed the mantle of Middle East Command in July 1941, replacing Wavell, General Sir James Marshall-Cornwall, commanding garrison forces in the Nile Delta, was instructed to begin digging a series of defences anchored, in the north on El Alamein. From that point the place was rapidly to become a household name as it has since remained.

In this strategy there was nothing outstandingly innovative and the plan was essentially conventional. It was intended to create a divisional strongpoint with its right anchored on the sea and enjoying the advantages gained from the modest heights of Tel el Alamein and two other hills, Tel el Eisa and Tel Mukkhad. Holding this high ground in the north afforded the Allies control of the terrain toward the Axis-held Miteiriya and Kidney Ridges. The higher elevation these eminences represented created a strong defensive position running north – south. The field was in fact quite narrow; a bare ten miles lay between the British Front Line and the Axis rear along the line of the Rahman track. Analogies between Alamein and a Great War battlefield are by no means far-fetched. Given the nature of the ground and the forces involved any attempted breakthrough would essentially involve a grinding battle of attrition.

Some fifteen miles south-west, the General sited his second linear defence concentrated around the rise of Quaret el Abd. This offered excellent visibility, most particularly to the north. Though the ground between the two high points was generally fairly level it was broken, just south of one of the desert depressions or 'Deir', in this case the Deir el Shein, by the swell of Ruweisat Ridge which lay on an east – west axis. Prior to 2nd El Alamein the tactical position was that, while the Allies held the greater part of the ridge, the Axis had a firm foothold on its western extremity. As a feature the ridge did not constitute any kind of real obstacle, sandwiched between two regions of level ground, hard and solid to the south, rather flakier to the north. Along the southern rim of the table south of Ruweisat Ridge another feature, what came to be known as Bare Ridge, ran eastwards for a dozen miles from Quaret el Abd. It then swung in a more northerly direction through Alam el Halfa till it finally merged into the eastern flank of the main ridge just south of the station at El Ruweisat. Possession of these insignificant looking ridges would be crucial to both sides during the 1st Battle of El Alamein, Alam Halfa and 2nd Battle of Alamein[36].

Moving south, it was necessary to ensure the pass through cliffs into the Quattara Depression at Naqb abu Dweis was adequately defended. This was high ground and troops dug in would enjoy an impregnable position. Conversely, such forces could be of little value otherwise, as that which inhibited an attacker from breaking in equally served to prevent them from breaking out. Between this position and that forming the centre the ground was rugged and precipitous. North of Gebel Kalakh a narrow throat of easy going gave access to a more even plain, hard and flat. North of this feature a line of depressions ran south-east from the vicinity of Quaret el Abd twenty miles to Deir el Ragil. On the southern flank high ground went towards Quaret el Himeimat before sloping eastwards to Samaket Gaballa. From here the terrain declined toward the rim of the Quattara Depression with the foul, infested swamps of El Maghra Oasis.[37]

This position was intended to provide a defensible line rather than necessarily offering a springboard for attack. The nature of the ground and the obstacles it presented would leave an attacker, that is to say an attacker reliant on armour, with three principal options. A northerly corridor lay between the railway line and the rise of Ruweisat Ridge. In the centre the attacker could seek to force entry north of Quaret el Abd then drive east along the southern flank of the ridge to the north of Alam Halfa. To the south he might aim to burst through to the north of Gebel Kalakh, Himeimat and Samaket Gaballa. Each of these approaches offered good going and the opportunity to outflank heavily defended areas. These 'boxes' could then be dealt with one at a time and were too far distant to provide interlocking fire support. The redoubts would thus swiftly become traps in a

Kesselschacht[38] battle. The nature of the Desert War implied that to extend the width of the individual strongpoints would require far greater resources and there was always the question of how to safely protect vulnerable soft-skinned transport. For the defensive strategy to have any prospect of success it was vital that sufficient reserves of tanks, at least two armoured divisions, be deployed to plug the gaps and engage any enemy breaking in.

This was no accidental battleground, a second Ypres around which armies simply collided. The Auk had chosen well. His line was relatively narrow with both flanks refused. It made best use of the available high ground and afforded good observation. The line barred any attack from the west and secured the gateway to the Delta, for the next stop line rested virtually on the Nile. Certain preparatory moves had been undertaken as far back as 1940 when the threat from Graziani's army appeared most potent. These preliminaries were curtailed after the rout but further works were undertaken in the spring of 1941 before matters really got going that autumn after the Gazala fighting. Three large boxes were now prepared. The first, most northerly, being around Alamein and intended to house a full division. The two additional positions, Deir el Quattara and the Jebel Kerag were each intended to hold a brigade. These positions were systematically strengthened by the construction of concrete pillboxes to hold AT guns and trench lines, secured with extensive wiring, the laying of mines and, in some instances, anti-tank ditches.

Field hospitals, command centres, stores and communications were housed underground, each served by water piped from reservoirs in the north fed via a pipeline from the Nile. With such large forces dispersed over a wide area the single coast road was both inadequate and exposed as a single line of supply. Consequently, a series of 'Sommerfield' tracks were constructed to remedy the defect. A total of eleven new airstrips were laid out. Mines, which had not featured significantly in the earlier battles, were becoming increasingly important (see appendix 1). Both sides now relied heavily on minefields and, as the armies surged back and forth the fields changed hands so that new were laid on top of old. The area west of El Alamein thus became a dense and interlocking web of deadly mines, a major hazard for whoever sough to advance and one which had to be overcome before there could be any prospect of success.

Prelude

For most of them there is a grave in the sand, perhaps a few rocks piled over them, their names in a hurried pencil-scrawl upon a cross made of petrol cases. For some there is no cross: only a mound of sand that the wind will soon soften and gently erase.

Captain Sean Fielding

It could be argued that the fall of France and the evacuation at Dunkirk, apparently catastrophic, did, in fact, confer an element of strategic advantage upon Britain. Freed from the dire attrition of obligations to continental allies, such as had enmeshed Imperial forces during the Great War with the meat grinder of the Western Front, Britain could fall back upon her traditional strengths. These were an all powerful navy and a resolute air force that had, in the summer of 1940, successfully defied the *Luftwaffe's* best efforts. Germany's failure to crush Britain presented the Nazi high command with a limited range of strategic options. To all intents and purposes the war in the west was won, as Hitler intimated when writing to Mussolini[1] all that remained was the final push against a moribund and defeated England. Similar assurances were offered to the Russians who appear to have been more sceptical. The key question for Berlin was whether they could afford to turn the swollen and victorious Wehrmacht east to settle with Russia while the British Empire, technically at least, was still in the ring.

Strategic Options

War on two fronts was the strategic nightmare which had haunted German military planners since the end of the nineteenth century. The opening moves of the Great War in the late summer of 1914 had been carefully choreographed to achieve a swift victory in the west before the Kaiser's legions had to turn and face the slower but monolithic threat from Russia. Hitler was in no doubt that, to achieve the eastern border of his greater Reich, he would have to deal with Stalin and the Red army. It was merely a question of when. Hitler, therefore, had to decide if he could afford to leave an impotent but undefeated Britain in his rear or should he bide his time, consolidate his resources, particularly in the air, so he could finally crush the RAF and make the prospect of invasion real enough to force Churchill to negotiate a peace.

Hitler had yet, through diplomacy, to 'sell' the concept of Greater Germany to the world at large and particularly to the Americans. He was obviously aware that Britain's hope of any renewed offensive capacity lay with the United States and Russia, the unlikeliest of bedfellows. Even before the aerial defeat of the *Luftwaffe*, Hitler had laid out his reasoning to his generals:

> In the event that invasion does not take place, our efforts must be directed to the elimina-tion of all factors that let England hope for a change in the situation – Britain's hope lies in Russia and the United States. If Russia drops out of the picture, America too is lost for Britain, because the elimination of Russia would greatly increase Japan's power in the Far East. Decision: Russia's destruction must therefore be made a part of the struggle – the sooner Russia is crushed the better.[2]

Admiral Raeder, who headed the Kriegsmarine, put forward another option which was to attack Britain and bring her finally to her knees, not through an assault on England but by striking at her empire. The string of defeats in Norway and France had convinced the Axis powers that the British Empire was a rotten hulk, a bankrupt corporation, just waiting for the receivers to move in:

> The British have always considered the Mediterranean the pivot of their world empire [Raeder wrote] … While the air and submarine war is being fought out between Germany and Britain, Italy, surrounded by British power, is fast becoming the main target of attack. Britain always attempts to strangle the weaker enemy. The Italians have not yet realised the danger when they refuse our help … The Mediterranean question must be cleared up during the winter months … The seizure of Gibraltar … The dispatch of German forces to Dakar and the Canary Islands … Close co-operation with Vichy … Having secured her western flank by these measures Germany would support the Italians in a campaign to capture the Suez Canal and advance through Palestine and Syria. If we reach that point Turkey will be in our power. The Russian problem will then appear in a different light. Fundamentally Russia is afraid of Germany. It is doubtful whether an advance against Russia in the north will then be necessary.[3]

With the collapse of France the strategic position in the Mediterranean had changed significantly. It was French naval power that would have secured the western end and the position of the colonies in North Africa and, particularly, Syria was now critical. Would Vichy remain neutral or align with the conqueror thus exerting further pressure on the overstretched British? The Tripartite Alliance which linked Japan's far eastern power to the Axis and which was agreed in September 1940, would, in Ribbentrop's confident assertion, keep America firmly focused on the Pacific and deter any overt intervention in Europe. With Raeder's concept in mind Hitler made overtures both to Franco in Spain and Petain in Vichy. After a tortuous nine hour meeting with the Spanish Generalissimo at Hendaye, the Führer declared that he'd rather have several teeth removed than repeat the experience! Franco was lukewarm and expected any commitment to be rewarded by the distribution of French colonies in North Africa. This was not something calculated to appeal to Vichy.

If it was made known that their participation in a combined attack on British interests would result in a hiving off of territory to fascist Spain, then where was their incentive? Hitler, showing no great enthusiasm himself, could only suggest that the French could be compensated by the grant of captured British provinces. Franco, cannily, remained sceptical over Axis prospects of finally defeating Britain. There was also the question of the oil which in war, as Clemenceau pronounced, 'is as necessary as blood'.[4] Without an adequate and continuous supply of crude oil no state could meet the huge demands of modern warfare. In 1939 Britain was importing some 9 million tons of crude, the bulk of which flowed from Iran, Iraq and the USA. By early 1941 oil reserves had fallen to alarmingly low levels, a failure of supply would force Britain to seek terms as surely as a renewed and successful air offensive.

The Matter of Oil Resources

It was estimated, by the Petroleum Board, that between spring of 1940 and 1941 some 14 million tons of oil would be required. The USA could be counted on to supply less than half of this and oil producers were not swayed by Anglophile considerations. They wanted cash on the barrel; precious dollars that Britain could ill afford to disburse. The Shah of Iran had seized on the urgency to extort fresh concessions. Supplies from the USA were subject to sickening wastage through U-Boat attacks. As the Vichy administration in Syria stood adjacent to the vital oilfields in the Middle East and the vulnerable, key refinery at Haifa, their sympathies were of some concern. In a memorandum of 3 August 1940, the Colonial Office provided a neat precis of the position:

> Our first aim on the collapse of France was to induce the French colonies to fight on as our allies. We established close contact with the local French administrations and offered substantial financial inducements. The reaction leaves no doubt that there are French elements ready to rally to our side. But the Vichy government is in a position to exercise strong pressure on the local officials who have been in a defeatist and wavering frame of mind; and there is no doubt that the official policy of the local administrations is now one of obedience to Vichy and refusal to co-operate with us.[5]

This was hardly encouraging. If French naval power, based in the North African ports, was to be added to that of the formidable Italian fleet then the balance of naval power in the Mediterranean would be upset. Oil tankers sailing from Iran would be vulnerable and Britain's entire position in the Middle East under serious threat. Already Mussolini was massing troops in Cyrenaica for a thrust into Egypt, their numbers vastly exceeding those of the defenders. In November 1940 the Fleet Air Arm sallied against Italian capital ships sheltering in Taranto and scored a signal success. A further engagement off Cape Spartivento on 27 November reinforced British superiority but the threat from a compliant Vichy remained.

Germany too, had concerns over its own supply of oil, every bit as pressing as England's. Lacking natural resources and the advantages of an established international network, starved of cash reserves by the crippling burden of war debt she looked eastwards to the Balkans and the rich Romanian oilfields around Ploesti. By clever and ruthless economic manipulation Germany had succeeded in exerting a measure of fiscal control over her Balkan suppliers. This dependency was not lost on Britain whose own experts had forecast a crisis of supply. At the outbreak of hostilities Germans had reserves totalling some 3 million tons of crude, yet demand over each of the following three years was predicted to nearer 10 million tons. To avoid shortfalls Germany was obliged to increase imports from Russia and to make use of captured stocks. The possibility of a British attack on the Ploesti oilfields was a tactical nightmare which loomed large in the minds of German planners – such an offensive had been considered but the practical difficulties were considerable. To facilitate aerial bombardment the British would need to utilise forward bases located on either Greek or Turkish soil.

It is highly probable that Hitler, at this stage, was not seeking any direct military involvement in the Balkans. The area had no immediate strategic importance beyond the need to secure Germany's oil supply. The Führer was reluctant to become embroiled in the morass of Balkan politics at a time when his attention was fixed on the east. Added to the traditional swirl of antipathies were the fresh sores opened by the re-drafting of the maps, undertaken by the victorious allies in 1918, dividing the carcass of the old Habsburg Empire. Yugoslavia was a composite state comprising a mix of races and faiths and dominated by the Orthodox Serbs. Hungary smarted from the loss of Transylvania, ceded to Romania from whom the Soviets also sought to recover Bessarabia. Rising tensions between Hungary and Romania so alarmed Hitler that he became personally involved, bullying the squabbling parties into acceptance of German arbitration. The resulting enforced settlement, the Vienna Award, cost the Romanians dear but restored some semblance of calm. The Nazis refused to take chances, however, and from September 1940 their military presence around the vital oilfields, with the acquiescence of a compliant regime, was steadily increased.

No sooner has the hapless Romanians been stripped of territories in Transylvania than the Bulgarians began pestering for the acquisition of Southern Dobrudja. Once again Hitler obliged Bucharest to submit though he did, this time, offer the guarantee that no further limbs would be shorn from Romania's reduced torso. Such arbitrary re-drawing of Balkan borders naturally antagonised the Russians, who were accustomed to reserving this prerogative to themselves. Russian Foreign Minister Molotov was quick to reprove the German ambassador for a perceived violation of their Non Aggression Pact. The very last thing Hitler sought, at this point, was to provide the Soviets with a casus belli. War there would be but only when Germany was ready and her armies fully deployed.

Italian Aims

Aside from possible British aggression, the other factor which alarmed Hitler was the likely intentions of his Italian ally. Il Duce was steadily becoming disaffected with the relegation of his country's role in the war. Where were the great gains he had hoped for, the triumphal marches of fascist armies through captured Allied dependencies? Now very much the junior partner in the Axis Alliance, Mussolini was hungry for spoils. The relationship between the two states was further strained by a clear element of mistrust. The Germans, or at least some in the high command, were deeply suspicious of their ally's competence in the intelligence war, to the extent that outright treachery was mooted.[6] Aware that Italy was looking covetously at Greece, Hitler took pains to ensure his fellow dictator was aware that Germany was steadfastly opposed to any military adventure. In August 1940 Von Ribbentrop had warned the Italian ambassador that Greece was not on anyone's agenda. Despite this, suspicions, all too well founded as it turned out, persisted in the face of a string of bland denials.

In all of this, the posture of the Americans was crucial. President Roosevelt was convinced of the evils of fascism and the need to sustain the British war effort. Initially the majority of the electorate was, at best, lukewarm and opposed to any firm commitment. The President was constrained to keep most of his discussions with Churchill out of the public arena, especially as he was obliged to fight an election in the autumn of 1940. Despite abundant and growing evidence of Nazi tyranny and wholesale oppression, Germany still enjoyed the support of a vociferous minority in the USA. The aviator Charles Lindbergh acted as the focus for a group styled 'America First'. Fiercely isolationist and dismissive of British prospects, it openly advocated an accord with Hitler and the Nazis. Joseph Kennedy and the Irish lobby within Roosevelt's own party, were rabid Anglophobes.

As ambassador to St James', Kennedy was less than a popular success, seeking to gain personal business advantage as a condition precedent to continued aid and openly touting for an armistice. The President was considerably embarrassed and recalled Kennedy. Repellent as his attitude and conduct were, he was not, by any means, in a minority; many US industrialists shared his leanings. Gerhard Westrick, a German agent with a trade attaché cover, liaised with numerous leading figures from the sphere of business and commerce, offering significant trading opportunities for US businesses with the Greater German Reich. A number of key industrial figures appeared convinced by his blandishments.[7] By the close of 1940, a year of serial disasters for England, livened only by the twin deliverance of Dunkirk and the Battle of Britain, the war cabinet was desperate for US support, without which sustaining the war effort was beyond the beleaguered and depleted capital of the state and its Empire. Churchill penned an eloquent and detailed essay to Roosevelt, stressing the need for unencumbered aid:

> I believe you will agree that it would be wrong in principle and mutually disadvantageous in effect, if at the height of this struggle Great Britain were to be divested of all saleable assets, so that after the victory is won with our blood, civilisation saved, and the time gained for the United States to be armed against all eventualities, we should stand stripped to the bone.[8]

This passionate plea touched a continuing chord in the President and became the inspiration for the subsequent Lend-Lease. More immediately and within a couple of days, Roosevelt had dispatched his personal representative, Colonel William Donovan, to liaise directly with Churchill. 'Big Bill' was a larger than life character, latterly a successful Wall Street lawyer he had abandoned the brief for the sword at his President's request even though their politics were, in many areas, incompatible. A much decorated veteran of the Western Front, Donovan had maintained a finger in the counter intelligence pie and was a firm advocate of the Allied cause. He would go on to found the US equivalent to SOE, the OSS which would, in due course during the emergence of the Cold War grow into the omnipotent Central Intelligence Agency.

Having met and conferred with Churchill in London, Donovan proceeded on a grand tour of Eastern Europe including the Bulgarian capital of Sofia, then on to Belgrade, where he spoke with Prince Paul, then to North Africa for discussions with the representatives of Vichy. His message to the War Cabinet was a simple one and typically forthright. If Britain wished to restore and maintain its foundering credibility with the Americans then some form of successful military venture had to be undertaken on the European mainland. Clearly France, the Low Countries and Scandinavia were beyond the Empire's much depleted resources, this left the Balkans, deadly melting pot and graveyard of spent alliances.

It was this need, coupled with the spectre of an Italian offensive that triggered Churchill's interest in Greece. If Britain, for a limited military commitment, could facilitate the defeat of Il Duce's strutting legions then this might achieve the necessary resonance across the Atlantic. Mussolini's designs were scarcely secret. Since the annexation of Albania in 1939, the Italian shared a common border with the Greeks and there had been an escalating tide of provocation since. In addition to a series of stage-managed border 'incidents', the Greek cruiser *Helle* had been brazenly torpedoed in an utterly unprovoked attack.

Hitler had met his Italian counterpart in October 1940 at the Brenner Pass in the wake of the German defeat over the skies of southern England. Mussolini was in high good humour as their talked ranged over a sweeping agenda. He might have been less jovial had he realised that the Führer had already taken the decision to beef up the German presence in Romania, to the extent that the whole country became an occupied territory, a key shift of policy he chose not to share. Some two weeks prior to the summit, Hitler had issued a directive setting out the defined objectives:

> To the world their [the military mission's] tasks will be to guide friendly Romania in organising and instructing her forces. The real tasks – which must not become apparent either to the Romanians or to our own troops – will be: To protect the oil district … To prepare for deployment from Romanian bases … in case a war with Soviet Russia is forced upon us.[9]

Il Duce roared with impotent rage when he finally learnt of the order and he blazed that he would behave in like manner – that Hitler would read of his projected invasion of Greece in the newspapers! He then gave orders for the invasion plans to be put in hand immediately. Consequently General Metaxas, de facto dictator, was awoken in the early hours of 29 October 1940 to be presented with an Italian ultimatum. He was accused by the ambassador, Count Grazzi, of aiding and abetting the British, Italy's enemy. As quid pro quo Mussolini now demanded free access to and passage over Greece sovereign territory for his troops. Anything less than complete acquiescence would be considered an act of war. Inevitably, as anticipated, Metaxas refused to see his country so summarily shorn of nationhood. Within a couple of hours Italian troops had crossed the frontier. That same morning Hitler arrived for a further summit in Florence to be met by Mussolini, who, grinning like a mountebank, promptly postured: 'Führer, we march.'

2

'Compass':
June 1940 – March 1941

Today we have naming of parts, Yesterday,
We had daily cleaning. And tomorrow morning,
We shall have what to do after firing. But today,
Today we shall have naming of parts. Japonica
Glistens like coral in all of the neighbouring gardens,
And today we have naming of parts.

Henry Reed

On the balmy evening of 10 June 1940 the Italian dictator preened from the central balcony of the Palazzo Venezia in Rome. To a roaring crowd he announced that Italy was now at war with 'the sterile and declining nations of Britain and France' – pure mummery which would cost his country dear. Niall Barr, in his consummate study of the El Alamein battles, describes Il Duce's policy as entirely opportunistic and this is undoubtedly correct. His notion was that of the 'Parallel War', Italy would fight alongside Germany but in pursuit of her own territorial ambitions. In this, Mussolini had greater faith in his own potential than his ally Hitler. If Britain, by comparison, was equally unprepared for war there had been some efforts made to link both strategic and tactical thinking in the vital Mediterranean theatre. As early as June of that year the joint commanders had established a liaison group; Lieutenant-General Archibald Wavell, Admiral Sir Andrew Cunningham and Air Marshall Sir William Mitchell.[1]

'Egypt's the place'

These senior officers saw quite clearly that there was a need to closely coordinate their respective arms where they were jointly responsible for so vast a territory, over 2,000 square miles with Wavell, following his appointment on 2 August 1939, as Commander in Chief. His task was an unenviable one, responsible for the defence not only of Egypt but also that of Sudan, Palestine, Transjordan, Cyprus, British Somaliland, Aden and Iraq. In Egypt, he could deploy the 36,000 soldiers of General O'Connor's Western Desert Force. A trained and mobile formation, desert-hardened but still short of equipment, facing them, in Italian

Cyrenaica, stood the 140,000 men of Marshall Graziani's 10th Army. In East Africa, a further 130,000 Italians confronted barely a tenth that number of British and Imperial troops.[2]

Italy was not the only foe. With the fall of France in June 1940, General Mittelhauser, who had replaced Weygand in the Middle East, appeared likely to accept the armistice terms and side with Vichy, contrary to British interests. The subsequent decision to sink the French fleet by bombardment at Mers el Kebir and Oran did little to improve relations. Mittelhauser was in turn succeeded by the virulently Anglophobic Fougere. Egypt was the key to the British strategic position. Only here, facing the Italians, could offensive action be undertaken. Harried from Norway and driven ignominiously from France, Britain lacked any other base for aggression. Egypt was also the key which could unlock the approaches to the Suez Canal and the oilfields of Iraq. From Il Duce's perspective, the earlier British failures against Germany suggested the time was ripe for the Italian fleet, which significantly outmatched the Royal Navy presence in theatre, to wrest control of the Eastern Mediterranean. Graziani's 10th Army could sweep through Egypt, taking Alexandria and Cairo before reaching the Canal.

Marshall Graziani, with other senior officers, had extreme doubts about the capacity of the Italian army, despite the apparent superiority in numbers, to mount a successful offensive. General Giuseppe Mancinelli had seen the Wehrmacht in action and gloomily noted the contrast:

> In 1938, the division, through the unhappy initiative of the then Chief of Staff ... had been transformed from 'ternary' to 'binary': this meant that the infantry component had been reduced from three to two regiments. This was a strange operation which certainly did not do any good to the general efficiency of the army. In the new units, the infantry-artillery ratio had been raised but the result could not be considered satisfactory since the division became too small a unit to be able to undertake and successfully terminate a tactical action of any importance; it was subject to quick deterioration and was incapable of any prolonged effort ... In general the problem of mechanisation, or more appropriately non-mechanisation, of our army, represented one of the largest gaps in our organisation, a canker which excluded any capacity for large manoeuvres ...[3]

The general concluded with some cynicism, but probably correctly, that the reduction in divisional strength had been a ruse to feed Il Duce's posturing by 'an apparently miraculous multiplication of the forces at his disposal'. Wavell, for his part, foresaw the likely Italian aims which he summarised in a detailed paper submitted just prior to his appointment. Italy, he predicted, would seek to dominate the Mediterranean as surely as Germany had crushed Northern Europe beneath the jackboot. To forestall Mussolini, defensive action alone would not avail, Wavell saw both the need and the opportunity to trounce the Italians and then secure a foothold on the European mainland. If the Mediterranean theatre could not encompass the defeat of Germany, it might be the means and the place whereby that process could begin. Wavell identified four clear strategic aims:

1. To secure control by an advance into Italian held territory
2. To secure control of the Eastern Mediterranean
3. To clear the Red Sea
4. To develop land action in South-East Europe[4]

Despite the apparently unstoppable triumphs of Axis arms Hitler was poised to make a major strategic blunder by diverting his attention eastwards and focusing on the forthcoming trial against Soviet Russia. Though his position in the west seemed secure this was rank folly while Britain remained undefeated:

> But if there were no prospect of a successful decision against Germany herself there was a subsidiary theatre where British forces could be employed to harass the enemy and perhaps inflict serious damage. Italy's entry into the war had turned the Middle East into an active theatre of operations. As a centre of gravity of British forces it was second only to the United Kingdom itself.[5]

The Führer had railed against First World War generals who elected to fight on two fronts. He now proposed to do the same and thus handed the beleaguered British a priceless gift. Even as France was about to fall Wavell, in a further study, had spelt out how the Middle East had become the 'centre of strategic gravity':

> 1. Oil, shipping, air power, sea power are the keys to this war and they are interdependent. Air power and naval power cannot function without oil. Oil, except very limited quantities, cannot be brought to the destination without shipping. Shipping requires the protection of naval power and air power.
> 2. We have access to practically all the world's supply of oil. We have most of the shipping. We have naval power. We have potentially the greatest air power when developed. *Therefore we are bound to win the war.*[6]

In 1945, Goering admitted that 'not invading Spain and North Africa in 1940' had constituted a fatal blunder.[7] From the British perspective and to hard-pressed Imperial forces in 1940, the situation appeared very far from rosy. Wavell's resources were stretched perilously thin and he was palpably short of materiel. 7th Armoured Division possessed only four tank regiments. 4th Indian Division was short of a full brigade of infantry and generally deficient in guns. The New Zealand Division was scarcely more than at brigade strength. Of the 27,500 troops deployed in Palestine, there was only a single British brigade and two extra battalions already marked for service elsewhere. These difficulties notwithstanding General O'Connor, when he assumed command of Western Desert Force in June 1940, found the Commander-in-Chief already had ideas for an offensive.

To create a viable infrastructure to fuel such an enterprise it was necessary to construct port rail and road facilities, lay hundreds of miles of water piping, lay out desert airstrips, establish supply dumps and depots, stockpile vast quantities of petrol, foodstuffs, clothing, tentage and all manner of supplies. Hospitals, workshops, tank repair facilities all had to be planned and constructed. This vast tail of rear echelon, orchestrated by the Royal Army Ordnance Corps and Royal Army Service Corps, was the very lifeblood of desert warfare without which the mobile columns at the front could never have functioned. The Desert was always a thinly populated canvas compared with the enormous armies deployed in Russia but numbers alone were not of the essence. The essentials were mobility and firepower, something which Churchill, with his outmoded notions of a form of colonial warfare, could not fully comprehend.

This vast logistical effort was underpinned by supplies from the UK, USA/Canada and India. British shipping could not move freely in the Mediterranean while the Axis, sailing from Brindisi or Taranto, had easy access to Tripoli or Benghazi. Easy but not secure, British submarines, warships and planes could issue from Malta and Alexandria. In May 1941, an attempt by the Germans to reinforce their airborne landings on Crete by sea met with disaster beneath the guns of British warships but those same ships paid a fearful price running the gauntlet of German fighter-bombers. The distance from Britain, around the shoulder of Africa, past the Cape of Good Hope and then via the Red Sea to Suez was 12,000 miles, a huge distance but less perilous than the Mediterranean, particularly once the menace of Italian submarines cruising the Red Sea had been dealt with.[8] From the New World the distance was only 200 miles greater than from the UK; even India was 3,000 miles away. The small and constricted port of Suez was not the end of the chain, supplies till had to reach the front:

> If you cabled for something, it might and usually did, take two or three months to manufacture and collect at an English port, a week to load (if bombing did not interfere), ten weeks at the lowest at sea, another two weeks perhaps to unload it at a small and most congested port, a day or two at a Base Depot, and from there four or five hundred miles by rail or road to the fighting troops in the desert.[9]

'Fox killed in the open'

Marshall Balbo, when writing to Il Duce after the fall of France, put his finger on the difficulties confronting an Italian army preparing for offensive operations in the Western Desert:

> It is not the number of men which causes me anxiety, but their weapons. With two big formations equipped with limited and very old pieces of artillery, lacking in anti-tank and ant-aircraft weapons, I need to be able to depend on the closing of ways of access to Tripolitania, and on the perimeters of Tobruk and Bardia. To have fortified works without adequate weapons is an absurdity. Another urgent necessity is anti-aircraft defences – batteries and organisation. It is useless to send more thousands of men if then we cannot supply them with the indispensable requirements to move and fight.[10] Count Ciano, Mussolini's son in law, put it rather more succinctly – 'May God help Italy.'[11]

Marshall Graziani arrived in North Africa towards the end of June 1940, Balbo being already dead.[12] He was under pressure from Mussolini to begin offensive operations but hamstrung by the same perceived difficulties as had afflicted his predecessor. He therefore confined his deployment to a slow build up of forces between Tobruk and Bardia. On 10 August, he received a communication from the Dictator intimating that the invasion of Britain 'has been decided upon'. Not wishing to be yet again sidelined and outshone by his Teutonic allies, Mussolini gave his General most specific instructions: 'Well, the day on which the first platoon of German soldiers touches British territory, you will simultaneously attack. Once again, I repeat that there are no territorial objectives, it is not a question of aiming for Alexandria, nor even for Sollum. I am only asking you to attack the British forces facing you.'[13]

A campaign without objectives has limited appeal. Both Wavell and O'Connor, despite the odds and apparent difficulties, were becoming clear in theirs. O'Connor was an officer of known dash and initiative, undaunted by the task which confronted him. Indeed offensive operations had already commenced; 11th and 7th Hussars with the élan of their light cavalry forbears had been enthusiastically 'biffing' the enemy. At home in the desert, the cavalrymen used their armoured cars as the eyes and ears of O'Connor's army. In a succession of raids they beat up enemy quarters at Forts Maddalena and Capuzzo. The former fell virtually without a fight though the latter proved a much harder nut. In Churchill's words the Hussars typified the romantic notion of the desert soldier: 'lean, bronzed, desert-hardened and truly mechanised'.[14]

It is fair to assert that the British, despite the innumerable discomforts, were always more at home in desert conditions. By late June, the LRDG had been established. This and the later Special Air Service, would prove not only invaluable as information gatherers but a potent thorn in the side of the Axis armies. Their epic marches and daring raids meant LRDG punched well above their weight. These pioneers of modern Special Forces, heavy with the aura of romance, proved natural successors to Doughty, Burton and T. E. Lawrence. Theirs was a brand of buccaneering that appealed strongly to Churchill.

Wavell, unfortunately, did not. His son conceded after the war that 'nobody would call my father a chatty general'. Wavell's reserve clashed with Churchill's loquacity and unfortunate penchant for dishing out tactical instructions. These were matters for the Commander in Chief at any time and generally based on a wholly fallacious understanding. The prime minister found Wavell aloof and independent, though the latter responded to Churchill's enthusiasm for offensive action in North Africa and in his boldness when he subsequently diverted supply. Nonetheless, the level of interference in tactical matters rankled: 'Winston did not trust me to run my own show and was set on his ideas.' Even the brilliant success of 'Compass' did not affect the prime minister's view. He dealt both churlishly and unfairly with a subordinate whose abilities and conduct merited far better treatment.

In the event, Wavell used those elements of Churchill's instructions which made tactical sense and disregarded the rest, 'a good deal of it'. His thinking was already more aggressive than that of his political superior and he was actively planning a thrust into Cyrenaica. He advised the prime minister that he needed adequate air cover both to defend Egypt and Alexandria and he urgently required a second armoured division. O'Connor was assisted in his detailed planning by Major-General Eric Dorman-Smith ('Chink') one of the most interesting commanders of the desert campaigns. Intellectually gifted, a friend of such eminent writers as Ernest Hemingway, but lacking in patience with those less favoured, mercurial, inclined to provoke extreme reactions, either highly favourable (Liddel-Hart) or vituperative (Alanbrooke) his successful philandering might have coloured some views. Nonetheless, the planning for 'Compass' was bold and imaginative. Rommel was later to intimate he thought Wavell's handling of this initial campaign showed real genius. Churchill was already fretting as the British had now been forced out of Somaliland in the face of enormous odds and the Italians were attacking both in the Sudan and on the fringes of Kenya. Cunningham's ships were making their presence felt and denying the Axis any hegemony in the Eastern Mediterranean but the Italian Navy remained a potent threat.

The forthcoming offensive, Operation 'Compass' had four clearly defined objectives:

1. The capture of Sidi Barrani
2. The capture and occupation of Bardia
3. The capture of Tobruk
4. An advance on Derna[15]

O'Connor's forces were mainly dug in around Mersa Matruh as, on 13 September 1940, Graziani finally lumbered into action. 10th Army advanced some sixty miles into Egypt to reach Sidi Barrani and Sofafi. No major clashes occurred and the Italians seemed, having reached their objectives within three days, in no hurry to advance further. From the British perspective this loss of ground was trifling except that the forward air bases were forfeit. This was serious in that British fighters would no longer be able to reach Malta, necessitating the island's reinforcement with additional planes. Graziani now proceeded simply to dig in, constructing a series of forward camps and establishing his HQ and administration.

This was not quite what Il Duce had intended but of course the planned invasion of Britain was now stillborn and the Italian dictator was beginning to focus his enmity upon Greece, where he espied another easy victory. In November, he received a rude check when the British raid on Taranto inflicted grievous loss on his warships. Wavell meanwhile, continued with his planning, favouring a short, sharp offensive of perhaps five days duration to eject the enemy from the Sidi Barrani, Buq Buq, Sofafi area. His subordinate was, however, already thinking in terms of a more decisive blow:

> General O'Connor had already been thinking on these lines but had come to the con-
> clusion that to attack the strongly held Sofafi group of camps simultaneously with the
> coastal group would involve too great a dispersion of the available forces. He proposed
> instead to attack first the centre group of camps, leaving those on the extreme flanks to be
> watched and dealt with later. The important supply and water centre of Buq Buq would
> be a profitable objective for raids; and when the enemy's administrative arrangements
> were thoroughly dislocated would be the moment to encircle Sofafi. This plan meant that

the main attacking force must pass through the gap, fifteen miles wide, which existed between Nibeiwa and Rabia; from now on it would be necessary to ensure this gap was kept open.[16]

The plan was indeed bold: '... the Western Desert Force was to be thrust into the heart of the enemy's position. There was a risk of discovery and heavy loss from air attack.'[17] Italian forward defences at Nibeiwa were overrun in fine style though elements of the garrison, including its gallant commander, fell at their guns; 4,000 prisoners were taken:

> The whole 'Compass' plan showed not only great imagination but a firm determination to do the utmost with the resources available. The role of 7th Armoured Division was not, of course, a new one to them; but to 4th Indian Division the operation had several novel features, yet the confidence and enthusiasm of the troops, when they learned what they had to do, could not have been greater.[18]

So swift was the Italian collapse as the British chased them down their own newly constructed highway the Via della Vittoria, that comparisons to the hunt seemed justified. As one Guards officer famously remarked: 'We have about 5 acres of officers and 200 acres of other ranks.'[19] It was not all one-sided; the Italians could fight hard and well. Captain Rea Leakey recorded the carnage when one of his cruiser tanks took a hit, its radio still functioning:

> The driver was killed by the first shot and the commander, our newest young officer, had one of his hands shattered. The driver's foot still rested on the accelerator and the tank continued ... Suddenly [the commander] yelled, 'The tank's on fire' ... Before the two in the turret could bale out they had to open the hatches ... [They] were stuck fast. Then all we heard were the most terrible screams of agony; they were being burned alive while their tomb of fire still went on towards the enemy.[20]

The campaign was one of a series of sweeping encirclements and successful assaults on defended positions unable, due to their siting, to provide mutually supporting fire. Here was a lesson for the British. On 5 January 1941, Bardia fell and 40,000 further prisoners were taken. Not even the determined commander of the doomed garrison Lieutenant-General Annibale 'Electric Whiskers' Bergonzoli[21] could delay the collapse. On the 22nd Tobruk was stormed, netting a further 25,000 Italians. The hunting metaphors, of which Wavell was so fond, were by no means inappropriate: '... Hunt is still going but first racing burst over, hounds brought to their noses, huntsmen must cast and second horses badly wanted. It may be necessary to dig this fox.'[22] O'Connor had made good use of his Infantry (I) tanks. These Matildas were slow and, as with all British tanks of this time, under-gunned but they were heavily armoured and impervious to much that was thrown at them.

O'Connor had also established all-arms coordination and, having taken and kept the initiative, he now had the opportunity to destroy the fleeing remnants of 10th Army. 7th Armoured, with the dashing 11th Hussars, led the flanking charge through Mechili, Msus and Antelat towards Beda Fomm and Sidi Saleh while the Australians, who had replaced 4th Indian Division,[23] pushed forward along the coast. The Italians appeared to have a particular horror of these Australian 'barbarians' whom the British had 'unleashed' into the Desert. These 'barbarians' were certainly astonished at the level of creature comforts their enemies had enjoyed till their rude awakening. War correspondent Alan Moorehead observed:

> Officers' beds laid out with clean sheets, chests of drawers filled with linen and an abundance of fine clothing of every kind. Uniforms heavy with gold lace and decked with the medals and colours of the parade ground … pale blue sashes and belts finished with great tassels and feathered and embroidered hats and capes … great blue cavalry cloaks that swathed a man to the ankles, and dressing tables … strewn with scents and silver mounted brushes.[24] Or, as one digger more earthily commented: 'The Tel Aviv police gave us a better fight.'[25]

By noon on 5 February, the Hussars had interdicted the enemy's line of retreat, firmly astride the road over which the Italians must pass. The odds were formidable, at least ten to one, but the light cavalry held their ground in bitter fighting till the 7th Hussars came up and the jaws of the trap closed inexorably. Next day witnessed more desperate attacks to break the ring; 100 light Italian tanks were knocked out. Their frantic attacks continued in darkness and into the following day before white flags began to appear, steadily and then in droves. The battle was over and, as O'Connor with suitable understatement reported: 'I think this may be termed a complete victory as none of the enemy escaped.'[26] Or, as he wrote to the Commander-in-Chief, still firmly posted in the hunting field, 'fox killed in the open' – colourful perhaps but largely justified.

British troops, surveying the ground, could swiftly appreciate the scale of the disaster which had befallen their enemies:

> After we had gone a few miles south … we came upon the scene of the campaign's last great battle … an imposing mess of shattered Italian tanks, abandoned guns and derelict lorries. There was the familiar sight of hordes of prisoners being rounded up; processions of staff cars, containing General Bergonzoli and his entourage, passed up the road towards Benghazi.[27]

At last after a string of dismal defeats and hurried evacuations, Britain had a victory, a complete and magnificent triumph over vastly superior odds. Il Duce's dreams of empire crumbled in the desert wind:

> In the three days from 9th to 11th December the Western Desert Force captured no fewer than 38,300 Italian and Libyan prisoners, 237 guns and 73 light and medium tanks. The total of captured vehicles was never recorded, but more than a thousand were counted. The British casualties were 624 killed, wounded and missing.[28]

In the two months duration of 'Compass', British and Dominion forces had advanced over 500 miles, captured a staggering total of 130,000 of their enemies, taken 400 tanks, twice as many guns, had destroyed 150 enemy aircraft and secured all of their objectives. Total losses were around 2,000 killed, wounded and missing. As Churchill himself phrased it after the initial successes: 'It looks as if these people [the Italians] were corn ripe for the sickle.'[29] O'Connor was desperate to capitalise on the moment and sweep onward to Sirte and Tripoli but the emerging demands of Greece and the Balkans acted as a brake. This must be the great 'what if' of the Desert War. Rommel for one was in no doubt: 'If Wavell had now continued his advance into Tripolitania, no resistance worthy of the name could have been mounted against him – so well had his superbly planned offensive succeeded.'[30]

O'Connor was equally adamant: 'In my opinion the operation would not only have been possible, but would have had every chance of success provided all three Services gave their maximum support and were not deflected by other commitments.'[31] Whether this would in fact have been possible and how such gains might have been sustained remains a matter of conjecture. A very new breed of fox was, however, set to emerge, one whose presence would transform the nature of the Desert War. Corelli Barnett has dubbed O'Connor as the 'Forgotten Victor' – fittingly so for whatever came after should not obscure the worth and achievement of 'Compass', a very signal triumph.

Another Breed of Fox

By the time the dust had settled over Bardia on 5 January, Hitler had taken the decision to intervene on behalf of his crumbling ally. He could not countenance a total collapse of the Italian position in North Africa. Major-General Hans von Funck was sent to carry out an analysis and gloomily reported that the proposed injection of German forces would not suffice to stem the rot. Hitler had already issued Directive no. 22 of 11 January determining that Tripolitania must be held and that a special military 'blocking force' would be deployed, Operation 'Sunflower'. This infusion of German troops would enjoy air support from *Fliegerkorps X* which was to be moved to Sicily. This formation was already trained in air attack upon shipping and quickly made its presence felt, inflicting considerable damage on the aircraft carrier *Illustrious*. The *Luftwaffe* squadrons could also strike at British depots and targets in North Africa. If the British could strike at the Axis in the Eastern Mediterranean then, deprived of any other opportunities in the west, Hitler could riposte:

> On December 10th a formal order was issued allotting air units to bases in southern Italy for operation '*Mittelmeer*'. (It is to be noted that there was no intention of sending any German units to Egypt or Cyrenaica until the Italians should have secured the use of Matruh.) The force selected was *Fliegerkorps X* from Norway, many of whose units had specialised in operations against shipping.[32]

The Führer had decided to send 5th Light Motorised Division, replete with anti-tank guns and later added 15th Panzer to the deployment to beef up its offensive capabilities.

A further two Italian divisions, Ariete Armoured and Trento Motorised, were to be dispatched to make up, at least in part, the Italians catastrophic losses during 'Compass'. In February, the Führer appointed Lieutenant-General Erwin Rommel to command. The Desert Fox thus enters stage, a player who would tax the hounds rather more sorely than his predecessors.

Logistics were the determinant of success in the desert war. Life and campaigning in the arid expanses were only possible because of mechanisation and a supply chain that could move, deliver and maintain the vast stocks of every element that was needed to keep a modern, mobile force in the field. The further an army advanced the more tenuous the supply chain and rapid advance brought a risk that the army might completely outrun its own supply, thus severing that vital umbilical chord and grinding to a fatal halt. Clausewitz observed, and this long before mechanised warfare, that the advantages accruing to an attacking forced diminished over time, were expended; surprise, morale, concentration of resources, initiative cannot be maintained indefinitely. Those advantages enjoyed by the defender are not so susceptible to attrition and the closer he is forced back upon his own base areas the easier his re-supply becomes. This 'seesaw' or 'pendulum' effect was never more apparent than in the desert where the armies fought over such vast, sterile areas, habitually never more than fifty miles inland from the coast. Troops dubbed such violent swings of fortune the 'Benghazi Stakes'.

3

A New Thermopylae:
March 1941 – May 1941

The sea at evening moves across the sand,
Under a reddening sky I watch the freedom of a band
Of soldiers who belong to me. Stripped bare
For bathing in the sea, they shout and run in the warm
air;
Their flesh worn by the trade of war, revives
And my mind toward the meaning of it strives

F. T. Prince

'As Mr. Churchill stated in his review of the campaign, the military authorities considered that there was a line which, given certain circumstances, could be successfully defended. The Greek campaign was not undertaken as a hopeless or suicidal operation. It turned out to be a rearguard action only ...'[1]

Given certain circumstances; the Official History does not define what these circumstances might have been and there has, with the inestimable benefit of hindsight, been a common perception among historians that the Greek adventure was a hare-brained notion from the start:

The decision to go to Greece was a political one, and from the point of view of a professional it was a military nonsense ... the diversion of resources to Greece including 6th and 7th Australian divisions, the New Zealand division, and part of the 2nd Army took away from General Wavell in Africa practically the whole of the fighting formations which were ready and equipped for operations, and therefore by going to Greece we endangered our entire position in the Middle East.[2]

The Balkans

Wavell, was from the outset, far from sanguine about Allied prospects in Greece; he was rightly concerned that the Italian build up in Libya where Marshall Graziani's huge army dwarfed his own, represented the major threat. The General was, while a consummate professional, not imbued with the gift for dealing with awkward political masters. At the outset the Italians had some 280,000 men, supported by 1,500 aircraft, Wavell's RAF support, headed by Sir Arthur Longmore, could barely muster 200 airworthy machines, many of these obsolete. Supply was by convoy taking the long route around the Cape of Good Hope and through the Red Sea, prone to attack by swift Italian destroyers and submarines. An overland air supply route over the trackless wastes of the Sahara was opened from Takoradi, each run an epic in itself. In his directive of 16 August 1940 the Prime Minister stressed the vital importance of defending Egypt, Wavell certainly would not demur but he identified the overriding need, not for men but materiel, aircraft, trucks and tanks. Quite correctly he had judged that the war in the desert would be one that was decided by firepower and mobility, supported by superiority in the air. The General's conclusions were accepted and the supply of equipment stepped up accordingly. Churchill's bold idea of sending a convoy through the Axis infested waters of the western Mediterranean, while extremely risky, paid off.

In Greece, a great surge of patriotic fervour, sufficient to unite the many disparate factions, even under the leadership of a despised autocrat such as Metaxas, rallied and took on the Italian invaders. Despite a shortage of just about everything and a haphazard supply chain, the ill-armed Greek conscripts swiftly brought Mussolini's seemingly irresistible juggernaut to an abrupt halt. The Italian troops were not equipped for an autumn campaign, their morale proved illusory and a determined counter-attack, launched in mid-November, began, very swiftly, to assume the proportions of a rout. Although Hitler was quick to criticise his hapless ally for the severity of the defeat he was not perhaps as opposed to the idea of a Balkan involvement as he might have appeared. The idea of a coordinated attack on Greece and an offensive in North Africa, aimed at the capture of Suez and thereby, imperilling Britain's entire position, was not unattractive.

As early as the summer of 1940 German planners at both OKH[3] and OKW,[4] the top tiers of the Nazi command structure had considered the possibility of supporting an Italian invasion of the Greek mainland with a simultaneous airborne assault on Crete. This would only be launched when Graziani's legions had succeeded in capturing Mersa Matruh in the second leg of the proposed desert offensive thus providing the Axis with forward airstrips and bringing the British fleet anchorage at Alexandria within bombing range. The naval base at Souda Bay on the north coast of Crete, just east of the island's administrative capital Chania, would be an invaluable asset in the war at sea, one which was presently available to the British. The scheme for proposed co-operation did not find favour with Il Duce who saw his dreams of imperial conquest coming to fruition purely as a result of Italian efforts, without the need for German intermeddling. As General Franz Halder sourly remarked the Italians 'do not want us'.[5]

As the Germans were tentatively touting the idea of a combined Balkans operation, the Greeks, in August, already alarmed by Italian sabre rattling and overt provocation had approached the British ambassador requesting assistance in the event, as now appeared likely, of an invasion. The subsequent report prepared by the Chiefs of Staff Committee and delivered to the War Cabinet on 9 September was unequivocal:

Even with the reinforcements at present contemplated, our land and air forces in the Middle East will be no more than sufficient to withstand a determined attack by Italian and German forces. Until the attack on Egypt has been finally defeated no forces will be available for assistance to Greece … no forces can be made available for assistance to Greece until the present threat to Egypt has been liquidated.[6]

The Campaign in Greece

The overwhelming weight of military advice was therefore, and from the outset, against any intervention in Greece; Britain's stock of military capital was simply too slender to face a fresh division of resources. Churchill, writing later, and with a fine eye for the useful benefits of hindsight, gives the wider political view:

We often hear military experts inculcate the doctrine of giving priority to the decisive theatre. There is a lot in this. But in war, this principle, like all others, is governed by facts and circumstances; otherwise strategy would be too easy. It would become a drill book and not an art; it would depend upon rules, and not on an ever changing scene.[7]

In 1940, a year of defeat and bare deliverance for Britain and her surviving allies, those brave fighters who had escaped from Poland, Czechoslovakia, Norway, Denmark, the Low Counties and France, in real terms few in numbers, the strategic position appeared to improve. The Greeks were busily trouncing the Italians, it seemed as though Albania could fall and British Fleet Air Arm Swordfish torpedo bombers scored a signal success against Il Duce's navy at harbour in Taranto. In the second week of December Wavell unleashed his desert offensive and inflicted s series of dramatic defeats on Graziani's army to the extent that the whole Italian position in North Africa began rapidly to unravel.[8]

The earlier confidence of the Axis leaders, preparing to act as receivers of a bankrupt British Empire, evaporated. In December both Bulgaria and Yugoslavia declined to join the Tripartite Alliance, worse the Russian attitude began to harden. In the course of a conference in Berlin Molotov displayed both caution and suspicion, even presuming to grill the Führer himself. A timely air raid by the RAF served to underline the fact of Britain's continuing defiance. When Stalin later confirmed his foreign minister's demands and intransigence Hitler realised that the time for 'Barbarossa'[9] was at hand. From now on German strategic considerations were to be driven by the need to plan and prepare for the invasion of Russia. The Balkans would thus be a sideshow only, a necessary sideshow and one which had the advantage of providing a cover for the German build up.

Collapse of the Italian position in both Greece and North Africa removed any argument over the question of German involvement. Hitler had to secure this southern flank before committing his forces to an all out attack on the Soviets. Thus, the *Wehrmacht* was being drawn into a Balkan campaign not by policy but as a consequence of diplomatic failure and, on Il Duce's part, military bungling. After a further, unsuccessful effort to interest Franco in an attack on Gibraltar Hitler was convinced of the need to intervene in Greece.

Churchill also had a fascination with the Balkans and the autumn successes against the Italians fuelled his interest in Greece where it might yet be possible to strike a blow against the Axis, such a blow as might serve to significantly bolster American enthusiasm for the Allied cause. The Prime Minister had convinced the Chiefs of Staff that a descent upon Rhodes, Mussolini's last Aegean bastion, might be accomplished by a mixed force of marines and commandos. In the event, this did not proceed.[10] Wavell, as GOC, had already re-iterated his earlier misgivings in a cable dated 2 November:

> As hostilities develop between Italy and Greece we must expect further, persistent calls for aid. It seems essential that we should be clear in our minds on this main issue now. We cannot from Middle East resources send sufficient air or land reinforcements to have any decisive influence on the course of the fighting in Greece. To send such forces from here or to divert reinforcements now on their way or approved would imperil our whole position in the Middle East and jeopardise plans for offensive operations. It would surely be bad strategy to allow ourselves to be diverted from this task and unwise to employ our forces in fragments in a theatre of war where they cannot be decisive ... [and later in a further communication of the following day] ... in general all Commanders-in-Chief are strongly of the opinion that the defence of Egypt is of paramount importance to our whole position in the Middle East. They consider that from the strategical point of view the security of Egypt is the most urgent commitment and must take precedence of attempts to prevent Greece being overrun.[11]

Buoyed by the sweeping successes of the December offensive, Eden, by January 1941, appeared far more willing to consider a deployment in the Balkans. Indeed Churchill now felt the Italians should not be pursued beyond the vital bastion of Tobruk. With the campaign, as he saw it virtually over a view that was supported by the South African General Smuts, attention could revert to the Balkans.

Wavell remained obdurate but he based his objections on the view that the German threat was more apparent than real, he might have been wiser to simply re-iterate that Britain lacked the necessary resources to embark on a Greek expedition. This flaw earned an immediate rebuke from Churchill who sharply reminded the Commander in Chief that his obligations were to carry out orders rather than determine policy. Thus chastened, Wavell seems to have taken the view that he had no choice but to comply with his instructions regardless of any misgivings.

Consequently, both he and Air Marshal Longmore were dispatched to Athens for a high level meeting with the Greek commanders. Wavell would not be disappointed to discover that the Commander in Chief, General Papagos, was far from enamoured of the concept of British intervention. He believed that a modest deployment of troops would achieve nothing and possibly only worsen the situation. Wavell was thus able to report a negative outcome and press on with his plans, already in hand, to pursue the beaten Italians as far as Benghazi. Though Churchill concurred he did not abandon the Greek venture and the sudden death of General Metaxas, who succumbed to a heart attack on 29 January, raised fresh possibilities. Anthony Eden, with the zeal of the convert and a desire to please, conceived the notion of a grand Balkan alliance, a united front that would be strong enough to thwart any Axis attempt to intervene further in Greece who would join with Britain, Turkey and Yugoslavia.

If the Turks were to be the eastern bastion with the Yugoslavs to the north then it was essential that the Greeks, in the vulnerable centre, were speedily and substantially reinforced. A fresh mission to Athens would therefore be necessary; this time headed by Eden rather than Wavell or Sir John Dill, the Chief of the Imperial General Staff, a shift of emphasis from the purely military to the overtly political. Even so Churchill, when writing to Wavell, intimated that if it was not possible to reach a working brief with the Greeks then all that could be done would be to salvage Crete and any other island bases which might be useful. When Eden met with Wavell, Dill, Longmore and Admiral Cunningham (Commander in Chief of the Mediterranean Fleet), in Cairo he once again found the General sceptical of the prospects for offensive military operations in the Balkan sector. Eden was not easily dissuaded and wrung a concession from the C in C that a scheme for the defence of Salonika be devised and put to the Greeks. Cunningham later noted that both he and Dill saw little to offer in this but held their counsel.

Salonika, Greece's second city and her great northern port, one which had seen much Allied military activity in the Great War, was the pivot upon which the proposed Balkan alliance must turn; it was also the only harbour other than Piraeus that could provide a base for an expeditionary force. To hold the city however, the Greeks would have to base their defensive line on the northern chain of Macedonian passes. Wavell privately felt that this would be a good deal further than they would wish to extend and might, hopefully, allow the whole idea to founder. He also expressed the clear need to have the Balkan allies on side before seeking a deployment around Salonika for, as matters stood, the Axis could invade long before any sufficient build up could be established and simply overrun the bridgehead. Wavell, who had already received a severe rebuff from Churchill, had also, even in the hour of his triumph in the desert, been subjected to a series of rather petty snubs and recurrent sniping. It was clear to him that he did not enjoy the Prime Minister's confidence and that his strategic assessments, invariably sound, were likely to be disregarded.

Eden did not feel constrained by such practical considerations, now convinced the proposed intervention could be made real. He conceded that the whole strategy constituted a 'gamble' but the risk was justified by the paramount need to be seen to be doing something to assist the Greeks. So fired was the Foreign Secretary by the urgency of his mission that, as his delegation flew on to Athens there was some hasty and disreputable shuffling of the resources Britain was able to commit.[12] At the Tatoi Conference and after some considerable haggling and a further inflation of the figures a form of accord was attained, though, as it transpired the Greeks were as nimble as the British in overestimating numbers. General Papagos was in favour of holding the northern line and thus securing Salonika but this would requite the disengagement of troops currently deployed in Albania, a difficult and uncertain matter.

Churchill, by 7 April, appeared to be having second thoughts and seeking to curb his Foreign Secretary's enthusiasm, cautioning that there was nothing to be gained from encouraging the Greeks to a doomed struggle if we had only troops in penny packets to offer. A further complication now arose in that some 80 per cent of the forces to be deployed in Greece were to be drawn from the Australian and New Zealand contingents but these were not directly under the orders of the C in C Middle East, nor for that matter, the War Cabinet. Acceptance of the strategic reasons for the deployment should, according to protocol, be sought beforehand from the Dominion governments.

In the event both Blamey and Freyberg were simply given their orders without reference to Canberra or Wellington. This highhandedness was to spark understandable resentment in the wake of the Greek and later the Cretan debacle. The official reasoning, outlined in a cable sent to the acting Prime Minister in Australia, was the need to form Eden's hoped for Balkan Front. The Greek Expedition suffered from the outset from a confusion of objectives and a raft of heroic assumptions which largely proved untenable. Both Eden and Papagos had wildly overestimated the numbers which would be available. The entire scheme was based on the concept of a Balkan Alliance which did not even begin, at this stage, to exist and was put forward in the teeth of opposition from all of the commanders involved, army, navy and air force. The decision to assist Greece was, from the outset, political rather than military. In practical terms the ability of either Britain or Greece being able to deliver the resources needed was, at best, highly questionable.

The question of where best to stand on the defensive was discussed at the Tatoi Conference. Here the bland eloquence of political assurance began to founder against the harsh reality of the topography. The first position was a line drawn along the Bulgarian Frontier which would safeguard Salonika or a rearward position buttressed by the slopes of Mount Olympus and the Vermion range – the Aliakmon Line, stronger but being some forty miles behind the first would mean the abandonment of Salonika. The Greeks, for understandable patriotic reasons wished to hold the frontier and deny the Germans the soil for which they had already fought so hard.

But to hold this it was necessary to have the support of Yugoslavia, the second bastion of Eden's proposed alliance. Militarily the British generals favoured the Aliakmon Line as the advanced position could easily be outflanked if the Germans attacked through Serb territory, a real possibility as the attitude of the Belgrade Government had yet to be ascertained. Despite the apparent confidence some of those present at the conference (as Freddy de Guingand confirms) were by no means sanguine at the prospects of holding the Aliakmon Line:

> We had a momentous conference at Tatoi, the King of Greece sitting at the head of the table with his prime minister on one side, and Papagos, his commander-in-chief on the other. And I was actually there when Eden asked Dill to inform the King of Greece and his cabinet his views as to whether we'd be successful if we intervened in Greece, and Dill got up and made a most optimistic statement that he felt we could hold the line in Northern Greece called the Aliakmon Line and prevent the Germans from getting deep into Greece. I remember I was absolutely shattered because all our own studies in the ground planning staff had shown that it wasn't possible, you'd never get the forces in sufficient strength there in time before the Germans would be there, in sufficient strength to come right down into Greece.[13]

One of the main weaknesses of the strategy determined at Tatoi was the reliance on the Yugoslavs at a time when the mood in Belgrade was unknown, as indeed was the view in Ankara, the third capital in Eden's three great pillars. The Turks, while conciliatory, were not easily drawn. They had no reason to invite German aggression and any vague assurances were clearly dependent upon them receiving quantities of aircraft and materiel which Britain was not placed to supply. The situation in Yugoslavia was even more uncertain; the country was a political creation, born of the dismemberment of Austria-Hungary after 1918. This uneasy mix of peoples was dominated by the Serbs who leaned toward Britain, their ally from the First War. There was, however, in Croatia a substantial minority who leaned toward Germany and, in February 1941, Hitler had made it clear to the Yugoslavs that he expected them to ally themselves unequivocally with the Axis.

Prince Paul, the Regent, treading a delicate path between to two protagonists, was inclined to accept the German accord with the assurance that Italy would not benefit at his country's expense. He was cautious, as he intimated, as he feared too overt a move toward the Axis could produce a backlash that would unseat his government. The Germans were not minded to temporise – it was a question of whether the Regent preferred an alliance or an occupation. At the same time he was fending off repeated calls from Britain with the result that his country stood unhappily poised in a continuing dichotomy.

The net result of this feverish diplomacy was entirely negative. Sir Anthony Eden's dream of a buttressed Balkan coalition was exposed as a chimera and the viability of the British military expedition to Greece fatally undermined before the first shots were fired. In London the War Cabinet was becoming alarmed; Eden's initiatives had been launched on the Prime Minister's sole authority but the bulldog refused to be cornered. Admitting that the expedition might prove a military blunder Churchill challenged his colleagues with the need, imperative, as he now saw it, to support the Greeks regardless of loss. The Cabinet backed off but with the important proviso that the expedition must receive the full endorsement of the dominion governments.

In the event, on 26 February the New Zealand administration concurred, buoyed by assurances from General Freyberg. It may certainly be said that the facts, particularly the prospects for Yugoslav and Turkish involvement may have been cast in a singularly optimistic light. R. G. Menzies, the Australian Prime Minister who had been present at the cabinet meeting, also urged agreement though he seems to have felt a greater degree of unease than this urging would suggest. He commented that the decision was being undertaken on the basis of assessment supplied from Middle East Command who had in fact expressed grave reservations about the whole scheme.

Some authors have argued that the concurrence of the Dominion governments was gained 'by a combination of misunderstanding, misleading information, and straight untruth'.[14] This may be unduly censorious and it is likely that Churchill adopted the same steamroller tactics as he did with his own colleagues. The Axis dictators had the considerable advantage of being accorded demigod status and were not troubled by having to cajole members drawn from an elected assembly and with differing political hues. Goering, in March 1941, observed with practised sycophancy that 'The Führer is a unique leader, a gift of God. The rest of us can only fall in behind.'[15]

By 13 December 1940 Hitler was outlining his plans for a Balkans campaign. This would begin in March 1941 and be expected to last no more than three weeks. Timing was everything for the divisions would soon be offered fresh employment elsewhere. The invasion of mainland Greece and the occupation of Bulgaria, codenamed '*Marita*' would be an exercise intended to secure the southern flank while the main issue was settled on the Russian Steppe. Even the deployment of General Rommel and his Afrika Corps expedition to Libya was merely intended to bolster the Italians and keep the British engaged rather than advance into Egypt and capture Suez. As Halder noted in February: 'The war in Africa need not bother us very much … but we must not risk the internal collapse of Italy, Italy must be saved from that. It will be necessary to send some help.'[16]

A dramatic development occurred on 26 March 1941 when an army coup unseated the Yugoslav Regent, took control of the person of the young King Peter II and established a Serbian dominated military regime. This course of events had been in part instigated by Big Bill Donovan who had tapped into Serbian Nationalist, anti-Axis sentiment in Belgrade and the key garrisons. Although the junta leaned now toward the allies, the generals were not so foolhardy as to hazard their tenuous grip on power by defying Germany. Although there were discussions with General Papagos early in April, these broke up in confusion but the die was already cast. Outraged at what he perceived as standard Balkan duplicity Hitler had, on 27 March, issued orders for the aptly named Operation Punishment.

It was now the turn of Yugoslavia to experience the full horrors of blitzkrieg with her airforce shot to pieces on the ground and her capital subjected to a murderous aerial bombardment that left the city transformed into rubble and 17,000 of her citizens dead in the ruins. The Yugoslav army had disintegrated even before the panzers arrived and on the morning of Sunday 6 April five full armoured divisions under General von List crossed the Greek frontier, together with two motorised, three mountain, eight infantry and the SS Adolf Hitler divisions. There was no Balkan Alliance but there was now a Balkan War.

> No one expected the Greek campaign to be anything but a disaster. Long before any official announcement was made it was known we had troops in Greece, and I could find no one of whatever kind who believed that the expedition would be successful; on the other hand nearly everyone felt it was our duty to intervene. It is generally recognised that as yet we can't fight the Germans on the continent of Europe but at the same time 'we couldn't let the Greeks down'.[17]

As Salonika was too exposed for disembarkation, the majority of British and Dominion troops came ashore at Piraeus or further north at Volos which was closer to the forward post at Larissa. In total the forces dispatched totalled some 58,000 men of whom roughly 35,000 were front liners with the rest support and administrative personnel. The Dominion divisions were 10,000–15,000 strong at the outset, and took with them their own divisional artillery, mainly the highly effective 25-pounder field gun and the considerably less useful 2-pounder anti-tank gun, obsolete and generally ineffective against panzers. The Kiwis had their mechanised battalion equipped with light tanks and Bren carriers – the 'divisional cavalry regiment'. In addition to an anti-tank regiment the divisions were equipped with anti-tank rifles and brens, the men carried .303 Lee-Enfield bolt action rifles as their personal weapons, together with a few Thompson sub-machine guns, the ubiquitous 'tommy gun', a .45 calibre weapon which was capable of firing in bursts. A large number of trucks were available and the single British armoured division of 3,000–4,000 soldiers had around 100 tanks, together with field artillery, anti-tank and engineer formations. It also possessed some anti-tank rifles and light mortars.

From the outset the *Luftwaffe* enjoyed an almost unchallenged superiority. The lack of air cover was a constant nightmare for the hard pressed and weary troops on the ground – much criticism was levelled at the RAF ('Rare as Fairies' and other epithets). This was not due to faintheartedness – the planes were simply not available, the crucial element for the success of any modern campaign, adequate air support, was lacking from the very start.

> We marched and groaned beneath our load,
> Whilst Jerry bombed us off the road,
> He chased us here, he chased us there,
> The bastards chased us everywhere.
> And whilst he dropped his load of death,
> We cursed the bloody RAF,
> And when we heard the wireless news,
> When portly Winston aired his views –
> The RAF was now in Greece
> Fighting hard to win the peace;
> We scratched our heads and said "Pig's arse",
> For this to us was just a farce,
> For if in Greece the air force be –
> Then where the Bloody Hell are we?[18]

The initial Allied plan was that the three Greek divisions, under equipped, under strength and under supplied would be used as a blocking force to blunt the German onslaught. The remainder of the available Greek forces were enmeshed with the three Italian armies operating in Albania. This attempt at a holding action was never really a viable proposition and the blow launched on 6 April across the Bulgarian border and to the east of Salonika was delivered in overwhelming force, with full and close air support. Paratroops were dropped behind the Greek lines guarding the Rupel Pass but his early deployment of airborne troops was not a success, most of the detachment of 150 were killed or captured as the Greeks fought back with considerable gallantry. Nonetheless, Salonika fell within days.

Greece was, to all intents and purposes, a country with a near medieval infrastructure. A single railway line wound from Athens to Salonika, a narrow and highly vulnerable ribbon that connected the two principal cities. Roads were little more than tracks, unsuitable for motor vehicles and impassable in bad weather. The allied commander General 'Jumbo' Wilson was further hamstrung by the fact that, in order to satisfy the Greeks, still officially neutral, he was obliged to pretend he did not really exist, masquerading as a journalist! As war between Germany and Greece had not, prior to 6 April, been declared, the German legation in Athens was not troubled and the military observers were able to observe without interference. It was into this almost Ruritanian atmosphere that British and Dominion troops were disembarking:

> The Greeks hadn't declared war on Germany – it was an amazing thing. The fellows from the German embassy were quire openly walking about with us. There was a blackout in the town at night for aircraft and I remember going to the local night-spot a place called Maxime's – a sort of night club. And the fellows from the German Embassy were all there in civvies, drinking and laughing at us. There was a bit of trouble because one of our blokes got into the German Embassy and stole a pair of very expensive pyjamas. Nothing ever came of it to my knowledge because the Greeks declared war on Germany shortly there-after.[19]

The situation had the makings of comic opera but the consequences of this extraordinary lax security were serious enough – by 9 March OKW in Berlin had a full and accurate assessment of Allied strength and intentions. If Wilson's problems were not sufficient he struggled to exercise any proper form of command structure beset by logistical difficulties imposed by an unhealthy mix of Balkan politics, difficult terrain, poor communications and muddled objectives. These problems were further exacerbated by a lack of standardisation and co-operation between the forces at his disposal, each clinging rigidly to its own pre-determined structure. Brigadier 'Bruno' Brunskill, to whom was passed the poisoned chalice of coordinating the logistical effort, found initially that he was not able to move freely north of Larissa for fear of antagonising the Germans! His only reconnaissance was by air and he was obliged to rely on a single borrowed map. His efforts to blend Greek and Allied supply networks were doomed to failure.

The primitive state of the Greek national infrastructure further hamstrung the Allies, while the Germans had been able to create functioning airstrips in the occupied countries. To signal the type of interference the British might expect the *Luftwaffe* carried out a serious raid on the docks at Piraeus on the night of 7 April. One of their targets was the supply ship Clan Fraser – loaded with munitions. Brunskill, arriving by car to do what he could, found total chaos:

> To my dismay I saw the port was in flames. The fire on the *Clan Fraser* had taken such a hold there was no possibility of putting it out. There was not a Greek in sight nor any member of the crew. Red hot fragments from the ship had started fires wherever they dropped on buildings and more important on every ship, lighter and boat. No one seemed to be doing anything to save the ships. I found a small party of New Zealanders and we put out a few small fires with buckets of water.[20]

By the middle of March Allied battalions were digging in along the Aliakmon line but the plan was already crumbling. General Papagos was unwilling and largely unable to extricate his divisions from Albania, newly raised formations were hopelessly inadequate and under equipped. Wavell's expressed concerns over the vulnerability of the Allied defences proved entirely well founded. The line was also very thinly held and a vital corridor, through which the Germans could penetrate and thus turn the whole position, was virtually unmanned. Hitler was not blind to the strategic opportunities his sudden and violent occupation of Yugoslavia now presented.

Now there was no alternative but to withdraw and Wilson extricated his forces from the trap which the Aliakmon line had become to establish a new position which, in the east, would stretch from the anchor of Mount Olympus to the Serbian border. In the course of the withdrawal the Greek Macedonian divisions began to disintegrate, a whiff of treachery was also in the air.[21] This proved to be the beginning of a series of extended rearguard actions into which the campaign deteriorated, faced with the continuous advance of an enemy with an overwhelming superiority of men, guns and armoured vehicles, his advance closely supported at every stage by the siren wail of the Stukas and the murderous strafing runs of Me109s.

M. Koryzis, the Greek Prime Minister, on hearing from Papagos (as did Wilson) that the Greek armies had reached the limit of their endurance, chose the moment to end his political career by blowing his brains out. His commander in chief, now becoming anxious to spare his country further suffering in the face of inevitable capitulation, suggested to Wilson that it was time for the Allies to withdraw, *sauve qui peut*. This was the news that Wavell must have dreaded, all his worst fears were confirmed and the War Cabinet accepted the inevitable endorsing the order for an evacuation. It was now just a question of how many could be saved from the gathering debacle.

On the ground Wilson faced the unenviable task of attempting a fighting withdrawal from the ruptured position around Mount Olympus to a shorter line of no more than fifty miles and running from the heroic outpost at Thermopylae to the Gulf of Corinth. Even when they reached their new positions the Allies were as exposed as ever. Wavell now flew to Athens to take stock of the unfolding disaster and to confer with both Wilson and the Greeks. The King was already preparing to evacuate his court and entourage to Crete and, after receiving their Commander in Chiefs pessimistic report of 21 April, the War Cabinet confirmed the order to withdraw. It was none too soon for the Thermopylae line was now looking untenable; many units had lost much or all of their artillery and anti-tank weapons and casualties, principally caused by air attacks, were mounting. Evacuation, in the teeth of German hegemony in the skies was problematic; Piraeus was impractical which meant that the withdrawal would have to be accomplished through the necklace of small harbours further south in the Peloponnese. All heavy equipment would have to be rendered useless and abandoned. Movement for the fighting formations was only permitted at night with the troops filtering down to their evacuation points. Non combatant units had to take their chances during the lengthening spring days, easy meat for the prowling Stukas.

On 22 April the Greeks formally surrendered and by the 30th evacuation by sea from the beaches was largely complete, despite a successful attempt by German paratroops to seize a vital crossing at Corinth by a coup de main. The Navy, not for the first or last time, had delivered the rump of the army, some 80 per cent, from certain death or capture.

Behind them the defeated army left all of their vehicles, heavy guns, armour and anti-tank weapons, with great quantities of small arms, spares and supplies. While the evacuation was a brilliant operation superbly handled by the Navy, it remained a perilous operation with the departing ships, once the sun had risen, exposed to the fury of the *Luftwaffe*. At 17.54 hrs on 25 April some 5,000 men from the 19th Brigade were landed at Souda Bay, the first contingent of Wilson's battered evacuees: 'They had very little in the way of arms or personal equipment; they were dirty, ill organised, with no proper chain of command existing, 'bomb-shy' and conscious of their recent defeat.'[22] Crete; the backwater, ill manned, barely considered was about to become the new front line.

The Fall of Crete

With Greece lost, the focus of the Mediterranean conflict shifted to Crete, a mere 200 miles from Alexandria, most southerly of the Greek islands, no stranger to conflict. The Allied forces on the island, very nearly 30,000 strong were spread along the narrow ribbon of the settled north coast, on which were located the principal towns and strategically important airfields. For both sides the forthcoming battle was largely unnecessary as the island had little serious strategic value. The invasion, Operation 'Mercury', was remarkable for three elements:[23] it was the first attempt to invade solely from the air by paratroops and airborne infantry,[24] Ultra intelligence played an important role and[25] the civilian population participated enthusiastically in the Allied effort, to their very considerable cost.

Bernard Freyburg had been persuaded to command the garrison which, overall, was in a poor state of readiness and fatally hamstrung by the total Axis air superiority. Hitler, for his part, was anxious to get the business done so that he could direct resources eastwards for Barbarossa. Axis intelligence was faulty in the extreme and the opening phases of the attack, on 20 May, resulted in heavy loss. New Zealanders, defending Maleme airstrip, gave a first class account of themselves and the landings at Rethymnon, Chania and Heraklion were met with stiff and successful resistance. A failure by senior officers to appreciate the significance of Maleme and a preoccupation with a possible seaborne reinforcement led to disastrous mistakes and the battered *fallschirmjager* were able to consolidate a toehold which was to prove the turning point.

Though victory had been in the Allies' grasp it was thrown away and the battle ended with a nightmare trek over the spine of the mountains and down the precipitous gorge to Sfakia on the southern flank where the RN, once again, came to the rescue and evacuated many thousands of survivors. Again, though battle casualties were few, some 10,000 went into the bag and a vast haul of transport, stores, material and arms fell into Axis hands. By 31 May the evacuation was complete and the long, bitter occupation of Crete began. Italian forces had, at the last minute, landed in the eastern part of the island so Il Duce could claim fatuous credit for the Axis Pyrrhic victory.

4

'Brevity' & 'Battleaxe':
May 1941 – July 1941

Who for some vague thought
Of honour fell,
Nor why he fought
Could clearly tell

Patric Dickinson

What will history say in passing its verdict on me? If I am successful here, then everybody
else will claim all the glory … but if I fail then everybody will be after my blood

Erwin Rommel

Rommel owed his appointment to a personal relationship with the Führer and the
perceived charisma observed by Josef Goebbels. The exploits of his 'Ghost' Division
in France and his own fondness for self-promotion had contributed to the general's
rise. His tactical abilities, relentless and ruthless energy, boldness and decisiveness
were qualities that would ensure his desert legend. Hampered by the fact he was
outside the patrician loop of staff-college generals and his unwillingness to tolerate
fools or abide by orders he considered incorrect won him few friends at OKW. Both
Von Brauchitsch and Halder had made it perfectly plain his role was defensive and
subordinate to the Italian C in C, General Gariboldi. The forces he had were all
that he would get. There would be no more and he must not consider plans for an
offensive until 15th Panzer were deployed in theatre. His superiors, unlike Rommel
himself, were privy to plans for *Barbarossa* – the invasion of Russia, compared to
which North Africa was the merest of sideshows. The deployment was strictly a
blocking move, *sperrverband*. Despite these stern admonitions the Fox was keen to
make his bite felt and had already determined 'to depart from my instructions to
confine myself to a reconnaissance and to take the command at the front into my own
hands as soon as possible'.[1]

Not a Step Further Back

Rommel was not destined to enjoy good relations with the Italians. That necessary talent for patient diplomacy was simply not in his nature. Gariboldi, who had succeeded Graziani, was not in favour of early offensives and chided Rommel on his lack of desert experience. Nonetheless, his position was strengthened when Il Duce instructed that all motorised Italian units should be placed under Rommel's immediate command. The General's newly appointed aide de camp, Lieutenant Schmidt, witnessed the disembarkation of the first formations which would finally form the *Panzerarmee*. Pressed, brushed and gleaming, the soon-to-be desert veterans drove through the streets of Tripoli. As Schmidt noted, their Italian hosts showed little enthusiasm:

> It was a bright sunny day, but the Italian population did not seem to show a great deal of interest in this display of might ... Singly and at regular intervals the Panzers clattered and rattled by. They made a devil of a noise on the macadamized streets ... I began to wonder at the extraordinary number of Panzers passing, and to regret that I had not counted them from the beginning. After quarter of an hour I noticed a fault in one of the chains of a heavy Mark IV Panzer, which somehow looked familiar to me ... Only then did the penny drop ...[2]

The fox was already in action, parading his armour in a caracole around the streets to convince British eyes that he was stronger than he was. Soon, he had Volkswagen cars padded and disguised to fool aerial observers. For these German troops coming ashore in distant Africa this was a new theatre of war. Unlike the British, Italians and French they did not have years of occupation. As might be expected, they immediately discovered difficulties with items of kit, wood burning stoves in a country without wood and twin-wheeled trucks designed for European roads and trackways.[3] Nonetheless, as Naill Barr points out, their tactics for tank warfare, in a land so suited to the use of armour, were already worked out; had been tested initially, on a limited basis in Poland and then decisively against France.[4] The three divisional formations, 15th & 21st Panzer (forming DAK), with 90th Light Division,[5] were already fully mechanised all-arms units[6] and blessed with the inestimable advantage of superb communications.[7] These men were already part of an elite force which had won such stunning victories in Poland and France, the *Panzerwaffe*.[8]

As OKW had cautioned Rommel not to contemplate serious offensive action until 15th Panzer arrived in May, Wavell too believed no attacks could be launched just then. In this he and Halder were mistaken; both had equally underestimated Rommel. While he had clear respect for Wavell as an opponent this did not extend to his superior whom Rommel regarded as a mere pen pusher. Relations between him and Halder were always strained. When the latter subsequently dispatched Von Paulus to report on the alarming developments in Africa he observed that this was 'perhaps the only man with enough influence to head off this soldier gone stark mad'.[9]

General O'Connor had been evacuated from the front to undergo treatment in Egypt for a stomach condition and his replacement was Sir Philip Neame VC. As he did not expect an attack before May, Wavell considered that a single infantry division, supported by one armoured brigade, should be sufficient to consolidate the British grip on Cyrenaica while forces were diverted to Greece and Abyssinia. Wavell's chief difficulty was the vast sphere of his fiefdom where demands were coming in from so many quarters. The debacle in Greece led to the further catastrophe in Crete.[10] The campaign in Abyssinia was followed by others, firstly in Iraq and then in Syria.

> He [Wavell] had had to decide upon the least strength required to make the western front of Egypt secure, and then to provide the largest possible force for Greece or Turkey. Naturally the one requirement directly affected the other. The decision had to be made quickly, soon after the middle of February, and the consequent moves and reorganisations began at once. At that time General Wavell thought that the force he was allotting to Cyrenaica could deal with anything the enemy was likely to do before May; thereafter the Germans would become appreciably stronger, but so also would the British.[11]

In March then Neame had 2nd Armoured Division's support group around Mersa Brega, with 3rd Armoured Brigade stationed some five miles north-east. The British tanks were in poor shape, worn out by the rigours of earlier fighting. Many were non-runners, the rest in urgent need of servicing and repair. A quantity of captured Italian light tanks had been pressed into service but these were of limited effectiveness. Two brigades of infantry from 9th Australian Division were dug in east of Benghazi while a third occupied Tobruk. An Indian motorised brigade held Mechili. Rommel was poised to strike. He had 5th Light Division with eighty PzKw Marks III and IV, the Italian Ariete Armoured Division, additional Italian infantry and support from advance squadrons from *Fliegerkorps X.*

The Loss of Cyrenaica

Wavell was convinced Rommel would not be in a position to attack before May. His trust in Neame's abilities was limited:

> I found Neame pessimistic and asking for all kinds of reinforcements which I hadn't got. And his tactical dispositions were just crazy; he had put a brigade of Morshead's[12] 9th Australian Division out into the middle of the plain between El Agheila and Benghazi, with both flanks exposed … I came back anxious and depressed from this visit, but there was nothing much I could do about it. The movement to Greece was in full swing and I had nothing left in the bag. But I had forebodings and my confidence in Neame was shaken.[13]

On 24 March Rommel launched a probing raid on the British positions at El Agheila. This was entirely successful and justified his confidence in a more ambitious undertaking. Churchill sent a tremulous cable to Wavell: 'We are naturally concerned at rapid German advance to El Agheila. It is their habit to push on whenever they are not resisted. I presume you are only waiting for the tortoise to stick his head out far enough before chopping it off …'[14] Rommel could be described as many things but never as a tortoise. This was not an analogy likely to be applied again.

By the 31st of that same month, Rommel was about to confound both Neame and his own superiors at OKW. His advance began on that day, columns sweeping along the coastal route in the north, striking for Mechili through Andelat and Msus in the centre, and with Ariete cruising to the south in a wide flanking movement converging on Mechili. These dispersed, all arms groups were ideally suited to desert warfare and their deployment gave the lie to any assertion Rommel did not understand the nature and demands of the terrain. Like a battlefield conductor he led from the front, flying overhead in his Fiesler Storch light spotter, constantly urging his formations to 'push on'. His style was one of relentless insistence backed by personal leadership and intervention.

Such close and constant contact enabled him to direct the flow of battle to exploit opportunities. By 5 April Rommel had decided to concentrate his drive upon Mechili. The day before his troops had entered Benghazi and Neame was focusing upon withdrawal. This at least was sound, there was more to be gained from keeping forces intact than clinging onto ground. As Benghazi fell Wavell had sent the recovering O'Connor to bolster Neame:

> During the evening of 2nd April the Commander-in Chief sent for General O'Connor from Egypt with the intention of placing him in command in Cyrenaica because of his great experience of desert warfare. General O'Connor arrived by air next day, bringing with him Brigadier J. F. B. Combe, who had commanded the 11th Hussars and whose knowledge of the desert was unexcelled. After discussion with General O'Connor, who shared General Neame's view that the enemy was likely to make a move by the desert route, General Wavell decided to leave General Neame in command.[15]

On 7 April, a fresh reverse detonated when both generals, together with Brigadier Combe, were captured along with O'Connor's ADC 2nd Lieutenant Lord Ranfurly:

> 9 April 1941
> Jack Dent, General O'Connor's ADC came to see me. He'd just returned from the Desert. He told me that Dan [Ranfurly] and several Generals had set off in two cars and were last seen heading for a short-cut track behind Derna en route for Tobruk. He said an Australian who had gone that way had doubled back after finding a lot of cars stationary and hearing shouts. It was dark. For two days a big search was made for the Generals, to no avail. He told me Germans are now in the area and he thought it probable that a German commando had captured Dan and the Generals.[16].

Also on 7 April, Wavell reported gloomily to London and Churchill was quick to pick up on the Commander-in-Chief's earlier and outwardly more confident briefings – 'the War Cabinet decision regarding assistance to Greece had largely been founded on this appreciation'. Purest tosh of course, Wavell had opposed the Greek fiasco from the start and the prime minister was now preparing to offload responsibility for defeat in Cyrenaica. Churchill and Wavell were in accord, however, that the place which must be held was Tobruk, 'if we could hold the advance at Tobruk we would be well satisfied … Tobruk therefore seems to be a place to be held to the death'.[17] The Chiefs of Staff were in full agreement and Morshead, with 9th Australian Division, was entrusted with the defence while the shaken British regrouped around Mersa Matruh.

The Official History's account is a good deal more considered:

> General Wavell blamed no one but himself for the miscalculation … The truth is that the force allotted to the desert front could only have proved reasonably adequate if it had been up to strength in men and weapons – particularly serviceable tanks – and fully backed by the necessary transport, supply, and maintenance services to give it the freedom of action appropriate to its role … it was here that the simultaneous dispatch of an expedition to Greece had such serious consequences, for Greece was an under-developed country exhausted by war, and the British had to take with them every single thing they wanted.[18]

Rommel too, was aware of the significance of Tobruk and determined upon its capture. His own supplies were becoming a matter of acute concern and he could ill afford to permit a major Allied garrison to remain and threaten his rear. To maintain current efforts the Axis required some 50,000 tons of supplies every month. These were shipped by sea through Tripoli but less than 30,000 tons were arriving.[19] British activity from Malta and raids by the Royal Navy were taking their toll. The use of Tobruk and the elimination of the garrison would greatly ease this burden:

> On 6th April Mr. Eden and Sir John Dill … and the three Commanders-in-Chief met … They decided it was essential to stabilise the battle as far west as possible, mainly to reduce the air threat to the naval base at Alexandria, and because of the moral effect in Egypt. The best chance of holding the enemy was at Tobruk. Here there were large stocks of stores, a supply of water, and a port whose use would be invaluable to the enemy and should be denied to him.[20]

In attacking the Australians, well dug in and equally well prepared, Rommel discovered this was a new type of warfare, where mobility and firepower were not the determining factors. Each attack was repulsed in turn: 'In this assault we lost more than 1,200 men killed, wounded and missing. This shows how sharply the curve of casualties rises when one reverts from mobile to position warfare.'[21] Rommel writes that in mobile fighting what matters is materiel, the tanks and guns, without which the finest troops are impotent. Destruction of this materiel accomplishes the failure of the mobile force even though it may have suffered few battle casualties. This is the essence of desert tactics an appreciation of which Churchill had completely failed to comprehend. Men alone, as the Italians had discovered, were not enough; mobility and firepower were the keys. Nonetheless, the pendulum had swung again and Cyrenaica, so recently won, was now lost:

So ended the first attempt to hold 'the gateway of Cyrenaica'. This astonishingly rapid reversal of fortunes, only a few weeks after the decisive victory over the Italians naturally led to much anxious enquiry. Yet the reasons are not hard to discern, for General Wavell's estimate of when the enemy would be fit to undertake any major enterprise … seems to have been not unreasonable at the time. When it began to look like being too optimistic it was too late to do anything about it. The real disaster was that the sole British armoured brigade in Cyrenaica proved to be an armoured brigade in name only.[22]

Wavell was not alone in having critics; success breeds jealousy in the same way as defeat brings recriminations. Rommel had few friends in *OKW* and plenty of enemies, Halder in particular:

> In his frequent references to General Rommel Halder may have been influenced by the fact that Rommel was not a General who had made his way up the General Staff ladder; he had not even been chosen for his present post by the Army Command, but by Hitler himself. Halder noted savagely on 23rd April: '… Rommel has not sent in a single clear report, and I have a feeling that things are in a mess … All day long he rushes about between his widely scattered units and stages reconnaissance raids on which he fritters away his strength … and the piecemeal thrusts of weak armoured forces have been costly … His motor vehicles are in poor condition and many of the tank engines need replacing … Air transport cannot meet his senseless demands, primarily because of lack of fuel … It is essential to have the situation cleared up without delay.'[23]

Halder, like a prissy headmaster, decided to send out Von Paulus, a member of staff, to rein in this reckless prefect. Rommel could not comprehend why news of his successes was received with at best indifference if not downright disdain. Of course he did not know what was brewing, a conflict with Soviet Russia which would soon assume titanic proportions. He resented the constant snubs and bad-tempered efforts to keep him on a tight rein. As well as a constant soldier Rommel was a dutiful husband who habitually wrote to his beloved wife 'Dearest Lu' every day, as he did on 2 June:

> It was 107 degrees here yesterday, and that's quite some heat. Tanks standing in the sun go up to as much as 160 degrees, which is too hot to touch … My affair with the OKW is under way. Either they've got confidence in me or they haven't. If not, then I'm asking them to draw their own conclusions. I'm very intrigued to know what will come of it. It's easy enough to bellyache when you aren't sweating it out here.[24]

Wavell meanwhile had other ideas.

Wavell's Burden

Fate and Churchill would conspire to deny Wavell the stature he unquestionably merited. His burden was made far greater by the breadth of his responsibility and the fact he was constrained to divert slender resources to fight in several locations at once. That the British position in the Eastern Mediterranean and Middle East was held and did not crumble was, despite the disasters in Greece, Crete and North Africa, a remarkable success.

While the Desert War and the Greek debacle had been in full flow, British troops had been engaged against the Italians in East Africa. Here, the Duke of Aosta commanded perhaps 75,000 Italian troops with some 180,000 colonial levies. Having subdued Abyssinia (including Eritrea and Somalia) in 1936 Aosta's vastly superior forces were well placed to invade British Somaliland which fell in August 1940. Britain had recognised the exiled Haile Selassie and offered aid. Despite the impossible odds and the relatively small Imperial casualties (around 250) Churchill felt the loss of British Somaliland keenly and chose to blame Wavell. The retreat was in fact skilful and British forces withdrawn to the safety of Aden but this did not placate the prime minister – 'A bloody butcher's bill is not the sign of a good tactician' (Italian losses had exceeded 2,000).

Though the Sudan and Kenya were threatened, the Italians attempted no further major thrusts and their naval presence was quickly diminished and rendered impotent. In the midst of 'Compass', Wavell had to detach forces to mount a counter-offensive in East Africa. 4th and 5th Indian Divisions spearheaded the advance into Ethiopia on 19 January 1941. Six days later South African with 11th and 12th African Divisions attacked from the south. Led by Lieutenant-General Alan Cunningham, they swiftly overran Italian Somaliland while British Somaliland was liberated by an amphibious operation mounted from Aden. On 5 May Haile Selassie again entered his capital of Addis Ababa and, after a further eleven days, Aosta conceded defeat. Some 230,000 Italian troops were captured and the campaign ranks as a significant Allied victory, though guerrilla activity spluttered on till Italy's final collapse in 1943.

'I always disliked Iraq … the country, the people and the military commitment … it blew apart at the worst time for me.'[25] Thus Wavell summarised his views on a nation which fell within his remit and was, of course, vital to Britain's interest. In May 1941, a quartet of nationalist generals, 'the Golden Square' ousted the regent and installed Rashid Ali as premier. Their manifesto was one of full independence and they were willing to approach Germany to assist. Clearly, any such moves would constitute a clear threat to Britain's oil supply and troops were immediately deployed to secure Basra. The nationalists riposted by effectively laying siege to the major RAF base at Habbaniya. In the event aggressive action by the local commander obliged the nationalists to lift the siege and retire to Falluja.

As early as March 1941, Wavell had been attempting to hive off Iraq and have the responsibility grafted onto Auchinleck's Indian command. The disturbances in May came at a critical moment for Middle East command with Greece lost, Rommel squeezing in the Desert and the battle for Abyssinia raging. Auchinleck was completely in accord and the early operations in Iraq came under his aegis. Churchill, however, changed his perception and chose to view Iraq as part of Wavell's responsibilities, despite the latter's vociferous protests: 'I have consistently warned you [Chiefs of Staff] that no assistance could be given to Iraq from Palestine … merely asking for further trouble … My forces are stretched to the limit everywhere …'[26] These protests were entirely justified and a less biased critic than Churchill might have taken heed but Wavell's credit balance was already slipping into deficit.

British reinforcements from Palestine and Transjordan were thrown into the fight which quickly developed into a rout. From Falluja the crumbling nationalist forces were chased back to Baghdad and dispersed. The city was taken in a week and the former pro-British regime reinstated. Both Italy and Germany had drip fed piecemeal support but, more alarmingly, the Vichy forces in Syria had both assisted the Iraqi Nationalists and permitted the *Luftwaffe* to refuel there. The RAF had reacted with vigour but no sooner had the dust settled in Iraq than it was judged to be time for a reckoning in Syria.

Hopes that the Vichy forces might care to ally themselves with the Free French proved groundless and Gaullist propaganda had no discernible effect other than to irritate. On 7–8 June, Australian 7th Division with some British and Free French forces attacked, striking north into Syria and Lebanon from Palestine. Any notion that the rump of Vichy forces might quietly lay down their arms was swiftly confounded; well armed and determined, they put up a spirited resistance. The Australians were involved in heavy fighting on the banks of the Litani River and in Lebanon. By 21 June Imperial forces had wrested control of Damascus but more combat ensued in Lebanon before the Anglophobe General Dentz sued for an armistice. Terms were finally agreed at Acre, of crusading fame, on 13 July.

Thus, the operations in East Africa and Iraq had all been entirely successful but all drew resources away from the Western Desert and forced Wavell to shuffle his forces around like a high stakes gambler, and the stakes overall were very high indeed. It is hard to see how any commander could have achieved more given the scale and urgency of demands but Churchill's distrust of his Middle East commander was not clouded by reason. As John Strawson rather acidly observed in likening Wavell to a fit successor to Marlborough, 'he was serving a man who, family connection aside, thought of himself as an actual one'.[27]

Operation 'Brevity'

With the imminent arrival of 15th Panzer, Wavell recognised that his deficiency in armour would become even more telling. For once he and Churchill were on the same wavelength and the Prime Minister took the courageous decision to strip home defence of resources and send these, via the dangerous waters of the Mediterranean, to Alexandria. Operation 'Tiger' was thus an enormous gamble and also an unqualified success. Only one transport and its precious cargo were lost, the rest berthed on 12 May. Wavell would thus gain 238 new tanks and 43 Hurricane fighters. Churchill was inordinately proud of his 'Tiger Cubs' and hoped for great things to follow.

Von Paulus had reached North Africa on 27 April. While he reluctantly acquiesced to another, and equally unsuccessful, attempt on Tobruk he reported, undoubtedly as Halder would have wished, that the army was grossly over extended and should confine its role to the defensive. Von Paulus, unlike Rommel, was privy to *Barbarossa* – a campaign that would furnish him with his own catastrophic nemesis at Stalingrad. Ultra intercepts, picked up on the cable traffic, yielded intelligence that appeared to favour an early counter-offensive. 'The "Tiger" convoy would soon be arriving, but without waiting for it General

Wavell decided to strike a rapid blow in the Sollum area, and for this purpose allotted all the available armour, such as it was to the Western Desert Force.'[28]

Brigadier Gott was entrusted with undertaking Operation 'Brevity'. A limited offensive aimed at driving the Axis from Sollum and Capuzzo, wreaking as much havoc as possible and driving forwards towards Tobruk, as far as supply and prudence would permit. Any successes would form the curtain-raiser to a far more substantive blow, Operation 'Battleaxe' which Wavell was now planning. 'Strafer' Gott began well with Halfaya falling but Axis opposition stiffened and few other gains were achieved, those that were, including Halfaya, swiftly fell to counter-attacks. 'Brevity' was a failure, Rommel was not caught unawares: 'Intercepted signals had warned the Germans to expect an attack, which, when it came, caused some apprehension for it was thought to be the beginning of an attempt to relieve Tobruk and there was not enough transport to send forward strong reserves to deal with it.'[29]

Operation 'Battleaxe'

General Sir Noel Beresford-Peirse was to have command of 'Battleaxe' with 4th Indian Division (Messervy), now returned from service in East Africa and 7th Armoured Division, (Creagh). Messervy, with 4th Armoured Brigade in support, was to attack toward the Bardia, Sollum, Halfaya,[30] Capuzzo area while his open flank was covered by 4th and 7th Armoured Brigades. The intention was that the British armour would draw the Axis out into a decisive engagement. The date for the offensive to open was fixed for 15th June. Unlike his opponent, Beresford-Peirse maintained his HQ at Sidi Barrani some sixty miles from the action. Rommel was ready; he had some 200 tanks fit for service. He would not be taken by surprise. The objectives of 'Battleaxe' were threefold: A successful advance against the enemy in the Sollum – Capuzzo area, an advance towards Tobruk, coordinated with sorties by the garrison and exploitation of gains as opportunities arose.

Thus, Churchill's cherished 'Tiger Cubs' were blooded. 4th Indian Division could make little initial headway and, well dug-in, the dreaded 88mm flak guns took a fearful toll of both I tanks and cruisers. The Matilda, proof against much Axis ordnance, was no match, painfully slow and like all British tanks, fatally under-gunned; 'the means and methods that had done so well against the Italians were not good enough against the Germans'.[31] Having blunted the British attacks on 15 June, Rommel struck back the following day. Though 15th Panzer was stalled in the north, 5th Light Division was able to effect a minor breakthrough and push on towards Sidi Suleiman. Rommel, master tactician, was quick to see the potential 'the turning point of the battle'.[32] He ordered 15th Panzer to divert its main effort along the northern flank of the break-in. He also judged that Beresford-Peirse would launch his next thrust towards Capuzzo and resolved to strike first. Again, he was successful and an intercepted message from Creagh to HQ, requesting Beresford-Peirse to come forward, indicated the British were wavering.

Wavell had earlier reported to London in cautiously optimistic terms; the Guards had taken Capuzzo on the 15th – 'There is no reason to be dissatisfied with the progress made.'[33] By dawn on the 17th, however, the two arms of Rommel's pincer were approaching convergence. Creagh had warned, in his communication, that 7th Armoured's tanks were seriously depleted and British forces, still in the Capuzzo – Halfaya area, were at risk of encirclement. Such a clear loss of confidence acted as a further spur to Rommel. Wavell himself had arrived from Cairo and was with Beresford-Peirse when the message came in. Both now dashed to 7th Armoured HQ but the retreat was already underway. Messervy, after urgent communication with Creagh, had agreed with his pessimistic assessment and ordered a withdrawal. Wavell could do nothing other than concede and simply add that as many damaged vehicles should be got away as possible. After all the effort and optimism of Operation 'Tiger' the precious resources had mostly been expended to no avail. It was a bitter moment.

British losses had not been catastrophic, 122 killed, 588 wounded, 259 missing; 36 planes and 4 guns were lost. In terms of materiel, however, 64 Matildas and 27 Cruisers had been destroyed or abandoned on the field. In contrast, German losses, in terms of tanks, were only a fraction, perhaps 12 in all.[34] Wavell did not hesitate to take the blame upon himself, knowing with full certainty what the consequences must be: 'Fear this failure must add much to your anxieties. I was over-optimistic and should have advised you that 7th Armoured Division required more training before going into battle … I was impressed by the apparent need for immediate action.'

Churchill's reply cannot have come as any surprise: 'I have come to the conclusion that public interest will best be served by appointment of General Auchinleck to relieve you in command of Armies of Middle East.'[35] Wavell was to take over the Auk's command in India, his role in the desert war at an end. Rommel, who was always generous in his assessment of Wavell, ironically far more so than Churchill, was established as a desert commander of genius. He was perceived at possessing the 'Rommel touch' (*fingerspitzengefuhl*). His practice of restless leadership from the front contributed to this as did a team of excellent wireless intercept operators.[36] The legend of the 'Desert Fox' was set to grow.

5

'Crusader':
August 1941 – January 1942

The green Nile irrigates a barren region,
All the coarse palms are ankle-deep in sand;
No love roots deep, though easy loves are legion;
The heart's as hot and hungry as the hand.

In endless evenings, at the café table,
The soldier sips his thick sweet coffee up;
The dry grounds, like the moral to my fable,
Are bitter at the bottom of the cup.

G. S. Fraser

Hoist our Bannner highly
Our cause shall not be lost,
For we were the proud Eighth Army
Our emblem was the cross
Crusader knights of freedom,
Our country is our pride;
We won't forget those fallen
Who fell there by our side.
So hoist our banner highly,
Our cause shall not be lost;
For we were the proud Eighth Army
Our emblem was the cross.

'An Eighth Army Hymn' by Trooper T. Smith, 1st Holding Battalion RAC, (to the tune of 'Onward Christian Soldiers')

'Barbarossa'

Drang nach Osten – the strategic imperative to which Rommel was not privy, opening on 22 June 1941, transformed the nature of the global conflict as indeed did the bombing of Pearl Harbor and the entry of the US into the war on 7 December. Hitler had committed the fatal blunder of engaging in war on two fronts. The invasion of Soviet Russia, which triggered a titanic and bloody struggle, promised to bring relief to the hard-pressed British. In the desert, Auchinleck might feel he had time to garner his resources while, to OKW, the Axis effort was more of a sideshow than ever. With Russia attacked, however, Allied planners had cause to speculate what might happen if, as was anticipated, the Soviets collapsed and the road to the Caucasus and beyond was opened to the Panzers.

Rommel had other problems. Constant RAF attacks and the attentions of Force K[1] from Malta took a fearful toll of Axis shipping. From July to November some fifty vessels, 200,000 tons of shipping, were sunk. Auchinleck had made an impressive Commander-in-Chief in India and Churchill, as ever, had great expectations. The 8th Army, as Western Desert Force was now to be designated, would be led by General Alan Cunningham who had done such notable service in East Africa. The 'Auk' was helped by the stripping of East Africa from his sphere of responsibility and its becoming a separate command.[2] Less favourably, a deployment of *Fliegerkorps II* to Sicily empowered Kesselring to rain destruction upon Malta and ease Rommel's supply crisis. The entry of Japan into the war imposed yet further strain on limited British resources, diverting men and materiel from the Middle East.

Auchinleck immediately found himself constantly badgered by Churchill to launch an offensive. Winston had learnt nothing from past failures. His subsequent exhortation to victory, on the eve of 'Crusader', was stirring stuff:

> For the first time British and Empire troops will meet the Germans with an ample equipment in modern weapons of all kinds. The battle itself will affect the whole course of the war. Now is the time to strike the hardest blow yet struck for final victory, home and freedom. The Desert Army may add a page to history which will rank with Blenheim and with Waterloo. The eyes of all nations are upon you … May God uphold the right![3]

Knowing he would be under considerable pressure, Auchinleck was determined not to give way and court further disaster. In this, he had the support of the CIGS, Sir John Dill who had written privately to him on 26 June: 'The fault was not Wavell's except in so far as he did not resist the pressure from Whitehall with sufficient vigour … *You* should make it quite clear what risks are involved if a course of action is forced upon you which, from the military point of view, is undesirable …'[4] In July the President of the Board of Trade, Oliver Lyttelton, appointed as the War Cabinet's 'man on the spot' in Cairo, took up office and thereby relieved the C in C of a significant burden. He and Auchinleck established an early and cordial relationship. Despite continual badgering, the C in C refused to countenance any attack prior to 1 November. He would not commit till he felt he enjoyed an overall materiel supremacy of at least two to one. Though the Prime Minister might rant, even summoning Auchinleck back to the UK for a further browbeating, he would not be moved. As Churchill later wrote:

> He certainly shook my military advisers with all the detailed arguments he produced. I was myself unconvinced. But General Auchinleck's unquestioned abilities, his powers of exposition, his high, dignified and commanding personality, gave me the feeling that he might after all be right, and that even if wrong he was still the best man.[5]

It was now largely a race for adequate re-supply. With so many ships lost, Rommel's position was distinctly inferior as General Bayerlein confided: '… by the end of September, only a third of the troops and a seventh of the supplies which we needed had arrived'.[6] Rommel, as before, remained obsessed with the reduction of the Tobruk garrison where four Italian divisions, stiffened by three German battalions, were bogged down. Auchinleck was steadily building his strength with both armies looking at mid-November as the start date for further offensive action. Inside Tobruk, Major-General R. M. Scobie commanded 70th Division with an armoured brigade. To land his punch, Auchinleck now had two full army corps. Norrie commanded 30 Corps with 7th Armoured Division, 1st South African Division and 22nd Guards Brigade. 13 Corps, under Godwin-Austen, comprised 4th Indian and the New Zealand Divisions, with two tank brigades. The British could deploy up to 600 tanks with more on the way, a full third more than Rommel who had none in reserve. General Cruewell was in charge of the DAK with 15th Panzer (Neumann-Sylkow[7]) 21st Panzer[8] (von Ravenstein[9]) and 90th Light Division (Summermann[10]).

Throughout September and October the British build-up continued. These new arrivals found themselves heading into a barren and forbidding terrain:

> In some areas sandstorms are blowing and the desert is obscured in pallid, sunlit wooliness. We close the wooden compartment shutters, but the driving dust seeps through, and the atmosphere is like a fog … The desert, omnipresent, so saturates consciousness that it makes the mind as sterile as itself. It's only now you realise how much you normally live through the senses. Here there's nothing for them …'[11]

'Crusader' – High Hopes

'We have attacked in the Desert. Ironic to be fighting for territory we captured last year. I hate to think of so many friends struggling down there in the dust.'[12]

Cunningham's plan was that 30 Corps would attack in the north past Fort Maddalena (where the General's HQ would locate), push on to Gabr Saleh and towards Sidi Rezegh, seeking to pull the Axis armour into a decisive encounter. Once the Panzers had been tamed then the beleaguered garrison in Tobruk would mount a sally to link up. Meanwhile 13 Corps would advance to the south of Sidi Omar and deal with Axis forces manning the frontier zone. The experience of desert warfare would show that success turned upon two key tactical elements; all-arms integration within formations and the need to concentrate armoured forces. Singleness of aim should drive the delivery of force.

The 8th Army commander's plan, and he had no real experience of handling large armoured formations, had compromised the all arms role to satisfy concentration of armour. Fears that the uncovered flank of 13 Corps was unduly exposed were only relieved when an armoured brigade from 30 Corps was detached to provide cover. Cunningham, whose HQ was some eighty miles to the rear of the main action, was a general who believed that once the plan was translated into action he must depend upon his subordinates to harvest the fruits. Rommel, of course, was very much the opposite, a commander who led, in one instance during this battle, literally from the front. This dashing style also had it limitations, leaving the *Panzerarmee* virtually leaderless during a critical period in the fighting.

To support 'Crusader' a substantial infrastructure had been created, 160 miles of pipe had been laid, seven pumping stations and nine reservoirs constructed. All of this vast logistical effort was being fed in to win ground no one would normally have deemed worth fighting over, yet now the destiny of the warring nations was being hammered out in this barren waste. On 16/17 November, as formations of 8th Army advanced to their start lines, something like 100,000 men, 600 tanks and some 5,000 support vehicles were on the move.[13] Any brigade with 1,000 vehicles in its train, allowing for no more then 10 per mile, would have a tail nearly 100 miles in length, a vast, slow, choking caravanserai, consuming terrific quantities of fuel at an alarming rate. Vehicles would also break down, experience punctures, overheat; a planner's nightmare! Howard Kippenburger, then a battalion commander recalled:

> This great approach march will always be remembered by those who took part in it though the details are vague in memory. The whole Eight Army, Seventh Armoured Division, First South African Division, and the Second New Zealand and Fourth Indian Divisions moved westwards in an enormous column, the armour leading. The army moved south of Sidi Barrani, past the desolate Italian camps of the previous year, along the plateau south of the great escarpment, through the frontier wire into Libya …[14]

Ahead of the main thrust, on the night on 13/14 November a daring, if ill-starred, raid had been launched by 11th Commando under Lieutenant-Colonel Keyes, assisted by the experienced Colonel Laycock. Among the force objectives was an assault on Rommel's HQ which, in bald terms, equalled an assassination attempt. The raid failed and few survivors made it back to Allied lines. Countess Ranfurly recorded the news on 21 November: 'Bob Laycock's Commandos have raided Rommel's headquarters and it is rumoured that Geoffrey Keyes was killed and Bob is missing. By ill luck Rommel was away and so escaped capture or worse.'[15]

'Crusader' burst across the frontier on 18 November and sped forwards in a kind of dummy war; opposition was minimal and no immediate counter-punch developed. Rommel was still fixated on the impudent garrison of Tobruk and dismissed the offensive as a probing raid. He himself had earlier instigated just such a reconnaissance in force, 'Midsummer Night's Dream', to glean what he might of Auchinleck's intentions. By evening, 7th Armoured Brigade had reached Gabr Saleh, thrusting virtually unopposed. The Fox had been humbugged but, ironically, his very inertia had robbed Cunningham of the decisive clash of armour his plan demanded. 'The morning's reports strengthened General Cruewell's view that a British offensive was developing. Rommel, however, would have none of it …'[16]

Disconcerted, Cunningham proposed, on the second day, to split his armoured forces and seek out the foe. By now the Fox was alert and began to concentrate his own armour for a riposte. Gott, at this point commanding 7th Armoured Division, expressed the view that the moment was now ripe for a break-out from Tobruk. This was contrary to the previous planned assertion that the Panzers must first be humbled. Nonetheless, Cunningham agreed and the move was planned for morning on 21 November. Meanwhile, armoured units were colliding piecemeal in the tanker's equivalent of a 'soldier's battle'. Not the precise, staff-college business of ordered formations but a swirling, dust shrouded, grinding melee. Captain Sean Fielding vividly recalled: 'Round and about are many Italian tanks and some of ours … All very badly shot up and some with their dead still in them. The oddest details remain in one's mind. The commander of one Wop tank, lying dead beside his machine, had his fingers crossed; and he had absurdly small feet cased in new boots …'[17]

Despite the ferocity of these initial exchanges, the main armoured forces of both sides had yet to engage. Cunningham, nonetheless, appears to have considered that a major engagement had indeed occurred and was disposed to believe over-optimistic assessments of enemy losses.[18] Not only were these wildly exaggerated but DAK was still far more accomplished at retrieving damaged machines from the field and restoring them to battle-worthy. Reassured, Cunningham gave the order for the Tobruk break-out, codenamed 'Pop'. This threw into sharp relief the need to hold the tactically significant ridge at Sidi Rezegh which lay between Gabr Saleh and the town. This otherwise unremarkable feature would now become a boiling cauldron.

Rommel was aware of the significance of Sidi Rezegh, a mere twelve miles from the beleaguered citadel. More and more Axis armour was fed in as the battle for the ridge intensified, drawing in much of 8th Army's own tanks. The fighting was close and frightful, 7th Hussars were decimated while Jock Campbell performed prodigies of valour which earned him his well-merited VC. As tanks surged around the disputed higher ground that ring of Axis forces besieging the port remained unbroken: 'The sortie from Tobruk was opposed partly by Germans, and not entirely by Italians as had been expected. The enemy were well dug in behind wire and mines. They resisted stubbornly and brought down intense artillery and machine-gun fire …'[19]

Despite the fact that by evening on the 21st the break-out had been contained, Cunningham remained buoyant and Auchinleck was sending confident cables to London: 'It is authoritatively stated that the Libyan battle, which was at its height this afternoon, is going extremely well. The proportion of Axis tank casualties to British is authoritatively put at three to one. General Rommel, the German commander, is trying to break through, but his situation is becoming more unfavourable …'[20]

Though Rommel had been obliged to divide his available forces, he was far from defeated. Even as Churchill was drafting a victory address the Fox struck back on the

22nd, sending his Panzers in a flanking arc to strike at Sidi Rezegh from the west. This manoeuvre netted tactical gains and various support units were overrun. Throughout the next day fighting raged unabated, a rough and savage collision of armoured leviathans, wheeling and blazing. Fritz Bayerlein described the action from an Axis perspective:

> Guns of all kinds and sizes laid a curtain of fire in front of the attacking tanks and there seemed almost no hope of making any progress in the face of this fire-spewing barrier. Tank after tank split open in the hail of shells. Our entire artillery had to be thrown in to silence the enemy guns one by one. However, by the late afternoon we had managed to punch a few holes in the front. The tank attack moved forward again and tank duels of tremendous intensity developed deep in the battlefield. In fluctuating fighting, tank against tank, tank against gun or anti-tank nest, sometimes in frontal, sometimes in flank-ing assault, using every trick of mobile warfare and tank tactics, the enemy was finally forced back into a confined area.[21]

Tanks were shot to pieces, other simply broke down; both sides suffered loss and wrecks littered the scarred waste like primeval skeletons. The New Zealanders suffered grievous loss, though less than the South Africans. Jock Campbell was still on hand to rally, exhort and lead but Allies losses were significant, there was no victory in sight.

> The fighting about Tobruk and Sidi Rezegh which began on 21st November, and lasted with few pauses for three days, was the fiercest yet seen in the desert. Round Sidi Rezegh airfield in particular the action was unbelievably confused, and the rapid changes in the situation, the smoke and the dust, the sudden appearances of tanks first from one direction and then from another, made great demands of the junior leaders. They certainly did not fail …[22]

One Allied witness likened the great swirling melee to:

> … a naval battle, something of a medieval cavalry charge, but all speeded up madly as you might speed up a cinema film … Inside that frantic jumble, tanks were duelling with tanks in running, almost hand to hand fights, firing nearly point blank, twisting, dodging, sprinting with screaming treads and whining engines that rose to a shriek as they changed gear. As each new tank loomed up ahead gunners were swinging the muzzles of their guns automatically, eyes strained behind their goggles, fighting through the smoke and dust to discriminate friend from foe …[23]

With that daring and tactical insight which would guarantee the endurance of his legend, Rommel planned a counterstroke of breathtaking audacity, one which sent shudders through his more cautious subordinates. He had resolved to draw off some of his forces from the furnace of Sidi Rezegh and strike towards Egypt. This was at the very moment Cunningham was suffering something of a personal crisis. On the 23rd, alarmed by the heavy losses particularly in armour, he had broached the possibility of breaking off the action and retreating. This was not something the 'Auk' was prepared to countenance. By next day the C in C had decided to remove his 8h Army commander and appoint Ritchie in his stead. Now Rommel was leading his spearhead eastwards, leading very much from the front, the epitome of daring and gallantry, if not perhaps of prudence. Under his personal command he led the remnants of 15th Panzer and Ariete. The blow threatened to sever 30 Corps line of retreat and swept through rear echelons like the grim reaper. Cruewell, his reservations dismissed, was ordered to send 21st Panzer to drive 13 Corps back onto the web of frontier minefields. For both sides this was to be the crisis.

'Crusader' – Ritchie Takes Command

In his memoir of the desert war ... Douglas[24] used what seemed to be the perfect literal metaphor of protection, the belly of a Crusader tank ... That was his home ... the limited apprehension of the world that a moving tank allows. He likens the view to that rendered by 'a camera obscura or a silent film ... Men shout, vehicles move, aeroplanes fly over; and all soundlessly, the noise of the tank being continuous perhaps for hours on end, the effect is of silence ... an illimitably strange land, quite unrelated to real life. The illusion is breached when the crew halt beside a burnt out shell and the scorched remains of its occupants'.[25]

Whether this [Rommel's gambit] was a good decision is an interesting point. There can be no doubt that the moment had come to exploit the success gained around Sidi Rezegh; the question was how to do it. Cruewell on the other hand, saw a chance of wiping out the British armoured force altogether ... But when Cruewell made his report on the morning of 24th November it must have seemed to Rommel that although the British armour could not be written off it could be disregarded for the time being.[26]

Auchinleck, despite the seriousness of the situation, did not lose his nerve and Rommel's sweeping gambit soon ran into difficulties. Ariete could not get past the South Africans while 21st Panzer could make no headway against 4th Indian Division. Freyberg and the New Zealanders were fighting hard for Tobruk though, as the New Zealand Official History confirms, their casualties were high:

There was an enormous number of dead and wounded all over the battlefield. A significant feature was the sight of many men who had been hit by solid shot of anti-tank guns, fired at point blank range. These projectiles had torn large portions of flesh from the bodies of their unfortunate victims and it would be hard to imagine a more unpleasant sight or a more heavily contested battlefield.[27]

During the Crusader fighting one factor which had told significantly in favour of the British was air superiority. The Desert Air Force was flying effective sorties against Axis ground forces, denying Rommel the comfort of 'flying artillery' which had shielded and aided previous operations. The DAK diary for 25 November reflects a mounting frustration: 'Continuous heavy raids in the Sidi Omar area. Heavy losses among our troops. Where are the German fighters?'[28] Within 8th Army, news of Cunningham's replacement produced no outpourings of grief. Robert Crisp[29] recorded:

> General Cunningham had been relieved of the command of the Eighth Army and had been replaced by General Ritchie. This was a shock to all of us, but not really a surprise. Even right down at the bottom of the ladder, it was impossible not to be aware of the absence of firm direction and purpose from above. Everybody welcomed the change as the beginning of an era of greater decisiveness. Nobody had ever heard of Ritchie.[30]

On 27 November, union with 70th Division was effected, the heroic garrison finally relieved. British armoured forces at Sidi Rezegh, despite their fearful pounding, were reorganising and still very much in the fight. Rommel's units by contrast were equally battered but now dispersed and vulnerable. At DAK Headquarters Colonel Westphal had already assumed responsibility for the recall of 21st Panzer, Rommel now out of touch, though, on flying back that evening he tacitly approved and began drawing back 15th Panzer as well.

> So ended General Rommel's spectacular stroke. Without compelling the British to alter their plans it had caused some temporary embarrassment and local confusion. It failed completely in its purpose of relieving the frontier troops. The Germans lost at least thirty of their hundred tanks, while the British armour was given a chance to refit – a chance of which good use was made.[31]

His priority now was to try and re-establish the ring around Tobruk. From 28 November, there was more savage combat around El Duda, Belhammed and Sidi Rezegh. Ground was taken, lost and retaken; both sides sustained further, heavy losses. As November drew to a close, German armour was battering the remnant of the New Zealanders, unsupported by Allied tanks. Freyberg was pushed back, his division's casualties dreadful, Tobruk was again encircled. The battle was by now one of attrition, a fight in which the Allies were better placed but Rommel was not yet ready to withdraw. On 2 December he threw his battered formations back into the fight for a further five days of murderous intensity. An officer of 3rd RTR recalled the numbing drain of constant battle:

> I can truthfully say that none of us had more than the vaguest idea where we were from day to day and hour to hour, or what was happening either to our own forces or the enemy's ... There was no such thing as advance and retreat. We roared off to areas of threat or engagement depending on the urgency of the information. We chased mirages and were chased by mirages. Every few hours a landmark of a name would punch our memories, with an elusive familiarity, and we would recall a forgotten early incident or a battle fought there days before that was now part of a past so near in time but so distant in event.[32]

In the relative comfort and security of the Delta, unheard of places such as Sidi Rezegh seemed very distant and the actions there confusing in the extreme: 'A big tank battle is raging in the Desert near Sidi Rezegh. I think the Sherwood Rangers may be involved. Perhaps, after all, I am lucky that Dan is a prisoner and not in the midst of this turmoil … I am afraid we are not yet as well armed as the Germans – their Mark 3 and 4 guns are excellent and they have the awful 88mm gun.'[33]

The end of November was a crucial time: 'Crusader' was a long way from being over, but an important stage had been reached: The British were able to introduce fresh troops and the enemy was not.'[34]

By 7 December the pace of attrition had forced Rommel to recognise the need for a withdrawal. Both sides continued to incur casualties but the Allies could replenish at a far faster rate. They had greater reserves, this steady grinding down was not a fight DAK could win. Consequently, Rommel proposed to retire upon a fixed, defensive line running south from Gazala. The British, scenting victory, swooped after, hard upon the heels of the retreating Axis. By the 16th a further retirement became expedient and by 22 December, as 1941 drew to a close, the Axis forces had fallen back as far as Beda Fomm and Antelat. Further withdrawals, firstly to Agedabia and finally El Agheila followed and, though constantly harassed, the rearguard provided an effective screen. By now both sides were equally exhausted.

Swings of the Pendulum

'Crusader' was a British victory, in that Tobruk was relieved, the enemy was driven from Cyrenaica with heavy losses, and all the Axis troops holding positions on the Egyptian frontier were destroyed or captured. This all took longer than expected, however, and in doing it the British exhausted themselves.'[35] Winter quarters in the Western Desert were generally disagreeable:

> Flies produced more casualties than the Germans. It is impossible to describe, without suspicion of exaggeration, how thickly they used to surround us. Most of us ate a meal with a handkerchief or piece of paper in one hand and our food in the other. While we tried to get the food to our mouths, free from flies, we waved the other hand about wildly; even so we ate many hundreds of flies. They settled on food like a cloud and no amount of waving about disturbed them. They could clean jam and butter from a slice of bread much quicker than we could eat it … it can be realised how serious the menace of flies was considered when I say that, even in remote parts of the Desert, one came across notices saying 'Kill that fly, or he will kill you'.[36]

The pendulum had indeed swung but this placed fresh difficulties in the path of 8th Army. As a direct result of this strategic shift, 8th Army was that much further away from it supply base and its communications were that much more attenuated. Conversely, the army which had retreated was so much closer to its own base, thus supply and replenishment was that much easier. Technically, 8th Army had won the day and 'Crusader' ranks as a British victory. It was dearly bought. Allied losses in killed wounded and missing, were in the region of 18,000, while the Axis lost 20,000 more. Both lost heavily in tanks and guns. 'Thus the British had succeeded in their object of clearing Cyrenaica of the enemy, though not by means of a rapid stroke, as had been planned, but only after a long and costly struggle which consumed so many of their resources that by the time they reached the western end of Cyrenaica their blow was spent.'[37]

Though the Desert Air Force had been in the ascendant throughout, ground to air cooperation was by no means yet perfected: 'British superiority in the air made the failure to make full use of the day-bombers all the more disappointing.'[38] Similarly DAK did not enjoy close support and cooperation from the *Luftwaffe*: '… contrary to an impression widely held at the time, the enemy did not have a highly organised and efficient system of army/air cooperation; the British had at least laid the foundations of a system and were bent on making it work although they had not yet overcome all of the difficulties.'[39]

Cyrenaica was indeed re-taken but, in the Far East, there had been serious reverses; both *Prince of Wales* and *Repulse* had been lost to Japanese air attack. The Russians had been defeated in a series of epic *Kesselschlact* or Cauldron battles and the Germans were at the gates of Moscow. Malta was under tremendous pressure and Rommel's prospects of adequate re-supply that much brighter. The Desert Fox was again restive and not intending to sit on the defensive. On 17 January he confided in his daily letter home: 'The situation is developing to our advantage … and I'm full of plans that I daren't say anything about round here. They'd think me crazy. But I'm not; I simply see a bit further than they do. But you know me.'[40]

6

'Msus Stakes' & 'Gazala Gallop': January 1942 – June 1942

But by a day's travelling you reach a new world
The vegetation is of iron
Dead tanks, gun barrels split like celery
The metal brambles have no flowers or berries
And there are all sorts of manure, you can imagine
The dead themselves, their boots, clothes and possessions
Clinging to the ground, a man with no head
Has a packet of chocolate and a souvenir of Tripoli.

Keith Douglas

In those moments in between of what is
And what was meant to be.
There in silence you will find me.
A faceless face, an unknown name.
The unknown soldier, my simple grave.
There friends and family came not visiting.
There my widow could not weep for me.

In life I was not alone.
In life, I was not unknown.
I had a wife, a son, a home.

The Unknown Soldier by Samantha Kelly

The Fox & the Pendulum

On the surface, it appeared that the 'Crusader' battles had resulted in a significant victory for 8th Army but this was largely illusory and the thinning of British dispositions left the gains in Cyrenaica, so dearly won, again at hazard. Auchinleck was proceeding to plan 'Acrobat' – a further attack upon the remaining Axis hold on Tripolitania. Strung out in

winter quarters the army had few fixed defences and penny packet garrisons; a doleful lack
of concentration. The 7th Armoured Division had been withdrawn for a much needed refit
and 1st Armoured, who lacked their fellow tankers battlefield experience, were put in to
plug the gap. Supply lines were tenuous and inadequate, plus there remained the problem
of Malta. 8th Army required the island fortress still in British hands to continue the fight
but, to protect Malta, needed to maintain forward aerodromes in Cyrenaica.

> To supply the 13th Corps and its attached troops … required some 1,400 tons [of supplies]
> a day. The average daily amounts received at Tobruk by sea and by lorry convoys … togeth-
> er came to 1,150 tons … there was thus a shortfall of some 250 tons on daily needs alone …
> The fact is the administrative resources of 8th Army were now stretched to the limit.[1]

Rommel had also noted these deficiencies and a subtle shift in the balance of resources
provided him with an opportunity which he, as arch-opportunist, was not about to ignore:
'… At a staff conference held on 12th January his senior intelligence officer, Major F. W.
von Mellenthin, predicted that for the next fortnight the Axis forces would be slightly
stronger than the British immediately opposed to them.'[2] On 21 January, the Desert Fox
threw two strong columns into an attack, one advancing along the coast road, the other
swinging in a flanking arc, north of Wadi el Faregh. Caught off-guard and dispersed,
British units began to fall back. General Ritchie was, at this time, far to the rear in Cairo
and disposed to regard these moves as nothing more than a raid or reconnaissance in force.
He and Auchinleck did not detect the tremors of disquiet that commanders on the ground
were experiencing. Early cables suggested the situation might be ripe for a strong riposte.

It has been said of military matters that 'too often the capacity to advance is identified
with the desirability of advancing'.[3] Never was this truer than in the Desert War and
the reality was that Rommel had seized and was maintaining the initiative. DAK had
also perfected its offensive tactics as Panzer officer Heinz Schmidt recorded: '… With
our twelve anti-tank guns we leap-frogged from one vantage point to another, while our
panzers, stationary and hull-down, if possible, provided protective fire. Then we would
establish ourselves to give them protective fire while they swept on again …'[4]

By the 24th the 'Auk' was sending signals in an altogether more sober tone. Rommel
was still advancing, his own supply difficulties notwithstanding. When one officer had the
nerve to point out fuel stocks were critical, he received the curt advice: 'Well go and get it
[fuel] from the British'. Within a day there were plans to evacuate Benghazi, producing
a rather plaintive cry from Whitehall: '… why should they all be off so quickly?'[5] Both
Ritchie and Auchinleck flew to the front but the local commanders, their instincts more
finely tuned, were preparing for withdrawal. 4th Indian Division was pulling out from
Benghazi as 1st Armoured prepared to regroup near Mechili.

Swift as a terrier, Rommel, alerted by wireless intercepts, planned a double-headed
thrust. One pincer swept along the coast road while the second, the Fox in the lead, pushed
over higher ground to sweep around and come upon the port from the south-east. A
dummy lunge toward Mechili was intended to fool Ritchie and succeeded. He dispatched
his armour leaving Benghazi exposed. General Tuker, commanding 4th Indian Division,

whose appreciation of the unfolding tactical situation jibed with that of his superiors, lamented: 'We rang Army – and learnt to our consternation that the whole of the eastern flank had gone off on a wild goose chase after a phantom force of enemy armour falsely reported to be moving on Mechili … Dispersion, dispersion, dispersion.'[6]

Von Mellenthin, commenting on the effectiveness of the panzer tactics and the speed of the British withdrawals, observed scathingly: 'the pursuit attained a speed of fifteen miles an hour and the British fled madly over the desert in one of the most extraordinary routs of the war'.[7] If Ritchie was groping in the fog of war thrown up by his brilliant opponent, Rommel himself faced other enemies much nearer home. General Bastico had become alarmed because the limited spoiling attack, to which he had agreed, was turning into a full-blown offensive of which he strongly disapproved. He signalled his fears to *Comando Supremo* and asked that General Rommel should be made to take a more realistic view. This brought Cavallero to Rommel's Headquarters on 23 January, accompanied by Field-Marshal Kesselring and bearing a directive from Mussolini. In this it was stated that there was 'no immediate prospect of sending supplies and reinforcements to Africa in the face of present British naval and air opposition'.[8]

In short, Rommel was to halt further attacks and establish a defensive position. Despite the weight of the delegation ranged against him, he demurred and reminded his superiors that only the Führer himself could apply restraint. Besides, as he contemptuously added, most of the fighting would be done by Germans. Kesselring, who was inclined to back Cavallero and was no particular admirer of Rommel, could not move the General and the party were sent packing, Smiling Albert now 'growling' in frustration.

Meanwhile, and without armour, Tuker could not maintain a viable defence and quite rightly withdrew. 7th Indian Brigade was garrisoning the port while the remainder of the division was holding a line east of Barce. These troops encountered the sweeping arm of Rommel's flanking move in a series of sharp encounters and escaped the net only with difficulty. Sergeant Grey DCM, MM of the Cameron Highlanders found himself in the thick of the confused fighting, at one point made prisoner. His captors, including a German and an Italian officer, expected him to lead them to his comrades:

… There seemed no alternative, so I pointed to my left … I started off up the hill, with the officers on either side and, stumbling in the dark, managed to bring my platoon well on to my flank. Then I aimed for their position, which I could just distinguish in the dark. I heard a Jock say, 'Here the b*****s come.' Then the Italian said: 'Shout to them to surrender!' So I shouted: 'McGeough, McGeough!' (I knew he was a good shot), got within ten yards of them, shouted 'Shoot!' and fell flat. The boys shot and got the German in the head and the Italian in the stomach.[9]

On 29 January Rommel rode triumphantly into Benghazi while the 8th Army scattered back to a defensive position astride the line from Gazala in the north to Bir Hacheim: '… back in fact to the very place where, only seven weeks before, General Rommel had broken away because he judged the tactical balance to be against him.'[10] Early in February, Godwin-Austen, commanding 13 Corps asked to be relieved. He considered Ritchie's intermeddling in his decisions had eroded his position to an intolerable degree. This may have left a bitter taste as the corps commander had likely had his finger more firmly on the pulse than his superior. This need not imply that all was entirely well 'on the other side of the wire':

> ... The [Axis] chain of command creaked from time to time, but the firm hand of general Rommel made up for its many weaknesses. He was not the commander in chief, it is true, but he was emphatically the man whose views mattered, for he did what he felt to be militarily right in spite of the frequent protests of his superior, General Bastico. And then, having made up his own mind on the policy, he had a habit of becoming a tactical leader, and by taking command personally at the most important spot, ensuring that his ideas were carried out.[11]

Rommel's own post mortem on the fighting up till early February, forming a portion of his official report, while allowing for some artful editing, contains a very fair assessment of British shortcomings:

> The assembly of all the forces for the autumn offensive was cleverly concealed (wireless deception was also used) and was favoured by the weather. The attack therefore came as a complete surprise, but although the British command showed skill and prudence in preparing the offensive they were less successful when it came to carrying it out. Disregarding the fundamental principle of employing all available forces at the most critical point ... Never anywhere at any time during the fighting in Libya did the British High Command concentrate all its available forces at the decisive point ... British troops fought well on the whole though they never attained the same impetus as the Germans when attacking ... The military result was that the British 8th Army was so severely beaten that it was incapable of further large-scale operations for months afterwards.[12]

Despite being penned by the enemy this was by no means an overly-harsh assessment. Throughout the 'Msus Stakes' the 8th Army had been hamstrung by inaccurate intelligence, uncertainties of supply, inadequate training and a total lack of flexibility. The retreat resulted in the loss of 1,400 men, 70 tanks and 40 guns.[13] Operation 'Acrobat' was now a distant dream and Malta was weakened by the loss of forward airfields. This reverse came at a singularly bad moment for the War Cabinet. It is easy to criticise Churchill for his abrasive and often unreasonable attitude, yet the burden he carried was a mighty one. The entry of the US into the war had yet to make an impact while the crisis in the Far East deepened with Singapore threatened. Malta was under terrific pressure and plans for 'Gymnast' – joint Anglo-American landings to capture French North African colonies had to be shelved. After a week's siege the unthinkable happened and Singapore fell, a savage blow.

General Sir Alan Brooke, now CIGS confided to his journal: '... It was his [Churchill's] darkest hour ... The weight of his burden would have crushed any other man'.[14] By late February, Brooke was warning that Malta's position was extremely precarious and the outcome doubtful, 'unless we could recapture Benghazi before May at the very latest'.[15] On 29 January, Auchinleck had sent a cautious if not disingenuous cable: 'It must be admitted that the enemy has succeeded beyond his expectations and mine and that his tactics have been skilful and bold.'[16] His next communication, a bare 24 hours later, sounded a rather more dolorous note: 'I am reluctantly compelled to [the] conclusion that to meet German armoured forces with any reasonable hope of decisive success our armoured forces, as at present equipped, and led must have at least two to one superiority.'[17]

This was not at all what the War Cabinet wished to hear. Rommel, on the other hand, appeared to have near magic insight, the Nelsonian 'touch and take'. He displayed the remarkable ability to convert limited tactical successes into major gains. His policy of leading from the front, though fraught with risks, had so far paid handsome dividends. Even though 8th Army command might be depressing the War Cabinet with what appeared to be excessive caution, Auchinleck and Ritchie were if anything understating British weaknesses. The policy of senior officers to lead from a distance placed a greater burden on corps and divisional commanders. When the latter painted a sombre picture of the true state of their units, these assessments, though valid, were hardly ever greeted with rapture. Messervy, when reporting his tanks to be in far worse state than Ritchie was wont to assume, felt his observations considered 'subversive'.[18] Tuker was no less outspoken: '... You will notice also that the principle of security was neglected, for nowhere west of Tobruk was there a firm base on which 13 Corps could fall back, or behind which it could be ready for a counter-offensive'.[19]

The Gazala Line

On 26 February, the Prime Minister sent a peevish telegram to the C in C Middle East: 'According to our figures, you have substantial superiority in the air, in armour and in other forces ... The supply of Malta is causing us increasing anxiety ... Pray let me hear from you.'[20] To afford the island fortress much needed relief, Whitehall needed an offensive in mid-March or early April at the latest. Auchinleck would not agree a date before the middle part of May. Lyttelton had meanwhile returned to England to become Minister of Production, his successor as Minister of State in Cairo was the Australian Richard Casey. A part of Auchinleck's difficulties was the mechanical inferiority of his tanks. Simply to have more machines than your opponent was of no consequence if those you had were unreliable. British tanks, particularly the Crusader, were markedly outclassed by German models and mechanically unsound to boot. Lyttelton was acutely aware of these shortcomings:

> On top of this mechanical failure must be reckoned the superior gun position of the German tanks ... the Germans had developed a better form of tactic in the employment of their armoured formations; their tanks moved slowly from position to position waiting till they had discovered the location of our artillery and anti-tank weapons ... They kept out of range of the latter and suffered little damage from the former.[21]

Churchill, though he railed at the bad designs, continued to press Auchinleck for an early offensive and the 'Auk', to his credit, remained obdurate. A snappish exchange of cables ensued: 'We consider [3 March] that an attempt to drive the Germans out of Cyrenaica in the next few weeks is not only imperative for the safety of Malta on which so much depends, but holds out the only hope of fighting a battle while the enemy is still comparatively weak …'[22] 'We are agreed [8 March] that in spite of the risks you mention you would be right to attack the enemy and fight a major battle.'[23]

When the Auk refused to bend and refused to hazard Egypt to succour Malta, he was summarily ordered home. He demurred, leaving Churchill with the choice of either 'backing him or sacking him'. Brooke and other wise counsels prevailed against the latter course and Auchinleck won his breathing space. Clement Attlee had been nominated to chair an enquiry into the mechanical defects of the British tanks which found the C in C's concerns fully justified. The model had been rushed into production with expediency put ahead of thoroughness. The Prime Minister's personal emissaries, Sir Stafford Cripps and General Sir Archibald Nye, vice CIGS, were minded to side with Auchinleck. Their representations earned a sarcastic reply:

I have heard from the Lord Privy Seal [Cripps]. I do not wonder everything was so pleasant, considering you seem to have accepted everything they said, and all _we_ have got to accept is the probable loss of Malta and the army standing idle, while the Russians are resisting the German counter-stroke desperately, and while the enemy is reinforcing himself in Libya faster than are we.[24]

Both Churchill and Auchinleck were right. The pressure on Malta was dreadful and the Russians were in deep difficulties, but for 8th Army to have mounted a hasty and ill-prepared assault would have been disastrous. Nye was not to be browbeaten either and the C in C had another eminent and persuasive ally in Brooke, who could argue his case in person. With grudging reluctance, Churchill was persuaded to agree to a date of 15 May as the earliest upon which an assault could be launched. Rommel was also subject to political restraint. Hitler and Mussolini held a conference in April when the strategy for Axis moves in North Africa was on the agenda. It was concluded that DAK should launch an attack on the Gazala Line at the earliest opportunity. So far so good, but this was to be a limited offensive, neither dictator would let the Fox completely slip the leash. Once the line was breached and, as a major secondary objective Tobruk re-captured, then the attack would be held till Malta was dealt with and the overall supply situation improved.

In Directive 32 Hitler had already set out a strategic vision for the erosion of the British position by a combined Axis advance through Libya, Bulgaria and the Caucasus. Von Brauchitsch[25] advocated the cautious line that operations in the Mediterranean and Western Desert should be more closely coordinated and Malta remained the key objective. British shipping had suffered considerable loss in the winter months, _Ark Royal_ had been torpedoed and sunk in November while, between February and May 1942, five destroyers, six supply vessels and a hospital ship had succumbed to air and U-Boat attacks.[26]

Auchinleck quickly found that he could not hope to meet his own deadline of mid-May. Mid-June looked possible but a delay till August could not be fully discounted.

Even Brooke found it difficult to maintain his dogged defence and his diary recounts an increasing frustration. Churchill was at his most venomous. A further, highly acrimonious exchange of cables followed but the C in C refused to be pushed on the basis Malta's peril justified the risk. Quite rightly, his attention was focused on defence of the Delta. Rommel, however, was about to decide the matter as he planned his attack for 26 May. Auchinleck was aware of his opponent's intention in terms of an offensive but not as to how and where he planned to deliver the main blow. The 8th Army was thus braced to expect an attack in the centre with a diversion to the south. British armour was deployed accordingly.

Rommel, disobligingly, intended his main assault to be directed in the south swinging on the pivot of Bir Hacheim, which he expected to overcome without undue difficulty. The attacks in the centre and north would, in the case of the former, be secondary and, in the latter instance, a mere feint. The Fox himself would lead the main armoured thrust in the south which would, having dealt with the Free French at Bir Hacheim, sweep around behind 8th Army and begin rolling up the line. Italian armour would attempt to batter through British minefields in the centre while Cruewell would command joint infantry forces in the north. General Tuker's lament over wide dispersion of Allied forces was well uttered but no heed had been taken. Ritchie's deployments were piecemeal and ill-considered. In the north 13 Corps was spread in a series of defensive 'boxes' with 30 Corps to the south disposed by brigades together with the bulk of available armour. Auchinleck, in all fairness, was not unaware of the current failures in British tactical doctrine:

> The experience of the winter fighting had taught General Auchinleck to decide upon two important changes in the organisation of the army. It was not only the enemy who had noticed that the British armour, artillery and infantry had often been unsuccessful in concerting their action on the battlefield. General Auchinleck accordingly made up his mind 'to associate the three arms more closely at all times and in all places'. He thought that the British type of armoured division would be better balanced if it had less armour and more infantry – like a German *Panzer* Division. In future, therefore, an armoured division would consist basically of one armoured brigade group and one motor brigade group. The former would contain three tank regiments, one motor battalion, and a regiment of field and anti-tank guns, and the latter three motor battalions and a similar artillery regiment. In addition, both types of brigade group would include light anti-aircraft artillery, engineers, and administrative units. The Army tank brigades, each of three regiments of 'I' tanks, would not form part of a division, but would continue to be allotted as the situation demanded.[27]

The C in C had also been pondering on the composition of brigade groups. He concluded that the various arms should be welded together on a permanent basis. Thus, the infantry division would comprise three brigade groups, each of three battalions with a regiment of field and anti-tank artillery with light AA guns, engineers and rear echelon.[28] In qualitative terms the British armour was still deficient. A new version of the Crusader tank had thicker frontal armour but was still plagued by reliability problems.[29] The German armour had also had the benefit of a makeover with improved case-hardened frontal protection. Only the US Stuart (dubbed 'Honey' by the British) with its 37mm gun could fire capped ammunition yet the newest variant of the PzKw III was fitted with a long, highly effective, 50cm gun. The under-gunned Allied tanks were at least now being reinforced by a new American model, the M3 Grant which carried a 75mm sponson mounted gun capable of firing both HE and AP.[30]

Rommel's offensive and the Battle of Gazala, dubbed 'the Gazala Stakes' by 8th Army, can be divided into three phases: (1) Rommel launches his flank attack, 26–29 May, attempting to overrun British defences from behind; (2) fighting in the 'Cauldron' – Rommel tries to re-supply and consolidate his forces and (3) the reduction of Bir Hacheim, and the pounding of British armour 11–13 June, followed by withdrawal from the Gazala line. A fourth and final phase of this battle was the subsequent storming of Tobruk. In the fighting 100,000 Allied troops, 849 tanks and 604 planes would face some 90,000 Axis with 561 tanks, (228 of which were of the inferior Italian sort) and 504 aircraft.

Bir Hacheim, the pivot upon which the Axis southerly attack was to turn, proved a far tougher nut than Rommel had anticipated. General Koenig's Free French put up a spirited and resilient defence. The task of battering these defences into submission was entrusted to Ariete Division. Nonetheless, the Panzers achieved a series of local successes, swatting a succession of ill-coordinated Allied units. By mid-morning they had swept over Messervy's HQ, netting the general and his staff. Though he soon made good his escape, the resultant confusion was disastrous. Rommel's two more northerly assaults both failed to break in stalled against minefields and determined resistance. The new Grant tanks and heavier punch of the 6-pounder AT guns made their presence felt. Failure to eliminate Bir Hacheim spoilt the smooth execution of his plan, supply lines were attenuated, vulnerable to marauding columns of light armour and armoured cars.

Despite the Axis potentially exposed position, Ritchie failed to concentrate his armour, an error which amazed his more nimble opponent: 'Ritchie had thrown his armour into the battle piecemeal and had thus given us the chance engaging them on each separate occasion with just about enough of our own tanks. This dispersal of the British armoured brigades was incomprehensible.'[31] Many of the Allied tank officers had approached this battle with far greater confidence than before believing the improved firepower of their Grants would even the odds. Colonel G. P. B Roberts, leading 3rd RTR described the fighting which subsequently took place south of El Adem: 'There they are – more than a hundred. Yes, twenty in the first line, and there are six, no eight lines, and more behind that in the distance; a whole ruddy Panzer Division is quite obviously in front of us. Damn it. This was not the plan at all – where the hell are the rest of the Brigade.'[32] Despite the odds the 75mm gun did good service in the melee: '75 gunner, enemy tank straight ahead receiving no attention – engage … Good shot that got him – same again.'[33]

Thrown in piecemeal fashion, 2nd and 22nd Armoured Brigades, despite gallant and costly efforts, were insufficient to stem the onslaught. DAK was now within an area known as the 'Knightsbridge' Box. British command failures permitted Rommel, whose position hemmed by 'mine marshes' and Bir Hacheim could and should have been dire, to concentrate his forces. During the 29th this consolidation proceeded with panzers massing between the Sidra and Aslagh Ridges, an inconspicuous span of barren desert soon to be dubbed, and with good reason, as the Cauldron.

The Cauldron

For Rommel this was the crisis. His armour was backed onto the British mine marsh, his support from the west had yet to penetrate. Bir Hacheim was not subdued and the supply situation critical. Resolute and concentrated attacks by properly directed British armour with artillery and infantry supports could have achieved success but no such concentration seemed possible. Instead, penny packet assaults without the necessary guns and men were fed in to the mincer. The Germans too suffered loss, senior officers such as Generals Gause and Westphal were wounded and Cruewell himself, recognised by both sides as a 'brave and energetic' leader, was captured on 29 May when his Storch spotter was shot down.

On 30 May, 150th Brigade, left horribly exposed, was overrun: 'Help did not arrive. At first light on 1 June the enemy attacked from all sides, and platoon by platoon the brigade was overrun and captured. The last sub-unit to go down was believed to be the platoon of the 5th Green Howards commanded by Captain Bert Dennis.'[34] It was not till 1–2 June that Ritchie decided to storm the Cauldron. As the Official History tersely records: '…British operations on the night of 1/2 June were a fiasco'.[35] The subsequent attack put in before dawn on the 5th – Operation 'Aberdeen' was a tragedy. 7th Armoured and 5th Indian Division stormed their objectives only to find they had missed the enemy and landed a blow in the air: '… evil consequences were to follow quickly'.[36] Exposed to relentless counter-attacks, several regiments and their supporting guns were decimated.

When the minefield barrier was finally breached and Axis support came through, Bir Hacheim was further isolated, pressure ratcheted to an irresistible level. On 9 June, the survivors, battered but unbowed, fought their way clear of the trap. Of the 3,600 who had begun the fight 2,700 escaped: 'The defence of Bir Hacheim had achieved several purposes. At the outset it had made longer and more difficult the enemy's temporary supply route; it had caused him many casualties; and it gave the British a chance to recover from their defeat in the Cauldron.'[37] Driver R. J. Crawford described how vulnerable supply columns of both sides were to the attentions of marauding armour:

> He [a survivor] described how they were moving up towards Bir Hakeim when they ran into the tank ambush. The tanks closed in from all sides, blazing away with their guns. The Bren guns of the supply column hardly had a chance to answer before the gunners were mown down. Then carnage was let loose as the tanks drove straight over the column, smashing lorries onto their sides in all directions. Within a few minutes the column was a mass of blazing wreckage with bodies strewn everywhere …

With this obstacle removed, Axis forces were freed for a further thrust, this time toward El Adem, with a demonstration to distract the British in 'Knightsbridge'. By dark on 11 June Rommel had attained El Adem having, once again, wrong-footed his opponents. Next day he moved in an attempt to surround the remnants of 2nd & 4th Armoured Brigades. There was now a very real risk the largely static infantry formations to the north could be surrounded and heavy clashes occurred in the vicinity of Rigel Ridge. Here the Scots Guards fought tenaciously, earning high praise from Rommel, by no means an easy general to impress. Nonetheless, relentless pressure and mounting losses forced the British from the higher ground, 22nd Armoured lost some two thirds of its tanks. On 11 June, Ritchie had been able to field some 300 machines, giving him a numerical superiority of two to one. Within two days, ground down by murderous combat and poor tactics, only 95 runners remained, the odds having thus swung heavily in favour of DAK.

As the Axis held the field, they were able to recover many of their damaged vehicles with customary efficiency, 8th Army could not and those left damaged were effectively written off. Despite this, British units were improving their overall rates of recovery and repair: 'Ever since the opening of the battle the British had striven hard to get damaged tanks into action again quickly.'[38] Many damaged vehicles were recovered and innumerable 'roadside repairs' successfully carried out. Casualties among experienced crews were nonetheless heavy, the tankers 'only too well aware of the shortcomings of their own tanks.'[39] The Crusader had an evil propensity for bursting into flames, immolating its crew. The lighter Stuarts, though agile, were only really suited to a reconnaissance role while the Grant which had achieved successes was hamstrung by its inability to take an effective hull-down position, limited traverse and a lack of effective AP shells.[40] The 2-pounder anti-tank gun, without AP and ballistic capped ammunition, was useless against the up-armoured panzers.

By 14 June, Ritchie was seeking permission to draw off, fall back to the frontier and save his forces from encirclement; Rommel was master of the central battlefield. This would imply the temporary abandonment of the Tobruk garrison which would again be isolated. Auchinleck was not yet ready to throw in the towel, insisting that further counter-attacks be launched to deny the approaches to Tobruk. As C in C he had to answer to the Prime Minister who was already querying his intentions: '…Presume there is no question in any case of giving up Tobruk?'[41] Rommel felt a surge of confidence which he transmitted in his daily correspondence to his wife on 15 June: 'The battle has been won and the enemy is breaking up …'[42]

Withdrawal in the face on an aggressive enemy is never a smooth business and the retreat of 8th Army inevitably produced a semblance of rout. Rommel would not relinquish pressure and struck toward the airfield at Gambut. The rump of 4th Armoured sallied out but was again badly mauled; control of events had passed irrevocably beyond Ritchie's grip. For Rommel, there was now the matter of his unfinished business with the defenders of Tobruk.

Nemesis of Tobruk

As early as January 1942, the joint Middle East commanders, Auchinleck, Cunningham and Tedder had agreed that Tobruk, if isolated, should not once again be defended. Militarily, this was eminently sensible but the place had become imbued with a great deal of political capital at a time when British arms had endured such a series of dismal defeats in Norway, France, Greece and Crete with such sharp reverses in the Western Desert. By 17 June, Rommel had secured Gambut airfield and beaten off the remnant of British armour.

Tobruk was again invested. Two days later there was still some ill-founded optimism that the perimeter could be held on the basis, or in the pious hope, that Axis forces would settle down for a lengthy siege. The situation now within the ring was very different from before. Hitherto strong defences had been denuded and pillaged to meet the exigencies of the now defunct Gazala Line and the garrison was badly placed to resist a sustained attack.

Rommel, scenting this weakness, unleashed the *Luftwaffe* who began blasting the fortress on 20 June as the precursor to a determined attack from the south-east. By 07.45 hrs the anti-tank ditch, equivalent to the medieval moat, had been breached and the perimeter was collapsing. There had been talk of a breakout should this occur but, in reality, no escape route was viable. Auchinleck's report to London, late on the 20th, sounded a note of impending catastrophe:

> Enemy attacked south-east face of Tobruk perimeter early morning after air bombard-ment and penetrated defences. By evening all our tanks reported knocked out and half our guns lost … Major-General Klopper commanding troops in Tobruk last night asked authority to fight his way out feeling apparently could not repeat not hold out. Ritchie agreed … Do not repeat not know how he proposes to do this and consider chances of success doubtful.[43]

Tobruk fell and 35,000 Allied soldiers passed into captivity; 2,000 tons of fuel and as many vehicles fell into Axis hands.[44] It was a disastrous defeat. The debacles in Greece and Crete combined had not witnessed such fearful loss. Churchill was in the United States, within the sanctum of the Oval Office, when the dread tidings arrived. Casey had already cabled a warning to Washington but this was a terrible blow; first Singapore and now Tobruk. It is unquestionably true that a lesser man than Churchill would have been broken. The news could not have come at a worse time when Britain was struggling to instil some measure of confidence in its ally. There is perhaps no more telling testimony to the Prime Minister's indomitable genius that he emerged still doggedly defiant even from this latest blow. The objective analysis provided by the US military attaché in Cairo, Colonel Bonner L. Fellers and reported on 20 June, was scarcely complimentary:

> With numerically superior forces, with tanks, planes, artillery, means of transport and reserves of every kind, the British army has twice failed to defeat the Axis forces in Libya. Under the present command and with the measures taken in a hit or miss fashion the granting of 'lend-lease' alone cannot ensure a victory. The Eighth Army has failed to maintain the morale of its troops; its tactical conceptions were always wrong, it neglected completely cooperation between the various arms; its reactions to the lightning changes of the battlefield were always slow.[45]

At the time it would have required a particular shade of optimism to disagree.

7

Mersa Matruh & First El Alamein: June 1942 – August 1942

Did you ever see a man bleed in sand? I
Asked him, did you ever see a soldier, a khaki
Hero with his life blood blotting entirely and quickly
Into the khaki sand? Did you ever see a man drown in Quicksand
Or, let alone a man, a tree or a bedstead?

Patrick Anderson

Excellent as our tactical achievements were in all theatres of war, there was not that solid strategic foundation which would have directed our tactical skill into the right channels.

Rommel: Krieg ohne Hass ['War without Hate']

On 25 June 1942 General Auchinleck, accompanied by Dorman-Smith, arrived from Cairo at Maaten Baggush, Ritchie's 8th Army HQ. It was not a social call; the army commander was curtly relieved of his post and Auchinleck, as C in C, assumed direct tactical control of 8th Army. Dorman-Smith – 'Chink' was to act as an unofficial chief of staff. On the flight from Cairo the two had discussed the current, dire position, concluding that the only course open was for a further tactical withdrawal to the El Alamein line 150 miles east of Mersa Matruh, where the army was attempting a stand. Wavell had previously identified the small port as the absolute 'last ditch' position for defence of the Delta. From here, enemy aircraft could strike at vital installations and civilian targets there. Ritchie was apparently stunned at the suddenness of his taking off, yet it was evident he was hopelessly out of his depth: 'General Ritchie had become accustomed to consult the Commander-in-Chief, not because he had not the strength of character to make decisions for himself, but possibly because he continued to think more as a staff officer than as a commander.'[1]

Mersa Matruh

In the bitter wake of the catastrophe at Tobruk, Roosevelt had made the generous and important gesture of offering 300 new Sherman tanks with a further 100 105mm self-propelled guns. General Marshall had further proposed sending the US 1st Armoured Division. Such relief was welcome but for Churchill, the bile of humiliation and defeat still rising, this must have smacked of the same condescension shown by Hitler when he first sent succour to his defeated ally.[2] Undeniably the situation of 8th Army was unenviable:

> British troops in the Western Desert were now the equivalent of three and two thirds infantry divisions weak in artillery; three armoured regiments of which two were partly trained and one was composite; two motor brigades and some armoured car regiments. The New Zealand Division was beginning to arrive at Matruh. Thus the force was not suitably composed for a campaign of manoeuvre.[3]

Despite the scale of the recent reverses, 8th Army HQ persisted in a degree of upbeat assessments whose optimistic tone rested on the belief that Rommel, for the moment, was spent and could not maintain his offensive. Given the British deficiency in mobile, armoured forces the policy was one which sought 'to delay the enemy at the frontier … while withdrawing the main body of 8th Army to the Matruh defences'.[4] 'Chink' had given the assembled war correspondents a bracing and confident briefing on 21 June. This was more propaganda than pragmatism of course but reflects his reliance on Clausewitz's principle of diminishing offensive capacity. If Rommel was not minded to agree then his nominal superiors at *Comando Supremo* most definitely were.

Bastico, with Kesselring, reminded their impetuous paladin that it was time to draw breath while the agreed strategy for Operation '*Herkules*', the reduction of Malta, was effected. Bastico, who like Rommel had now attained his field marshal's baton, demanded a halt. The Desert Fox, who modestly ascribed his successes solely to the valour of his troops, and who might have regarded his elevation as rather more hard won than that of his theoretical superior, simply declined this 'advice'. Kesselring, who had met with him on 21 June, achieved no more, doubtless he was again left 'growling'. As before, Rommel appealed directly to Rome and Berlin. For Il Duce, so deprived of laurels, there was the dazzling prospect of riding his white charger through the streets of conquered Alexandria, like a latter-day Caesar or Octavian. Hitler was receptive; after the Pyrrhic victory on Crete he had little enthusiasm for an assault upon Malta. He cabled his fellow dictator that it would be foolish to break off contact while 'the Goddess of Victory smiles'.[5] On 24 June Rommel received the green light, just as well perhaps as his forward units had already been advancing for the last two days!

The Fox, his hunter's instincts attuned, was poised to deliver what he believed to be the killing blow. Not just his magical touch but hard intelligence supported the decision. Colonel Fellers, who had been so scathing of the 8th Army's performance, was unwittingly providing the Axis with valuable information. He was that 'good source' referred to in Ultra decrypts as Italian Military Intelligence had cracked the US diplomatic cipher. Before he returned to the USA, toward the end of July, Fellers had provided them with key intelligence concerning losses in British armour: '… On 10 June there were only 133 tanks of all types in all the depots of the Middle East'.[6] After 25 July, the cipher was changed and this deadly leak sealed, but significant damage had been done.

In the circumstances, it is difficult to see what other course remained for Auchinleck, other than to take direct command. Ritchie was floundering and 8th Army left in a most parlous state. Brooke maintained his confidence in the 'Auk' and Churchill, who could be as magnanimous as he could be bullying, lent his hearty approval: 'I am so glad you have taken Command. Do not vex yourself with anything but the battle ...'[7] Nonetheless, Auchinleck had placed himself in an unenviable position in that he had delegated affairs in Cairo to his deputy Lieutenant-General Corbett which, to all intents and purposes, left Middle East Command without an overall guiding hand. In choosing Dorman-Smith as chief of staff, he found a subordinate of considerable intellectual capacity and strategic insight but one who, like himself, was not able to fully mesh with the army commanders themselves. These were frequently both confused and demoralised by orders they received but did not fully understand. Auchinleck commanded the army's resources but he did not control its soul, without which the sinews could not flex properly.

'Chink', whose views on his fellow officers tended to be unflattering, was made to 'writhe' when he learnt of Ritchie's dispositions for the defence of Matruh. It was as if 8th Army had learnt absolutely nothing from previous mistakes. Gott, with 13 Corps was to hold the perimeter around the port, with hastily dug and inadequate defences – inviting a repeat of Tobruk. 20 Corps was deployed twenty miles to the south astride an escarpment; Freyberg with his New Zealanders was posted 'in the middle of nowhere'. Remnants of 1st Armoured Division were lurking far to the south while the yawning gap between the two corps was patrolled by a brace of relatively weak mobile columns. Dorman Smith provided a more realistic appreciation:

> Correctly both of 8th Army's Corps should have been deployed for battle, shoulder to shoulder, on the open desert south of the northern escarpment, with only a token force in the Matruh defended perimeter. No heed should have been taken of the now previously prepared defensive positions or incomplete minefields. Had this been done and the armour moved from the southern flank into centrally located Army reserve, Rommel's impetuous advance would have met a powerful force in place of a vacuum dividing two strong but uncoordinated wings.[8]

Auchinleck was painfully aware of the political capital invested in the 'last ditch' position at Matruh. Britain's faltering credibility would slide yet further and there was the inevitable knock-on effect on civilian morale in the Delta, where anti-colonial sentiment was already hopeful of an Axis victory. He had thus decided to make a stand at Matruh while allowing his army the necessary flexibility to fall back toward the El Alamein position, perhaps the worst of both worlds as it implied any withdrawal would literally be under the enemy guns. This obvious difficulty would be compounded by the fact the principal Corps positions were so far apart. Battle was joined on 27 June when 90th Light pushed past 'Leathercol'[9] and 21st Panzer brushed aside 'Gleecol'.[10] The gap between 13 and 30 Corps now yawned with the Littorio Division trailing the German armour and the remainder of Italian XX Corps behind 90th Light Division. Caught in an isolated and exposed position 9th DLI, part of 151st Brigade was overrun, though Private Wakenshaw of the battalion gained a posthumous VC.[11] Auchinleck had intimated to both corps commanders, Gott and

Holmes, in Matruh that, should they deem a withdrawal necessary, they should do so in unison. Given the yawning gap between the two formations and the chronic unreliability of signals this was highly optimistic.

'Pike' was the code for retreat and both were to converge on Minqar Omar which lay some thirty miles east. Gott had already acted but his disengagement soon ran into difficulties. Though 1st Armoured withdrew smoothly, the New Zealanders ran into opposition. Freyberg had been wounded and Brigadier Inglis took over to find the division boxed in around Minqar Quaim. The Kiwis reacted vigorously, broke through the ring, inflicting loss upon the enemy. In Matruh, General Holmes was completely out of touch and was even planning a counter-attack. This came to nothing and by 28 June his corps was isolated and encircled. Holmes then planned for breakout: Both 50th and 10th Indian divisions would begin to move after 21.00 hrs and hasten south for thirty miles before swinging eastwards into the vicinity of Fuka.

British formations, thrown into brigade groups and moving in columns, endured a dangerous passage. Axis forces were already at Fuka where 21st Panzer had overrun the remnant of 29th Indian Brigade and a series of sharp, confused actions ensued. 10th Indian Division, in particular, suffered considerable casualties. Thus the decision to stand at Matruh had precipitated a further debacle and the *Panzerarmee* seemed unstoppable. In accordance with the notion of diminishing power of the offensive, Rommel should have run out of steam. The rule applied doubly in the desert where supply difficulties imposed such severe constraints but DAK had, in part, been sustained by captured materiel in Tobruk and more garnered in the wake of 8th Army's precipitate and frequently headlong retreats.

Prior to Rommel's offensive, supplies had been stockpiled for 'Acrobat' – the onward Allied rush into Tripolitania. Now, the hard-pressed rear echelon units of the RAOC and RASC struggled to salvage or destroy their precious stores in the confusion of defeat. Prodigies of deliverance were indeed effected but such was the scale and extent of the build-up that much still fell into Axis hands: 'The route was marked with great dumps of blazing stores. Everything that could not be removed was systematically destroyed. The night was lit by these beacons, until parts of the road were like a red daylight, with thin, ghostly streams of men and towering shadows of lorries sidling past like phantoms of an inferno.'[12]

If the Axis were doing well on the ground, their grasp of the skies was crumbling. Squadrons of Kesselring's planes were being fed into the endless mincer of the Eastern Front while sorties from Malta were exacting an increasing toll. For both sides, to be attacked from the air was a most disagreeable experience:

> During all these trips there were constant attacks by dive-bombers and Messerschmitts. These were bad enough when the column was at rest, and you could hear or see them com-ing. But it was much worse when the first indication you had of an attack was when the lorry in front of you blew up or the bullets smacked through your own windscreen.[13]

The *Luftwaffe* threat was diminishing at a time when the Desert Air Force was coming into its own, soon to be reinforced by B-24 'Liberator' bombers.[14] Though ground/air communications were still far from perfected, 'Mary' Coningham's[15] squadrons did excellent service. 8th Army was battered and depleted but the US tanks and self propelled guns were on their way, together with two fresh UK divisions, 44th (Home Counties) and 51st (Highland). The pendulum had not yet swung for the final time.

The El Alamein Position

Matruh had been another reverse for Allied arms yet, despite this setback, Auchinleck had kept the army in being. This, as he and Dorman-Smith had identified, was the prime objective. Only by preserving mobile field forces could the British position in the Middle East be saved. He had now gone beyond Wavell's 'worst case' and was considering how best to defend the Delta itself should he be pushed that far. Meanwhile there was the ground south of El Alamein, a strip of desert some thirty-eight miles in extent that lay between salt marsh and sea to the north and the impassable Qattara Depression, where no tank could tread. Here was ground that favoured a defensive battle, to be fought by an army markedly inferior in armour and less mobile than its opponent, one that needed time to rebuild and replenish.

For the most part this ground is featureless, till one reaches the rock-strewn hills that flank the waste of marsh and dune announcing the depression. Even these are no more than 700 feet above sea level but much nearer the sea are the twin eminences, rounded hillocks or 'tells' of which Tel el Eisa and Tel el Makh Khad would prove significant. The terrain is everywhere barren; loose, deepening sand alternating with unyielding rock which emerges in the narrow lateral ridges Miteirya, Ruweisat and Alam el Halfa. These insignificant features would assume considerable importance in the fighting to come and blood would be poured out in torrents to secure them. Once taken such features were heartbreakingly difficult to fortify, horribly exposed. In places the ground dipped into shallow depressions ('deirs'), natural saucers. That Auchinleck and Dorman-Smith should focus on the potential here was nothing revelatory, the Alamein position had been identified as a natural defence line for the Delta for some years beforehand.

Efforts at constructing a line of fortifications had been begun in the early days but operational priorities had relegated the endeavour. Initially, the plan had been for the creation of three heavily defended localities at El Alamein and the coast, at Bab el Qattara (Qaret el Abd) and at Naqb Abu Dweis. By the coast some positions were completed, wired and mined, in the centre there was rather less completed and in the south very little. Water supplies were, however, on hand along the axis of the intended front.[16]

'Chink' prepared a detailed assessment of the strategic imperatives at this time which, though it offered little guidance to the tactics to be employed in the forthcoming battle at Alamein, established 8th Army's key priorities. Supply was acknowledged to be critical; defence of the Red Sea ports would facilitate rebuilding the army's strength and thus its future mobility. At the same time, increased activity from Malta could damage the Axis. Dorman-Smith recognised that the Desert Air Force was becoming a force to be reckoned with and, for now, 'our only offensive weapon'.[17] That the army should fight at El Alamein was certain but it was to avoid any risk of encirclement and be prepared to fall back again to defend Cairo and Alexandria. This brisk assessment, strong on objectivity, could not disguise the fact that Alamein promised to be yet another debacle followed by a panicked flight to the Delta with all the damage to rear echelon and supply this would entail. It left the question of whether the Egyptians could be relied upon unanswered. The overall effect upon morale could only be detrimental.

Auchinleck's weakness was that he and Dorman-Smith were operating in a kind of vacuum. The army commanders could not readily divine his intent and the Auk did not issue any 'Backs to the Wall' oration and rallying cry. With his Indian Army background he did not possess the kind of informal but vital network that generally sustained the British Army. Employing 'Chink' as chief of staff, while a useful expedient at one level, created a further barrier. That it was his intention to keep the army in being come what may was sound and logical but this did not translate into language officers and men could understand and rally around. It seemed as if, outfought and depleted, they would once again be clinging to scratch positions in early expectation of a further, hurried withdrawal.

While the debacle at Matruh was unfolding, Churchill had again cabled the C in C to offer some helpful tips on generalship, tending to indicate how little the Prime Minister had learnt from the desert campaign thus far. He was incapable of understanding that the fluid and mobile nature of desert warfare was, above all, a battle of competing technologies. Put simplistically, the side which had the best tanks and in adequate numbers, together with commensurate strength in supporting arms would win. Heroic if pointless calls that 'every fit male be made to fight and die for victory',[18] meant nothing. The Italian collapse in the winter of 1940–1941 showed that simply deploying large masses of infantry, 'bayonets on the ground' had no place in this, most modern of modern wars. Given the circumstances, Auchinleck's reply was the very model of patient diplomacy:

> As to using all my manpower, I hope I am doing this, but infantry cannot win battles in the desert as long as the enemy has superiority in armour, and nothing can be said or done to change this fact. Guns and armour and just enough infantry to afford them and their supply organisation local protection is what is needed.[19]

Any hopes that the swing of the pendulum would cause Rommel to simply grind to a halt proved groundless. His juggernaut, thin on supply, men exhausted, machines overtaxed came on relentlessly. The 'good source' was still pumping out vital information. Von Mellenthin, on 30 June, received confirmation, via an intercept from A. C. Kirk the US ambassador, that Fellers felt the Axis could, within days, be at the very gates of Cairo.[20] In fulfilling this despondent prediction, Rommel was only too happy to oblige. Victory, as it seemed, was very close indeed. Battered, ground down and in no small part bemused, 8th Army was still far from beaten. The Desert Rats[21] were down but not out and their morale, despite such repeated pummellings, did not collapse. This resilience was a disappointment to Egyptian nationalists hoping for signs of cracking. The soldiers as ever found diversion in humour:

> One of our sergeants had seen a letter in the *Daily Mirror* asking if someone would be kind enough to send a dartboard to the writers. The signature on the letter was 'Lonely Outpost', and was from a gun-site which the author said was no fewer than three miles from the nearest village and five miles from the nearest public house. Our sergeant collected 10s from us and

sent the following letter to the _Daily Mirror_ for onward transmission to the 'Lonely Outpost': 'Dear Lonely Outpost – Please find enclosed ten shillings with which to buy a dartboard for you at the 'Lonely Outpost'. We can appreciate how lonely you must be, three miles from the nearest village and five miles from the nearest pub. We are three hundred miles from the nearest town and five hundred miles from the nearest pub. [Signed] DESERT RATS.'[22]

The First Battle of El Alamein – Rommel Attacks

Ever since the fall of Tobruk Field-Marshal Rommel had been striving to hustle the British and prevent them from forming a front behind which to absorb the land and air reinforcements they were likely to receive. General Auchinleck's object had been to keep the 8th Army in being. Although it had suffered severe losses in men and material and was much disorganised, it was bewildered rather than demoralised. Its framework still existed and the army was certainly capable of further efforts, as events were soon to show. But this did not alter the fact that it was now back in a 'last ditch' position. Rommel was certain to waste no time, no matter how exhausted his troops might be and no matter what they lacked – including the full support of their air force, which was still struggling to make its way forward. The task before the 8th Army and the Desert Air Force was clear; they must at all costs parry the blow that was surely coming.[23]

Rommel, on 30 June, was poised for the attack. His men were utterly weary and suffering from the customary shortage of supply. He did not pause but moved straight into the offensive. His limited reconnaissance was soon to be found wanting for he had failed to appreciate the strength of the South Africans dug in around El Alamein. His plan was that both 90th Light and DAK would charge the gap north of Deir el Abyad. While the Light Division would seek to replicate its earlier success in interdicting the coast road and thus isolating the Alamein garrison, DAK would sprint south to swing around behind 13 Corps. As ever the Italian formations were given a subordinate role, one division assaulting Alamein from the west, another behind 90th Light and the remainder trailing the panzers.

Matters did not go according to plan. Foul conditions delayed the progress of German armour and 90th Light bumped the Alamein defences and suffered under the intense weight of fire the South Africans brought down upon them. DAK found Deir el Shein unexpectedly held by 18th Infantry Brigade and a fierce battle erupted. Newly arrived and inexperienced, 18th Brigade had struggled to dig into the stony surface and had limited support. Nonetheless, the brigade fought hard against lengthening odds and with a crumbling perimeter, their few 'I' tanks and guns disabled. Despite a very gallant stand, the survivors were forced to surrender by evening on 1st July. The loss of the brigade was yet another blow and an intervention by 1st Armoured Division was so long delayed as to be too late. DAK had won another tactical victory but at the cost of a badly disrupted timetable.

90th Light, having extricated itself from this initial contact, sought to resume its headlong dash but intense fire from South African positions descended like a deluge and stopped any advance dead in its tracks. Desert Air Force was living up to its role as the main striking arm and the Axis sprint was grinding to a halt. DAK had suffered significant reported losses in available tank strength and its supply columns had been bombed incessantly. By 2 July Rommel was still making no progress and resolved to throw his armour behind the assault on the coast road.

Auchinleck had quickly appreciated that Allied outposts were exposed and moved to concentrate his forces. The Kiwis were given a more fluid role, their 6th Brigade pulled from Bab el Qattara with only a column remaining. The Indian Division was likewise to quit Qaret el Himeimat. As Rommel massed to attempt break-through at El Alamein 30 Corps would hold the line while 13 Corps launched a blow towards Deir el Abyad. Both sides attacked during the afternoon of 2 July. In the north, Pienaar's South Africans again resisted the Axis strike, aided by 'Robcol'[24] drawn from 10th Indian Division. 90th Light was again harassed by the incessant attentions of Desert Air Force and could make no headway. To the south and west, just beyond Ruweisat Ridge, British and German armour were heavily embroiled. At the end of a hard day's fighting, neither side could claim victory, but the Axis offensive had not progressed.

During the hours of darkness air attacks continued[25] till battle was rejoined on the morning of the 3rd. There was yet more heavy fighting south of Ruweisat Ridge. In the south, Freyberg's New Zealanders scored a signal success when they overran the artillery component of Ariete Division, netting a fine haul of prisoners and captured guns. 5th New Zealand Brigade was in action against the Brescia division at El Mreir. By now the Axis formations were severely ground down. Rommel reported his own divisions could only muster 1,000 or 1,200 men apiece[26] and incessant aerial bombardment was playing havoc with already overstretched supply lines. Skirmishing continued throughout 4 July but the main German effort was, for the moment, spent. It had been a failure.

Auchinleck, sensing the enemy was severely weakened, began to think in terms of turning the stalemate into a rout, proposing to unleash 13 Corps towards the Axis rear but the British armour, probing forward, was held by a scratch gun line. Next he planned a concentrated advance towards Deir el Shein but again this made little headway. SAS and LRDG were active against enemy airfields, destroying some aircraft on the ground. Rommel was in fact preparing to draw off his armour and the exhausted 90th Light leaving Italians to hold the line while the Germans drew breath and replenished. In this at last, the *Luftwaffe* was able to lend support and the high pitched screaming of Stukas again filled the desert air. Auchinleck, for his part, had now decided his main blow should fall in the north and concentrated his forces accordingly. This neatly foiled an attempt by 21st Panzer to catch the New Zealand Division and the intended Axis blow fell on empty ground. Meanwhile, Desert Air Force had switched to pounding long range targets and Axis held ports, while Coningham's fighters undertook a tactical bombing role.

Von Mellenthin was critical of his commander's performance; he believed any hope of a breakthrough had gone by 1 July and that operations:

> … were hopelessly prejudiced … Our one chance was to outmanoeuvre the enemy, but
> we had actually been drawn into a battle of attrition. 1st Armoured Division was given an
> extra day to reorganise, and when the Afrika Korps advanced on July 2 it found the British

armour strongly posted on Ruweisat Ridge and quite capable of beating off such attacks
as we could muster. The South African positions were strong, and 90th Light never had a
chance of breaking through them. The Desert Air Force commanded the battlefield.[27]

Having rightly judged the foe to be exhausted Auchinleck began a series of counter-
strokes, the first of which involved 30 Corps in an attempt to seize the rocky knolls of
Tel el Eisa and Tel el Makh Khad. Possession of these would facilitate further moves
southwards toward Deir el Shein and raids westwards against Axis airfields. 13 Corps was
to prevent any enemy reinforcement northwards and be ready to exploit opportunities. On
3 July, Morshead's 9th Australian Division had returned to the line and was now tasked
with taking Tel el Eisa while the South Africans stormed Tel el Makh Khad. Both had
armoured support and the attack at first light on 10 July was preceded by a 'hurricane
bombardment'. Both formations made good progress taking many Italians prisoner.

    Von Mellenthin, in charge of HQ while Rommel was absent and located only a few
miles up the coast, collected a makeshift battlegroup and held the line while the Desert
Fox brought up more reinforcements from 15th Panzer. A late counter-attack made some
progress but was seen off. The following day the Australians attacked again in a further
attempt to secure the entirety of their objective.

    Fighting on the ground was matched by the fury of combat in the air, skies crossed
with trails and bruised by the chatter of guns, Allied fighters duelling with Axis. For the
next three days Rommel sought to recover lost ground and eliminate the newly formed
salient but his attacks were repulsed and efforts to drive a wedge between the hills and the
Alamein box were equally abortive. The initiative now lay with 8th Army.

Auchinleck Counter-Attacks

Having got the Axis off-balance, Auchinleck decided to maintain pressure by striking
southwards against the long, lateral finger of Ruweisat Ridge. This otherwise unprepossessing
feature would witness hard fighting through 14–15 July, and again on the 21st. The OH dubs
these actions 1st and 2nd Ruweisat, both of which would highlight significant tactical
deficiencies in 8th Army, a lack of coordination between the attacking arms resulting in
tragic losses. The objective was straightforward, to storm the ridge and drive the enemy
from ground east of the Alamein – Abu Dweis track and north of the eminence.

    The task of securing the western flank of the ridge was given to 13 Corps while 30 Corps
was to take the eastern extremity and also strike southwards from this newly created salient
to take the hump of Miteirya Ridge. This was to be a night attack and 13 Corps would send
in two brigades of New Zealanders while 30 Corps deployed 5th Indian Brigade (from
5th Indian Division). Crucial armoured support for the Kiwis was to be provided by 1st
Armoured Division which would come up after first light – both Corps were to be on their
objectives by 04.30 hrs. To reach their target the New Zealanders had to cover some six
miles of ground in the dark. The attack, even once the enemy was alerted, was driven home
with great élan but, in the smoke and dust of a moonlit battle, many enemy posts were left

un-subdued. Some units became scattered and digging into the unyielding rock proved near impossible. Supporting arms, a few vital anti-tanks guns, were got up but much had not arrived. The remaining infantry sought to consolidate and, above all, dig in.

30 Corps' attack met with stiff resistance and there was some disorder, supporting armour was still distant. Italian defenders from Brescia and Pavia Divisions had been caught off-guard and numbers of them bolted to rear. A passing column of German tanks fell upon the NZ 22nd Battalion, swiftly dealt with the AT guns exposed on their portees and compelled several hundred survivors to capitulate. Efforts were made to get the British armour mobile and tanks were able to support a renewed assault by 5th Indian Brigade which partially succeeded in securing objectives on the ridge. Efforts to bring up supporting arms were frustrated by fire from enemy posts missed in the first rush. Only with the aid of a barrage were the reserve units able to begin filtering through.

With the Italians in disarray, Rommel had to assemble German units for the inevitable counter-attack, command of which was entrusted to Nehring. 4th New Zealand Brigade, with little or no support, was eventually overwhelmed and the western end of the ridge lost.[28] Next day, 16 July, the Germans attempted to drive off 5th Indian Brigade, who repulsed this and a subsequent attack. On the 17th Australian troops attacked southwards towards Miteirya Ridge, taking hundreds of Italian prisoners but were halted by heavy shelling and a German counterstroke.

In these actions, the New Zealand Division had fought hard and well but at considerable cost. They had stormed and taken their objectives but felt badly let down by their comrades in armour whom they blamed for leaving them so desperately exposed. This grudge and mutual incomprehension between infantry and tanks boded ill and was to bedevil 8th Army for some time. This was not due to faintheartedness on the tankers part but to a degree of misunderstanding as to the role and capabilities of armour which were far more constrained than the infantry might have imagined. Tank commanders, such as General Lumsden, were loath to restrict themselves to the infantry support role at the expense of mobility. Tanks should be free to act as the battle unfolded to seize opportunities while artillery and AT guns shielded the infantry.

Despite these costly setbacks, Auchinleck was convinced the Axis were close to breaking. The Italians had lost heavily in men and materiel; Rommel's panzers were ground down and diminished. The Auk now felt a further heavy blow in the centre might shatter them altogether. Overall, the Allied position was considerably better. Both the Australians and South Africans were in good shape, though the 5th Indian and New Zealand Divisions were reduced to a mere two brigades each. 1st and 7th Armoured Divisions, the latter being developed as a mixed battle-group,[29] were in strength. 7th Armoured had a hefty contingent of over sixty Grants in addition to Crusaders and Honeys. 161st Indian Motor Brigade and 23rd Armoured Brigade were arriving to swell the muster. The British might have initially lagged behind the Germans in developing the ability to recover damaged machines under battlefield conditions but this was changing:

There is one magnificent story of one REME recovery section who were ordered 'under pain of death' to get right up with the forward troops during the night, and be ready to

recover casualties when hell broke out next morning. The section did as ordered, and when
dawn broke both the enemy troops and our own troops looked from their positions to see
the REME section plumb in the centre of no-man's-land! It got back safely, too.[30]

For this fresh attack the main impetus fell on 13 Corps, to fracture the Axis at Deir el Shein
and Deir el Abyad then drive west. A feint would be launched in the south and 30 Corps
would ensure vigorous local action in its sector to keep enemy forces there tied down. Close
air support would be provided and Gott was intending that 5th Indian Division would
storm the western end of Ruweisat Ridge, where the New Zealanders had previously come
to grief. The Kiwis themselves were tasked to take the eastern rim of El Mreir saucer. Once
the infantry were on their objectives 1st Armoured Division would push westwards to a
further goal whereupon the brigades would follow up and consolidate. 22nd Armoured
Brigade was detailed to cover the southern flank of the attack while 2nd Armoured Brigade
was to interdict any initial counter-attacks once the attacking infantry were successful.

Gapping the minefields was entrusted to the infantry, though both brigades were
relatively inexperienced in this most difficult of tasks. Gott's plan appeared sound but a
key assumption was that the minefields could be detected and gapped in time to allow
23rd Armoured Brigade, whose role was to charge forward to the further objective, to pass
through. Despite the weight of artillery brought to bear, the New Zealand attack came to
bear a sad resemblance to that earlier tragedy. The infantry managed, in a night attack, to
gain their objectives but were left dispersed and without essential fire support. At first light
Axis armour struck back, easily eliminating the few AT guns available; the denouement
was inevitable, the infantry were overrun, artillery communications broke down and the
brigade suffered some 700 casualties.[31] 2nd Armoured did attempt relief but was stopped
by a mix of un-cleared mines and Axis fire.

161st Indian Motor Brigade's attack 'also experienced varying fortunes'. After hard fighting,
the assault battalions were either short of their objectives or driven off by vigorous counter-
attacks. Only when the reserve battalion was thrown in did the attack make headway. Major-
General A. H. Gatehouse was now in command of 1st Armoured Division, as Lumsden had
been wounded earlier. He was doubtful over committing 23rd Armoured Brigade when it
became clear the mines had not all been cleared and a viable gap had not been created. Gott
would not countenance calling off this part of the plan, however, as he believed the enemy
to be significantly wrong-footed. He therefore proposed that the line of advance should shift
southwards to cross an area believed, or rather hoped, to be free of Axis mines.

Two tank regiments were sent in. Both were heavily shelled and struck a host of
unexpected mines covering their supposedly clear approaches. Serious loss was incurred
before the objective was reached and then the survivors were furiously attacked. When
21st Panzer was thrown into the fight, the battered remnants withdrew, leaving forty tanks
wrecked and more badly damaged.[32] An attempt by 2nd Armoured Brigade to get through
to the New Zealanders isolated in the El Mreir Depression foundered in the face of
intense fire. A further twenty-one tanks were lost in the broil. Another night action, on 22
July, again launched by 5th Indian Division, aimed at finally securing the deadly Point 63
on Ruweisat Ridge, failed after a gallant and costly attempt. The infantryman's frustration

with his seemingly Olympian comrades in armour was largely based on ignorance of the tactical role and capabilities of Allied tanks. Observers like Robert Crawford who, as part of the logistical chain, could exercise a degree of understanding and objectivity were considerable less jaundiced:

> Their normal day in the forward area began before dawn, when they rose in time to get the tanks out of *laager* and deployed before daylight. No hot meal could be made, because all lights and fires were forbidden during the hours of darkness, while the tanks were in *laager* … The tanks moved out just before dawn, and spent the remainder of the hours of daylight deployed. If things were quiet, they prepared a hot meal at their battle station. But this was unusual rather than normal … When tank combats took place, our tank crews would watch the German tanks being refuelled and restocked with ammunition, behind a screen of anti-tank guns. Our tanks were impotent to do anything about this, as the anti-tank guns had them outranged … After the German tanks were ready, battle would be joined. Normally, it was a case of the German tanks trying to plaster our under-gunned tanks from beyond the effective range of our tank guns. We, for our part, tried to use our greater powers of manoeuvre by darting in and out, firing as we went.[33]

On 30 Corps' front, 22 July, the Australians again attacked. Fighting centred as before on the twin eminences of Tell el Eisa and Tell el Makh Khad. Early gains prompted a savage riposte and the Australians battled hard to hold ground won. Though they had some armoured support from 50th RTR, equipped with Valentines, liaison between the two arms was again patchy and twenty-three machines were knocked out for paltry return. Despite these costly reverses, Auchinleck was not yet ready to concede a stalemate, persisting in the belief the Axis were on the cusp of disintegration. This time, on 26 July, an attempt was to be launched by 30 Corps, beefed up with additional armour and infantry, to advance through the gap between Miteirya Ridge and Deir el Dhib. For its part 13 Corps, battered by previous exertions, would mount a convincing, full-scale diversion to the south.

To the South Africans fell the task of gapping the enemy's minefields south-east of the ridge. By 01.00 hrs the Australians were to have seized the eastern flank and then advance north and west. An infantry brigade would pass through the gaps to Deir el Dhib, gapping any further minefields encountered. Then it would be the turn of the armour to strike westwards. Some initial success was soon shrouded in a mist of confusion. The armour did not come up and, once again, the attacking infantry were left vulnerable, an opportunity the Germans never failed to exploit. 6th DLI and 5th East Yorks were overrun, as latterly were the survivors of 2/28th Australian battalion. As before, heavy fire prevented supporting arms from getting through, armoured support was ineffective and costly.

Fresh raids by LRDG/SAS accounted for further enemy aircraft and Desert Air Force continued to bomb the Axis without respite. Though these Special Forces actions were, in relative terms, mere pinpricks they did reduce the numbers of Axis aircraft and forced Rommel to divert resources into defending his airfields. Besides, this was precisely the type of Henty-esque derring-do the Prime Minister adored. Not only Churchill was impressed, soldiers of 8th Army were not immune from the charisma of these fabled desert warriors:

Of course, the super-saboteurs were our long range desert patrols. These were the super 'Desert Rats'. Stories were legion about their exploits ... No men were braver or fitter than those in these groups. Occasionally we actually saw them move out into 'the blue', but mostly they were as legendary as Lawrence of Arabia. They stayed out behind enemy lines for months at a time ... They were led by men of unrivalled knowledge of the Desert, and did untold material damage to German supplies, but their main contribution was in boosting our morale and lowering the German morale correspondingly. Whenever news came round their exploits, our tails went up like anything.[34]

By the end of July both sides were played out, swaying like punch-drunk fighters. Generals on both sides had demanded great sacrifices from their men and these had been freely made. It is hard to view this battle as anything other than a costly draw. Rommel's seemingly unstoppable run and the dismal series of 8th Army defeats had been halted. Mussolini could leave his stallion in stables for the moment. Indeed, the moment had most likely passed. First El Alamein must rank as an Allied defensive victory, though Auchinleck's efforts to break the Axis had, with the exception of 9th Division's northerly salient, foundered at high cost in men and materiel. Allied infantry, attacking at night, had shown competence and sustained valour but the vital support from armoured formations at dawn had not been forthcoming, leaving a wide and embittered breach between the two arms.

Driver Crawford of the RASC, who witnessed the 'tankies' in action was again more even-handed, even admiring in his assessment: 'In the earlier days they were outgunned time after time, but nothing could keep down their irrepressible spirits. How they fought in their 'cooking boxes' for hours on end I do not know. They would return from a foray wearing nothing but shorts, sun-tanned and begrimed, and looking like men from another world.[35]

As the front lines hardened, great belts of mines girded extensive positions and impeded any amount of free movement. Some writers have likened the process to the stalemate of trench warfare in the previous conflagration. It remained to be seen who might break the deadlock. Rommel had described the desert fighting as war without hate, and 8th Army observed its prisoners to be: '... a curious mixture of arrogance, belief in Hitler and surprise that the British had ever gone to war with them. They openly boasted that they were the finest soldiers in the world, and then added that the British were easily second best'.[36] The Germans were sometimes less punctilious toward Imperial troops who might not conform to their notions of racial superiority. Driver Crawford again:

> ... The enemy, having captured a Ghurka, shaved him and sent him back to the Ghurka lines. Shaving is, of course, against the Ghurka religion and is considered one of the greatest shames which can befall them. After telling his comrades what had happened, the Ghurka is alleged to have committed suicide. For the whole of that day the British officers were only just able to restrain the Ghurkas from going out to the enemy. The British officers cajoled and finally threatened the Ghurkas with all kinds of punishment ... When night came the Ghurkas lines emptied as though by the wave of a wand, and nothing was heard for some minutes. Then a great hullabaloo took place in the enemy lines, and the Ghurkas stole quietly back to their old positions. It was never known how many of the enemy died that night ...[37]

8

Alam Halfa:
August 1942 – September 1942

Here with the desert so austere that only
Flags live, plant out your flags upon the wind,
Red tattered bannerets that mark a lonely
Grave in the sand.

R. N. Currey

During this month of July [1942], when I was politically at my weakest and without a
gleam of military success, I had to procure from the United States the decision which,
for good or ill, dominated the next two years of the war, this was the abandonment of all
plans for crossing the Channel in 1942 and the occupation of French North Africa in the
autumn or winter by a large Anglo-American expedition.[1]

Thus Winston Churchill summed up the task confronting him in the wake of the Alamein
fighting. Though Rommel had been checked, he was not defeated and the threat from
Axis forces in the Western Desert remained potent. It was vital that, if the projected
invasion of the Vichy colonies Operation 'Torch' was to proceed, deadlock in the western
desert must be broken and Rommel's army along with it. Since the promising opening of
'Compass' in December 1940, Allied achievements had been modest and swiftly undone
by Axis ripostes. It appeared that British generalship, tactics, organisation and equipment
were all inferior. Observers now wondered of Auchinleck '... Has he anything left to
offer'.[2] For 'Torch' to succeed 'Acrobat' – the elimination of enemy forces in Cyrenaica and
Tripolitania would have to be exhumed, given new flesh and sinew. Churchill also had to
deal with Stalin. He needed to explain to the Soviet dictator why there could be no second
front in 1942, while still relying on the Russians entirely to bar the gates in the Caucasus.

Strategic Options

Auchinleck, though much concerned with the state of 8th Army, could never ignore other
threats which loomed over his wide satrapy. An Axis breakthrough in the north would be
calamitous, threatening Iran, Iraq and Syria, all volatile in themselves. As the soviets were

not in the habit of sharing plans it was difficult to ascertain if the northern front could be secured. The increasing demands of campaigning in the Far East, where one disaster followed another, also drained resources. Auchinleck simply did not have sufficient troops to fight in the desert while creating a viable defence to the north. The question was which constituted the greater imperative, to hold Egypt or the Persian oilfields. By 12 July[3] Churchill cabled that, as it was impossible to do both, defeat of Axis forces in Cyrenaica must remain the absolute priority. Despite the considerable gains German offensives in southern Russia appeared to be achieving it was unlikely that a complete breakthrough could be anticipated before the onset of winter halted operations. The question, however, remained: could Auchinleck, increasingly perceived as spent force, deliver the long hoped for victory?

Both he and Dorman-Smith were painfully aware the 8th Army was not placed to deliver a decisive blow. Though Rommel had been halted, this was only a check and not a reverse. Allied efforts to assume the offensive in July had been, at best, disappointing. There were significant gaps in 8th Army tactical competence and these would have to be resolved. Dorman-Smith was confident that a renewed Axis offensive could be successfully countered and that a 'modern defensive battle'[4] could be waged in the El Alamein sector. Rommel did not have sufficient infantry reserves for a blow to the north, therefore he would be obliged to attempt another wide, flanking move from the south. At this time, Auchinleck wished to formally appoint Brigadier Freddie de Guingand as chief of staff, freeing Dorman-Smith to return to his preferred job in the Delta.

Though Dorman-Smith has been credited with much of the vital tactical thinking that proceeded during the latter part of July and early August this, as Neil Barr points out, would be to underestimate the importance of the work undertaken by the C in C himself with his two corps commanders. One of the key tenets of Auchinleck's new approach was to try and close the yawning chasm between infantry and tanks. His proposal was to overhaul the divisional structure to improve mobility and coordination. Thus the 'mobile' division would include one armoured and two infantry brigade formations.[5] Logical as this might seem, it rather betrays his own lack of understanding of and bonding with his subordinates. Both infantrymen and tankers regarded this new doctrine as heresy. Major-General Richard McCreery, who commanded the armoured forces in Middle East Command, was vehement. Armoured formations trained together and this developed their particular ethos and comradeship. The idea of beefing up each tank regiment with the addition of a further, fourth squadron was equally unpopular. For once, infantry officers like Major-General Wimberley, who commanded 51st Highland Division, were *ad idem* with their tank brethren.[6]

In spite of this, Auchinleck was far from being played out. His appreciation of 1 August, while conceding that major offensive operations were for the moment out of the question, provided that both army corps would undertake vigorous raiding, involving land sea and air resources, utilising the buccaneering talents of the LRDG and SAS. Such an active defence would disrupt Rommel's fragile supply lines and prepare for the day, probably not before mid-September, when a serious blow could be delivered. General Gott prepared a further appreciation, focused on the need to counter an Axis offensive which was feared for August. He identified the high ground of Alam Halfa Ridge as 'vital for any advance down the Coast to Alexandria – they [Alam Halfa and Gebel Bein Gabir] are also vital to us for holding our present positions'.[7] Gott, in fact, correctly anticipated Rommel's subsequent plan: 'An attack with Alam el Halfa as his first objective, going round anywhere south of the Alam Nyal ridge – subsequently cutting the road in the Hamman area and thrusting straight for Alexandria.'[8] Gott made full use of Ultra intercepts to assess Rommel's likely strength and Auchinleck left the detailed working up of Dorman-Smith's broad brush appreciation to him. In concept, Alam Halfa was Gott's battle.

Ramsden was also busy looking at plans for 30 Corps. Any battle in the northern sector would resemble 'break-in' battles mounted by the BEF in 1918. Ramsden was a veteran of that titanic conflict. He noted that, in the July operations, infantry had generally succeeded in mounting successful night attacks and gaining their objectives. What had then gone wrong was the subsequent failure of armoured support to come up and prevent these gains being overrun by local counter-attacks. Ramsden considered that anti-tank guns must accompany infantry to consolidate a viable defence. Armoured support must not be tardy and pockets of un-cleared enemy activity should never be left 'in rear'. The concentration of artillery effort had paid dividends and should be developed as should a matching reorganisation of sappers. This was a 'tight' battle rather than the fluid, fast moving offensive, a classic break-in of the 1918 mould.[9]

Auchinleck, when penning his own further appreciation a day later than the first, took all of his subordinates thinking into account. He examined the prospects for an offensive, in the north, centre and south. Each was fraught with difficulty but he echoed Ramsden in viewing the vicinity of Miteirya Ridge as most promising. A break-in here could corral the Axis forces in the north and expose those in the south. In essence, the plan for the forthcoming offensive comprised the following elements:

1. A major blow in the north.
2. Diversionary activity and phoney preparations to the south.
3. Disruption of enemy supply and communications.
4. To create a defended zone behind the main El Alamein line to defeat any Axis thrust from the south.
5. To ensure armoured forces were full prepared to exploit any breakthrough(s).[10]

This was to prove Auchinleck's legacy. Far from being washed-up he had, with his subordinates, produced the blueprint for final victory in the Western Desert, even though full credit has traditionally gone to his successor. No sooner was this appreciation committed to paper than 8th Army staff, under de Guingand's able control, began working up detailed plans. This would be the true 'tight' battle, planned in detail and intensively trained for. Previous operations had failed but the lessons derived from those mistakes would lay the groundwork for final success. It should be noted that Rommel, for all his brilliance, did not appear to learn from past errors. This defect would cost him dear and ensure his eventual defeat.

Hand in hand with the need for intense preparation and training, was recognition that key operations, particularly mine clearing, should be standardised. In consequence a clear doctrine for gapping and clearing mines emerged. This emphasised the need for intense artillery bombardment to smother the enemy gun line, followed by a creeping barrage and the establishment of forward positions enabling sappers to approach their task. Full fire support could thus be directed to cover the dangerous work of the mine clearance teams. As soon as possible the lead elements of the armour should advance to test the gap, supported by anti-tank guns. Behind this vanguard the main body with infantry support would then move forward, broadening the gap as required.[11]

Dorman-Smith had earlier applied his formidable theoretical capacity to the question of defence and was most ably seconded by Brigadier Kisch, chief engineering officer. The lessons of Gazala were plain. A series of isolated brigade boxes with little capacity for mutual support and a lack of defence in depth had provided Rommel with a perfect target. Though many thousands of mines had been laid, these were not necessarily under Allied guns and could therefore be gapped with impunity. Breadth and depth were the keys to fresh planning. In the north, from Alam Nayil to the coast a dense fortified zone was to be prepared; far thinner defences were employed further south to provide Rommel with the necessary incentive. These minefields would merely delay rather than frustrate. Two brigades from 7th Armoured Division, 4th Light Armoured and 7th Motorised were deployed as a screen. Their designated task was essentially to impose delay, to avoid being drawn into a battle of annihilation and lead the enemy on toward their own nemesis.

In terms of this defensive concept, these ideas championed by Dorman-Smith were considered innovative though, as Niall Barr points out, actually reflected no more than a continuation of the methods devised by Germany in Flanders in anticipation of Haig's summer offensive of 1917. The first line would comprise of thinly held outposts intended to do no more than give warning of a major attack. When the blow fell, these forward units would retire into the main defensive positions. These would contain battalion sized groups sufficiently proximate for mutual artillery support. Between these static bastions mobile groups of guns and tanks would be stationed in readiness for a counter-stroke. As Alam Halfa Ridge was recognised as a key Axis objective the slopes were heavily fortified. Behind the Alamein position a further major defence web was to be dug in the Delta itself. As sound as these ideas may seem they were not necessarily welcome, seen as carrying connotations of defeat and withdrawal.

Despite limited successes in the previous battle, Auchinleck had never been able to develop an easy and clear understanding with his subordinates. Dorman-Smith, for all his undoubted abilities, was more a part of the problem. He appears to have held most of his fellow officers in low regard, his clear intellectual grasp conferring a somewhat Olympian view, untrammelled by the realities and exigencies of actually commanding troops in the field. The instructions given to 30 Corps appeared ambiguous; was 8th Army defending or attacking? To the Australians the idea of thinning out their positions in the Tel el Eisa salient did not appeal at all. Morshead would be pushed into explaining reasons he did not himself understand as to why his officers and men should give up such hard won ground.[12]

Gott had no such qualms and proposed the New Zealanders would hold Alam Halfa. Inglis could certainly see the logic but was unhappy in the detail, feeling the two brigade sized boxes were vulnerable. Gott in turn accepted the validity of these concerns and, importantly, there was time for Inglis and Brigadier 'Pip' Roberts commanding 22nd Armoured Brigade to fully confer and develop a better understanding. 8th Army thus prepared for Rommel; they had not, however, prepared for Churchill.

Changes at the Top

On 3 August Churchill had left England bound for Cairo. He was not alone; Brooke, Wavell and Field Marshal Smuts were to join him. Though the Prime Minister had suffered immense frustrations over seemingly endless delays and disappointments, he had always been impressed by Auchinleck's many qualities and soldierly bearing. Nonetheless in the words of the OH:

> Mr Churchill and the C.I.G.S. now carried out a brisk programme of interviews and inspections in Cairo and the Western Desert. They met many senior army and air officers, including in particular General Gott, and visited the Australian and South African Divisions. On 6th August Mr. Churchill discussed his impressions with General Smuts, Mr. Casey and General Brooke. He concluded, and his advisors agreed, that a drastic and immediate change should be made to impart a new and vigorous impulse to the Army and restore confidence in the High Command.[13]

Auchinleck's perceived failure to deliver a knock-out blow had obviously weakened Churchill's negotiating position with the Americans. With agreement reached, it was absolutely imperative that 'Acrobat' be effectively revived. It seemed increasingly that 'the Auk' would not be able to deliver. Even Brooke, his patient champion, was beginning to lose confidence and the downbeat nature of the C in C's communications further undermined his position. Auchinleck lacked the ability both to weld his subordinates into an effective, cohesive team and also the knack of dealing with his political masters, where a blunt rendition of the true position was not always the best course.

Whatever his limitations, Auchinleck shouldered an immense burden from which he had never flinched. He may not have defeated Rommel but he had stopped him dead in his tracks. His direct command of 8th Army had been a decision forced upon him by circumstances and was undoubtedly the right one. He now recognised the need for a fresh pair of hands and favoured Gott. He opined that the officer appointed to command 8th Army must be 'a man of vigour and personality and have a most flexible and receptive mind. He must also be young, at any rate in mind and body, and be prepared to take advice and learn unless he has had previous Western Desert experience'.[14]

Brooke was keen to advance Montgomery, something of a protégé but someone who the CIGS believed could deliver, his rather unfortunate character notwithstanding. Though it was not immediately proposed to relieve Auchinleck the 'chill' as Dorman-Smith described the atmosphere[15] could clearly be felt when the Prime Minister arrived at Desert HQ and the Auk had no gift for courtly diplomacy. The interview which followed in the stuffy, fly-laden heat of the operations room was not a happy one. Dorman-Smith felt he and Auchinleck were alone with a 'caged gorilla'.[16] Churchill was more on 'transmit' than 'receive', brusquely demanding offensive action without really listening to the matters being explained. Reasoning was mere excuse and Winston was not disposed to listen. He pointedly went outside with his back to his two senior officers. It was not auspicious.

Progressing to 13 Corps the Prime Minister fastened on Gott and spent some time alone with him, forming a favourable impression. Gott's excellent fighting record, high personal courage and soldierly manner impressed Churchill at a time when he was clearly utterly disenchanted with the pairing of Auchinleck and Dorman-Smith. The mere fact the Auk, like Brooke, favoured Montgomery probably helped the PM decide upon Gott as new 8th Army commander.

For Auchinleck, the die was cast and he was to be replaced by Alexander, an excellent choice, a general who was imbued with an innate flair for difficult diplomacy. Churchill expected his new C in C to lead the onslaught against the Axis personally and proposed to hive off the 'northern' Iraq/Iran sector, leaving the C in C Middle East better placed to concentrate his energies in the Western Desert. Dorman-Smith and others who Churchill saw as tainted with the Auk's brush were to be cleared out. On 7 August Gott carried out his final briefing as a corps commander, ensuring his officers in 13 Corps knew exactly what was expected of them in the coming battle. Perhaps for the first time 8th Army had a precise understanding of the enemy's intentions with a clear, coherent and cohesive plan. Infantry, artillery and armour understood their roles and the roles of their supporting arms, the senior officers were familiar with each other, were confident and ready. It seemed a propitious moment for their charismatic commander to ascend the promotional ladder.

Gott then prepared to fly to Cairo, hoping for a few days leave before taking up the command he would never exercise. Random fate relegated Gott to one of history's tantalising 'what ifs'. His plane crashed and he was killed.[17] Not all in 8th Army mourned his sudden taking off.[18] Montgomery thus gained 8th Army as Brooke would have wished but ironically by default. Auchinleck, having been summarily removed was offered the truncated northern command, more of an insult than a compromise and understandably declined. Alexander, in taking over his new command, was blessedly free of the peripheral entanglements that had bedevilled his predecessors. He reinstated McCreery whom Auchinleck had dismissed and this proved a most judicious appointment. It is hard not to feel that the historical record has been unfair on Auchinleck. Much of what was subsequently achieved was due to his and Dorman-Smith's solid preparation. He had, above all, kept 8th Army in being. Without this, neither Alexander nor Montgomery could have succeeded in their designated roles. 'Monty', it has to be said, was not one to share the limelight. Alexander's instructions were plain and as set out in a directive on 10 August:

1. Your prime and main duty will be to take or destroy at the earliest opportunity the German-Italian Army commanded by Field-Marshal Rommel together with all its supplies and establishments in Egypt and Libya.

2. You will discharge or cause to be discharged such other duties as pertain to your Command without prejudice to the task described in paragraph 1 which must be considered paramount in His Majesty's interest.[19]

Monty was nevertheless very much the new broom. Unlike his predecessor he was very much part of the UK military establishment and knew which officers he wanted, men who he already knew. He was not shy over getting rid of those who did not fit the bill. Alexander had made it plain that there would be no further retreats and that established divisional formations would stay as they were. Both of these pronouncements produced collective sighs of relief. Morale was not low but it was obfuscated by uncertainty. This would now disappear:

> General Montgomery … set to work at once to inspire confidence and enthusiasm in his Army. His address to the officers of Army headquarters made a tremendous impact, of which word soon spread. The defence of Egypt lay at El Alamein, he said, and if the 8th Army could not stay there alive it would stay there dead. There would be no more backward looks.[20]

One of Monty's most remarkable and admirable traits was the air of absolute confidence he exuded, regardless of circumstance. Here was a commander who knew his business inside out, who had an almost 'Cromwellian' faith in himself and his men. In a whirlwind tour of the troops Monty cleared away the fustian and made plain his intentions. If Rommel attacked, 8th Army was ready. When that battle was won, another and offensive engagement would follow and this time the Allies would 'hit Rommel and his army for six right out of Africa'.[21] When Monty said it people believed him.

> I introduced myself to them [HQ staff] and said I wanted to see them and explain things. Certain orders had already been issued which they knew about, and more would follow. The order 'no withdrawal' involved a complete change of policy and they must understand what that policy was, because they would have to do the detailed staff work involved. If we were to fight where we stood the defences must have depth; all transport must be sent back to rear areas; ammunition, water, rations etc. must be stored in the forward areas. We needed more troops in the Eighth Army in order to make the 'no withdrawal' order a possibility. There were plenty of troops back in the Delta, preparing the defence of that area; but the defence of the cities of Egypt must be fought out here at El Alamein.[22]

With Gott's death a new corps commander was needed and Monty drafted in Lieutenant-General Brian Horrocks with whom he had previously worked while leading South-East Command. He had in fact given significant thought to the coming 'modern' defensive battle. He had also decided to retain de Guingand, whom he knew well, in place. A wise choice as the chief of staff possessed a flair for diplomacy which his commander most certainly did not:

> I had pondered deeply over what I had heard about armoured battles in the desert and it seemed to me that what Rommel liked was to get our armour to attack him; he then disposed of his own armour behind a screen of anti-tank guns, knocked out our tanks and

finally had the field to himself. I was determined that would not happen if Rommel decided to attack us before we were ready to launch a full-scale offensive against him. I would not allow our tanks to rush out at him; we would stand firm in the Alamein position, hold the Ruweisat and Alam Halfa Ridges securely, and let him beat up against them. We would fight a static battle and my forces would not move; his tanks would come up against our tanks dug-in in hull down positions at the western end of the Alam Halfa Ridge.[23]

As part of his new broom approach Montgomery proposed to concentrate the whole HQ function at Burg el Arab and promote closer liaison with the Desert Air Force. This had rather slipped during the course of the recent fighting.[24] 'Now the two Services were to work in double harness, and, as will be seen, in their first big test – at Alam el Halfa – their mutual confidence was to be renewed in an unmistakable manner.'[25] In tactical terms Montgomery was proposing nothing radical; rather he was maintaining the careful work done by Auchinleck, Dorman-Smith, Gott and Ramsden. What he did achieve was to give this detailed planning a clear and public face as far as 8th Army as a whole was concerned. In modern parlance he put a positive 'spin' on what, though sound, had appeared confused and inherently pessimistic. Monty was also helped by the fact the flow or armaments and equipment from both Britain and the US was continuing to build.[26]

The Battle of Alam Halfa

On 'the other side of the hill' there was less general cause for optimism. As matters improved for 8th Army the position overall of *Panzerarmee Afrika* was deteriorating. Rommel continued to suffer supply difficulties. Axis shipping was suffering heavily from the attentions of British planes and warships, the air route from Crete, while less risky, was cumbersome. Most supplies, once unloaded at Tobruk, had to be brought forward by road and the port received unending attention from British night-bombers, roughly fifty aircraft every 24 hours.[27] Axis intelligence forecast the arrival of a massive Allied convoy due at Suez in early September. If Rommel was to attack it had to be soon before the disparity became crushing. The full moon was due on 26 August. Clearly this was the moment to strike.

As Gott had predicted, the blow would fall in the south, a lightning rush through the moonlit dark of the empty desert, sweeping for thirty miles, past the bastion of Alam Halfa to expose 8th Army rear areas – this to be achieved by dawn and ambitious in the extreme. His right would be covered by his German and Italian mobile formations while Ariete and Littorio Divisions (Italian XX Corps), both armoured, moved on the left. 90th Light which had been out of the line to recuperate would take the northern shoulder of the assault. Surprise, speed and guaranteed mobility were the harbingers of success. Build-up would be accomplished in the hours of darkness with panzers hidden beneath camouflage during daylight. To keep 8th Army guessing the Italian forces in 30 Corps sector would mount diversionary raids. This was, of course, precisely what Auchinleck and now Montgomery had been expecting:

I decided to hold the Alam Halfa Ridge strongly with the 44th Division and to locate my tanks just south of its western end. Once I was sure that the enemy main thrust was being directed against the Alam Halfa Ridge, I planned to move the armour to the area between the west of the ridge and the New Zealand positions in the main Alamein line. I was so sure that the movement of my own armour would take place that I ordered it to be actually rehearsed; and when it *did* take place on the morning of 1st September I had some 400 tanks in position, dug in, and deployed behind a screen of 6-pounder anti-tank guns. The strictest orders were issued that that the armour was not to be loosed against Rommel's forces; it was not to move; the enemy was to be allowed to beat up against it and to suffer heavy casualties.[28]

Alam Halfa was, as both sides saw, the key. If Rommel could get safely past, his offensive stood a very good chance of achieving success. If he could not, if the Allies remained in possession, then his position would become untenable. The ridge completely dominated his lines of communication. Defences at Alam Halfa were beefed up accordingly and the newly arrived 44th Division was brought up with two brigades 131st and 133rd deployed, supported by divisional artillery, both field and anti-tank. 22nd Armoured brigade was massed at the western end. Alam Nayil was garrisoned by Freyberg's New Zealanders together with 132nd Brigade. Behind, to the north, stood 30 Corps reserve formation, in the shape of 23rd Armoured Brigade. Eastwards, toward Point 87, was stationed 8th Armoured Brigade. Further south the deployment of 4th Light Armoured and 7th Motor Brigade had already taken place. As described above, their role was to delay rather than engage; 7th Armoured Division would snap at the flank and heel of any eastward attack. The noose was laid. It merely remained for the Fox to obligingly extend his neck.

The turned-back left flank of the New Zealand Division formed a stiff shoulder which could remain in place without the support of the relatively weak 7th Armoured Division to the south. In rear of the New Zealand Division's position was the Alam el Halfa Ridge, originally chosen by General Auchinleck to be a defended locality, and now strongly fortified and held by the 44th Division. General Horrocks's plan was for the New Zealand and 44th Division to hold their ground to the last, while in the south the 7th Armoured Division, on its wide front, was to delay and harass the enemy as much as possible. It was so likely that the enemy would try to seize the Alam el Halfa Ridge that the 22nd Armoured Brigade was placed in dug-in positions at the western end, where the fire of its tanks and the 6-pdr anti-tank guns of its motor battalion could be united with that of the supporting artillery in a strong defensive fire plan.[29]

As ever, Rommel's prime concern was petrol. Insufficient supplies could be found to enable the attack to proceed on 26 August. Kesselring promised to release some 1,500 tons from his *Luftwaffe* stocks and the Italians promised more, their ships due to reach North Africa on 30 August:

Consumption had been greatly in excess of the amounts arriving by sea, and stocks of all kinds – particularly fuel and ammunition – were running dangerously low. Rommel reported on the 22nd that, if the *Panzerarmee* was to attack at the end of August, shipments of about 6,000 tons of fuel and 2,500 tons of ammunition must reach Libya by specified dates between 25th and 30th August. *Comando Supremo* promised to do everything possible, and sent seven ships, carrying 10,000 tons of fuel, half for the *Panzerarmee* and half aviation spirit for the *Luftwaffe*. (In the event four of the seven ships were sunk).[30]

Despite these depressing shortfalls Rommel could not afford to wait, the offensive would begin on 30 August regardless.

This then was be the date fixed for the attack and everything would hinge upon whether the initial objectives were gained during the night of 30–31 August, '… the DAK had seven hours in which to go thirty miles and be ready to advance again to the attack'.[31] As the tanks rumbled forwards in the light cloak of desert night they blundered into unseen British minefields of substantial depth. As pioneers moved forward to begin gapping, a storm of fire descended. Desert Air Force swooped and added a deluge of bombs. The two British harassing formations performed their roles perfectly. When the harsh glow of dawn spread over the bare landscape DAK was still far to the west of its initial objectives. Any element of surprise was now lost. Speed and élan would give way to attrition.

For the Desert Fox there was no good news. Two of his experienced senior officers were down: von Bismarck, commanding 21st Panzer had been killed by a mine and Nehring wounded by bomb blast. Bayerlein assumed temporary command of DAK as the drive eastwards struggled to gain momentum. Even at this early stage Rommel contemplated calling a halt but instead modified his plan of attack. Now, the panzers would not seek to pass to the east of Alam Halfa but turn north, aiming for Point 132 on the line of the ridge while the Italians made for Point 102 at Alam Bueit. If a breakthrough could be achieved then the Axis forcers could continue their drive to the coast passing the eastern edge of Ruweisat Ridge. At this time however, say noon on the 31st, both Ariete and Littorio were still held in the minefields and 90th Light halted around Deir el Munassib. It was time to tighten the noose.

Monty sent 23rd Armoured Brigade to cover the gap between the New Zealanders and 22nd Armoured. This was just the type of battle he had intended to fight, his armour hull down and in strength with the Axis doing the 'balaklavering'. Both German tank divisions now barged into this strong defence and an intense battle raged all afternoon: 'A fierce duel began in which the Royal Scots Greys, the 1st and 104th Regiments RHA, and part of the 44th Divisional Artillery joined to give the enemy tanks a hot reception.'[32] The British would not be lured from their positions and the battering cost Rommel dearly. As darkness again fell the panzers withdrew. Overall, they had achieved nothing.

Night brought no relief from prowling bombers that hammered the exposed attackers, seeking out transport and supply. The milky dark was suddenly livened by the incandescent drop of flares, laying bare the bones of the desert floor, throwing vehicles into stark relief.

A most important factor which forced his [Rommel's] eventual withdrawal was the action of the Desert Air Force … Army and Air Force worked on one plan, closely knitted together … A major factor in the overall air plan was Tedder's decision to send his

Wellingtons to bomb Tobruk behind Rommel's attack, in that his last quick hope of re-supply vanished.[33]

On 1 September 15th Panzer attempted to outflank 22nd Armoured Brigade but found its advance barred by 8th Armoured Brigade. Other Axis armoured formations scarcely moved, the Italians still mired in mines. Trieste and 90th Light, further north, managed some limited gains, insufficient to affect the outcome. It was now stalemate; as darkness fell Desert Air Force began its nightly ministrations:

> A night of continuous bombing left a pall of smoke from countless petrol fires and burning vehicles. Of this and the next few nights the DAK recorded that not only was the damage very great but officers and men were badly shaken and their fighting capacity considerably reduced by the enforced dispersal, lack of sleep, and the strain of waiting for the next bomb.[34]

Montgomery, true to his expressed doctrine, refused to be drawn but, with all Axis forces committed, he could afford to deplete 30 Corps to stiffen the line at Alam Halfa. South African 2nd Brigade was shifted to a position just above the line of the ridge while 5th Indian Brigade was placed under Freyberg. From the Delta he moved up 151st Brigade (50th Division) toward the eastern rim. The noose was tightening. British armour in the south was already nibbling at Rommel's exposed flank and Freyberg was ordered to prepare for a southwards thrust. Still on 1 September the Australians mounted a major raid from their salient, 'biffing' the German 164th Division and netting a haul of prisoners, some 140 in all, though at the cost of 135 casualties sustained.[35]

Desert Air Force, whose sorties continued relentlessly, was reinforced by several American bomber squadrons. The US Mitchells added the massive detonation of their 4,000 lb bombs to the wailing chorus of destruction. To add to Rommel's difficulties his promised fuel substantially failed to materialise. The Italians had suffered further losses at sea and what was delivered remained on the dockside. Kesselring also failed to make good on his promises. On 2 September, the Fox conceded the game was up and began a phased withdrawal back through the maze of the British minefields. He expected to be attacked in force but Montgomery would not be drawn, confining his armour to harassment and cutting up stragglers.

Though Rommel might have judged his opponent overly cautious, the British attacks in July had clearly indicated that 8th Army was not yet fully ready for the offensive role. Much additional training and preparation was needed. Time, despite any urgings he might receive from Whitehall, was on Montgomery's side: 'Although it was clear to General Montgomery that Rommel had shot his bolt, he resisted the temptation to start a general counter-attack. He judged the 8th Army to be unready, and going off at half-cock would only make it harder to prepare for the decisive blow he had in mind.'[36]

Even Freyberg's push, set for the night of 3–4 September, had very limited objectives, intended to do no more than close the minefield gaps as the Axis withdrew. At 23.00 hrs on the 3rd the attack went in with the inexperienced 132nd brigade suffering heavily from enemy fire.[37] '... The enemy reaction was immediate and violent'.[38] The newcomers had 'much difficulty' in reaching their start lines, being nearly an hour late by which time the Axis had ample notice: 'There was much straggling and general confusion, which took some time to sort out.'[39] This may be something of an understatement. Brigadier Robertson was disabled by wounds and Clifton, commanding 6th NZ Brigade, was captured when he ran into enemy positions while undertaking reconnaissance.

5th New Zealand Brigade, veterans of desert warfare reached their objectives after heavy fighting. Indeed the Maoris overran enemy rear areas, wreaking havoc. Next day the Axis counter-attacked in strength. This was seen off as was the next; guns and aircraft piled into the advancing enemy. Such was the intensity of the combat that Freyberg rightly concluded any further attempts by his Kiwis were pointless, casualties were already high.[40] His subsequent request to withdraw survivors was accepted by both Horrocks and Monty. The latter remained sanguine:

> ... Moreover, it suited me to have their [Axis] forces in strength on the southern flank since I was considering making my main blow, later on, on the northern part of the front. I remember Horrocks protesting to me that the enemy remained in possession of not only our original minefields but also of some good view points from which to observe his [13] corps area. I replied that he should get busy and make new minefields for his corps. As regards the observation points such as Himeimat, it suited me that Rommel should be able to have a good look at all the preparations for attack we were making on our southern flank: they were a feint.[41]

In assessing the results of this battle[42] the OH defines the effect on morale as being of greater importance than the material gains which were indeed insignificant: 'To the Axis the battle seemed to put an end to their hopes of reaching the Delta. To the British it appeared as a clear cut victory in which Rommel had been defeated at his own game.'[43] This must substantively be correct, 8th Army had won no new ground nor destroyed the *Panzerarmee Afrika* but it had fought Rommel to a standstill and obliged him to withdraw. The limited offensive operation with the closing of the minefield gap as its objective had failed but:

> ... What had been plain for all to see was the benefit of concentrating resources, which was made possible by a particularly accurate forecast of what Rommel was going to do. This meant that the enemy's striking force could be met on ground of the defenders' choice by a tremendous volume of fire: from the air with a rain of projectiles ranging from machine gun bullets to 4,000 lb bombs, and from the ground with the concentrated fire of field and medium artillery, anti-tank guns and the guns of dug in tanks, notably the Grants.[44]

8th Army had scored a signal defensive triumph. The task now was to convert this new confidence into an overwhelmingly successful attack.

9

Prelude:
September 1942 – October 1942

The Night lies with her body crookedly flung
In agony across the sharp hills;
By the fitful moon her nostrils are taut, quivering;
She is tensed in cold sweat and lonely fear,
Giving sudden birth in dark, sly, trodden places
To her unlawful issue, blind hideous death.

Richard Spender

If Auchinleck's appreciation of 2 August proved the blueprint for the successful outcome of the Second Battle of El Alamein, there can be no question that the plan was made flesh by Montgomery. 'I was interested to read in 1955 a book called *Panzer Battles* by Von Mellenthin ... He describes Alam Halfa as "the turning point of the desert war, and the first of a long series of defeats on every front which foreshadowed the defeat of Germany".'[1] Monty was never one to pass by an observation which gilded his own laurels but there is a certain truth in Von Mellenthin's assertion. After Alam Halfa, 8th Army would never taste defeat and the Axis fortunes in Africa began, inexorably, to wane towards extinction.

Montgomery came to the southern sector of the Alamein front at Alam Halfa, and one of the first things he asked was, when did we leave England and had we had any post? Not a single soldier had had a letter. Had we any NAAFI? We hadn't even seen the NAAFI. We were scrounging as much as we could from other units – cigarettes – and understandably, other units weren't prepared to give them away or even sell them. He wanted to know why our shirts were stained – because we had only one shirt, and there was sweat – and they were hard, like bloody cardboard. He wanted to know if we'd had any leave. Nobody had had any leave at that stage. He made sure his adjutants took note of everything. He wasn't talking to the officers – he was talking to the riflemen – he was sitting inside little dugouts with the lads.[2]

Monty Makes his Mark

Monty believed the battle had shown his subordinates the need for a clear guiding hand at the top, a degree of certainty absent from his predecessor's tenure: 'The Eighth Army consisted in the main of civilians in uniform, not of professional soldiers ... to command such men demanded not only a guiding mind but also a point of focus: or to put it another way, not only a master but a mascot. And I deliberately set about fulfilling this second requirement.'[3] Thus, Monty exercised his own particular genius for self-promotion, a trait he shared with his adversary:

He [Montgomery] was wearing this Australian hat, with all the badges that were around the brim, and a pair of 'Bombay bloomers' – KD[4] shorts, which were a lot wider than the normal. Now, dressed in that hat and shorts, and with his thin legs, he looked like match-sticks in a pair of boots. Very high-pitched voice – and he didn't look like a general at all.[5]

The famous Australian bush hat and equally celebrated black beret, replete with badges became the Monty trademarks: '... I readily admit that the occasion to become the necessary focus of their attention was also personally enjoyable'. Boosting his own profile was manna indeed to Monty and nobody can deny it was necessary. To win, 8th Army had to believe in its commander as one who could outfox the Fox: 'What started as a private joke with the tank regiment which gave it [the badge] became in the end the means by which I came to be recognised throughout the desert.'[6]

Montgomey was what I call a bit of a bullshitter, but I think that was part of his act, and very effective, I think. He had to publicise himself and build up a reputation against Rommel, whose reputation was extremely high. We all thought the world of Rommel. If you were opposite Rommel, you expected something to happen. He did have a very demoralising effect on British troops. He was a bloody good general.[7]

Victory, even one as limited as Alam Halfa, came after a long, seemingly unending series of disappointments and defeats. The battle had been fought out as 8th Army command had predicted. Monty recognised the need to focus on three 'essentials'. These were 'leadership, equipment and training'. The new 8th Army commander was better placed than his predecessors in that the flow of equipment was coming on. The new Sherman tank and 6-pounder anti-tank gun went a very long way to remedy previous imbalances. The former was a tank which could match the best of the Axis and the gun was a serious tank-killer with far more punch than the obsolete 2-pounder.

Monty was ruthless in jettisoning officers he felt were below standard. He had already brought in Horrocks to command 13 Corps and he now replaced Ramsden with Leese, an officer he knew well 'and I never regretted that choice'. 10 Corps, which he was building up as an Allied response to DAK, was grudgingly entrusted to Lumsden, currently commanding 1st Armoured. Lumsden was a less certain appointment, an officer of whom Monty had no prior experience and he had reservations. Having imported two new senior commanders from the UK, however, he or rather Alexander, felt a promotion 'from within' was politic. Harding[8] was moved up to lead 7th Armoured Division.

As gunnery would be a vital element in the forthcoming offensive, Monty sent for Brigadier S. C. Kirkman.[9] 'When I told this to a senior officer at GHQ, he remarked that the present man was a delightful person and was also a golf champion. I agreed he was delightful but added that unfortunately the game we were about to play was not golf.'[10] Monty also brought on some highly competent staff officers: Brigadier Sir Brian Robertson,[11] Lieutenant-Colonel Graham,[12] Brigadier Belchem.[13] He appointed 'Bill' Williams[14] as his intelligence chief: '... it was a conversation with him which gave me the idea which played a large part in winning the Battle of Alamein.'[15]

Out of the chaos of earlier retreats, the forced abandonment and destruction of materiel, order was re-emerging. With communication lines mercifully short and a great quantity of supply flooding into Suez, losses were being made good. From Alamein to the main depot at El Amiriya was a bare sixty miles[16] and links between there and Suez were functioning. As Niall Barr observes, Wavell's realisation that Egypt could be grown as a vast workhorse had, by 1942, become a tangible reality. The Delta was a thriving war-based economy. Food was grown and reared, combining with a sophisticated industrial expansion aimed at maximum war production. These vital functions, undertaken respectively by RASC and RAOC, provided Monty with the sinews of war in the desert.

Some 30,000 Egyptians now laboured to supply Middle East Command[17] and every output reduced the need for supply by sea. The range and quantity of items manufactured was prodigious:

> ... An immense variety of work ... in June 1942 the workshops [at Abbasia] had over 900 separate jobs in hand, from notice boards to AA mountings, from meat-safes to carriers for sterilised blood-bottles, from 12,000 crates for Molotov cocktails to 25,000 trestle tops for tables. Shell and ammunition gauges and extractors of all kinds, fire ladders, open sights for 25 pounders, chairs, covers for machine guns, magnetic detectors of A/T mines, hospital trolleys, jigs, pistons, saddlery, yakdans (the sheepskin jacket beloved of Eighth Army officers), swivelchairs for tanks, tool chests, steel tent pins, special armourers' instruments etc. were only a few of these varied and special requirements.[18]

The Adversaries

As ever, Churchill was anxious to see a decisive blow struck against Rommel's depleted forces whose supply situation remained constantly critical. Despite the growing gulf in resources, Axis formations remained glued to the forty-mile Alamein front. Here at least both flanks were secure and nowhere east of Tobruk was such favourable terrain to be found. The Prime Minister desperately needed a successful offensive prior to the Anglo-American landings and he needed the airfields of Cyrenaica freed to fly escorts for convoys to embattled Malta. Montgomery, stoutly supported by his chief, would not countenance an early and ill-judged operation. He wanted time not just to equip and plan but to carry out the training he rightly regarded as vital. Consequently, and as the spread of the full moon was necessary for mine clearance, he intimated he would not be prepared to attack till 23 October. This was not popular in Whitehall but, fully backed by Alexander and Brooke, Montgomery got his way.

To deliver this decisive blow Montgomery could deploy three armoured divisions, two armoured brigade groups, a single brigade of infantry tanks, seven UK and dominion infantry divisions, two Free French and one Greek brigade groups.[19] Rommel, by contrast, and in terms of his German units, could deploy only two armoured divisions, one motorised, one partly-motorised with a single parachute brigade. The Italians added two armoured divisions, one motorised, four infantry and one parachute.[20] The disparity was far greater than this bare summation may suggest. Axis formations were under-strength and suffering acute shortage of supply. The Allies were building a marked superiority in both armour and ordnance, including anti-tank capability.

10 Corps was a new formation and was born from Montgomery's desire to create a strong reserve, well provided with armour. His initial intention was to pull together 1st, 8th and 10th Armoured Divisions together with the New Zealanders. However, 8th Armoured, which could not be given a motorised infantry brigade, was split up instead. Freyberg's Kiwis were attached to 30 Corps to take part in the first phase of the attack, the break-in. For the forthcoming battle, brigade groups were abandoned with the exception of the French and Greek units. Divisions would remain as distinct entities and fight as divisions. In principle, brigades would not be detached, though inevitably this did occur as expediency dictated.

In the air the Allies also enjoyed greater strength with perhaps 500 and more serviceable fighters as against 150 German and 200 Italian. The Axis had dive-bombers but nothing to match the medium to heavy-bombing capability of Desert Air Force. The balance of power in the air, regarded as decisive in modern conflicts, had swung firmly in favour of the British. Axis losses during the Battle of Alam Halfa were mute testimony. Coningham's plan was to smother enemy advance airfields and prevent them interdicting Allied build-up. Air attack would be round the clock, relentless; Rommel's positions would also be subject to constant aerial observation. As 8th Army attacked, the Axis would be pounded incessantly, both forward and supply zones. Amphibious forces would be deployed to mount spoiling raids along the coast and shore parties prepared to occupy the ports once the break-out succeeded.

As mentioned, with the arrival of the long-heralded Shermans, 8th Army would have tanks equal to the best of their opponents. Though much criticised later in the war for its defects, the Sherman, with its 75mm gun which could shoot HE or AP shell, appeared a battle winner. A marked improvement on the Grant where the main armament was sponson mounted. An up-gunned variant of the Crusader, the Mark III, which carried the 6-pounder was also expected. This was better, though scarcely more reliable than before and still incapable of firing AP. That dangerous gulf which previous failures had opened up between armour and infantry had yet to be bridged but some, like driver John Crawford, maintained their admiration for the tankers:

We all liked the armoured brigade men. They had a touch of something that was different. They were proud of themselves and prouder still to claim the title of 'Queen of Battle', which had been held previously by the cavalry. We liked their buccaneering way of going about. They had confidence and cheekiness sticking out a mile … The officers were the most unmilitary looking men in the whole British Army. They wore little or no military uniform! Invariably they wandered round a golfing jacket and a pair of grey flannel bags [trousers]. Sometimes they deigned to wear a forage cap and could thus be distinguished as belonging to the army. But other than that they looked like so many civilians wandering about. It was quite a common sight to see the same figures going off with shotguns, when the brigade was at rest stations, for a day's shooting in the Desert![21]

As the build-up continued, Monty could field some 1,029 tanks of all sorts including 170 Grants, 252 Shermans and 78 Crusader Mark III's. Around 200 were in rear as ready replacements with a further 1,000 in workshops throughout the Delta.[22] By contrast, Rommel had 88 Mark III Specials and less than half as many Mark IV Specials, those mounting the long 75mm gun.[23] As the OH records 8th Army disposed of a 'formidable' artillery train. Some of the new US 105mm SP 'Priests' had arrived, together with less satisfactory British variants. Around 900 field and medium guns were in the line together with 554 2-pounder and 849 6-pounder anti-tank weapons.[24] Rommel, while he could not match this weight of shot, still had a powerful arsenal of Axis anti-tank guns, around 300 of all types excluding the all-powerful 88s of which he could field a further 86.[25]

Monty had emphasised the need for training, brutally highlighted by previous failures in offensive actions. Thinning out the front to train in rear would always be a difficult undertaking but the 8th Army commander would not be deflected. One of the vital exercises involved the business of 'passing large bodies of troops through minefields by night'. This represented a new face on the old problem of siege warfare, punching a 'practicable' breach through the enemy's walls, (see Appendix 1). To feed this great enterprise and to ensure the continuation of supply from depots in rear 8th Army built up a vast fleet of soft-skinned vehicles: three dozen companies of three tonners, six of tank-transporters, nine water transport companies, and one for bulk fuel, with seven in reserve.[26] With a ration strength of 231,000, the staggering total of 2,500 tons per day of foodstuffs was needed.[27]

Rommel, if depleted, was by no means impotent. The Fox knew the hounds, at some stage, must be unleashed and he prepared to defend his lair. Defence in depth was a concept the German Army understood well and one which it had perfected during the Great War. Moreover, the Allied build-up gave the Axis time to strengthen their, already formidable, defences. The front was defined by coastline to the north and impassable desert to the south. This line could not be outflanked, therefore it must be breached in a grinding battle of attrition. Rommel had provided a double mesh of mines all along the front. The belts were, at intervals, linked to form boxes. The defenders' role in any sector was simple, to hold the line for long enough to allow the armour time to come up. Part of his difficulties lay in that he had insufficient German troops to form the static garrison and he had proven doubts over some if not the majority of Italians. To stiffen the collective spine of his allies, Rommel mixed units along the line, down to battalion level, so that every Italian formation had intervening German troops to act as a brace.

His armour he kept to the rear, 15th Panzer in the north, 21st to the south. Littorio Armoured division was attached to the former and Ariete deployed before the latter, thus splitting Italian XX Corps. Both 90th Light and Trieste Motorised Division were left in the north, westwards along the coastline. From the Mediterranean shore to Miteirya Ridge 164th with Trento Divisions held the line. Southwards, as far as Deir el Shein and Ruweisat Ridge, was the responsibility of Bologna Division. Southwards again, Brescia was deployed around Bab el Qattara. These two Italian formations were stiffened by dispersed battalions of *Fallschirmjager* drawn from Ramcke's Brigade. Down to Qaret el Himeimat Italian paratroopers from Folgore and infantry of Pavia Division manned the front.

In line with established practice, the leading edge of the first dense belt of mines was held by outposts only, with additional positions in the 'mine marshes'. These were liberally sown with anti-tank and anti-personnel mines, complicated by a deadly spread of booby traps. There were as many as 445,000 mines in total, the majority intended to disable enemy armour.[28] The outposts were not garrisoned in strength, platoon or company sized units only, with a solid supply of anti-tank and machine guns. At a distance of perhaps a mile and a quarter behind lay the principal minefields, fronted by very strong defences. One battalion would be responsible for a section of the line, say a mile wide and over three times that in depth.[29] More and numerous anti-tank guns and plentiful machine guns studded these positions. The whole defended zone was anywhere between two and a half miles and four and a half miles deep with the main gun line behind. Regardless of 8th Army's numerical superiority and weight of armour, a very tough nut to crack.

An attack upon the forward, outpost line would certainly be heralded by a massive artillery bombardment followed by infantry assault. Though this might gain some ground such deep defences would slow the attack and give clear note of where it was directed. Surprise would be gone before the main positions could be assaulted. Clearly the purpose of infantry would be to blast a gap through which Allied armour could deploy. The depth of these defences and the potency of the anti-tank guns could contain and slow an armoured thrust until Axis tanks could be brought up to seal the breach. With such thorough preparations, Rommel had done everything possible to safeguard his army and prepare for the blow that must fall. By this time he was a sick man, lesser mortals would have been ground down long before, and only an iron will kept him in harness. Nonetheless, he was obliged to take sick-leave and return to Germany while General Stumme assumed temporary command in the field.

Stumme, if he was wary, was not unduly pessimistic. He was, of course, painfully aware of chronic shortages in supply and cautioned against unnecessary consumption of fuel or ammunition, that stocks of both had to be conserved as far as possible. He knew an offensive must be launched soon but incorrectly thought the weight of preparation in the chosen sector would provide ample warning. As reported early in October to Kesselring: '*Pz Army* thinks that the main weight of the enemy attack will be south of Ruweisat, and perhaps also on either side of the coast road.'[30] Aside from patrolling and desultory flashes of artillery, October was a relatively quiet month which enabled the Axis to concentrate on developing their defences to a most potent level.

Even with Rommel gone, morale had not sunk. Stumme and his subordinates were confident they could hold the line. By mid-month he had already laid down the basis for a planned counter-stroke should a successful break in occur south of Deir el Munassib, astride the ridge or further north. Stumme would use his infantry to contain the break-in

1. Erwin Rommel.

2. Bernard Law Montgomery.

This pages: 3, 4, 5 & 6. British troops in the Western Desert.

7 & 8. British troops in the Western Desert.

Right: 9. General Archibald Wavell.

Below: 10. Bren gunners of the King's Own Royal Regiment deployed defending their camp.

11. A mortar team also from the King's Own.

12. New Zealand troops in Bren gun practice.

13. Anti-aircraft gunners in readiness.

14. A touch of colour – infantry of the
Arab legion on the march in Jordan.

15. Indian troops ambush Italian armour.

16. Communications – a
telephone exchange dugout.

Above: 17. Underground command post.

Right: 18. The grin on the face of this British soldier may be for the benefit of camera but the morale of Eighth Army, though bruised was never shattered.

19. Sinking a well – the water supply as ever was vital.

20. British troops advance through the shattered walls of an Italian fort.

21. Italian POW's, including native troops march into captivity.

22. British armoured cars assail Fort Maddalena.

23. British guns in action.

24. An Italian tank knocked out in fierce fighting.

25. A wireless operator at work in a shallow pit.

26. A long line of Italian POW's marches into captivity a Chevrolet truck keeps pace.

27. British carriers move past the ruin of Fort Capuzzo.

28. British Valentine tanks in action.

29. A British howitzer pounding Italian positions.

30. Australian carriers moving forward, dispersed according to sound desert practice.

31. Recovered shell of Grant M3 tank.

32. Rommel's Grave.

33. Montgomery's grave.

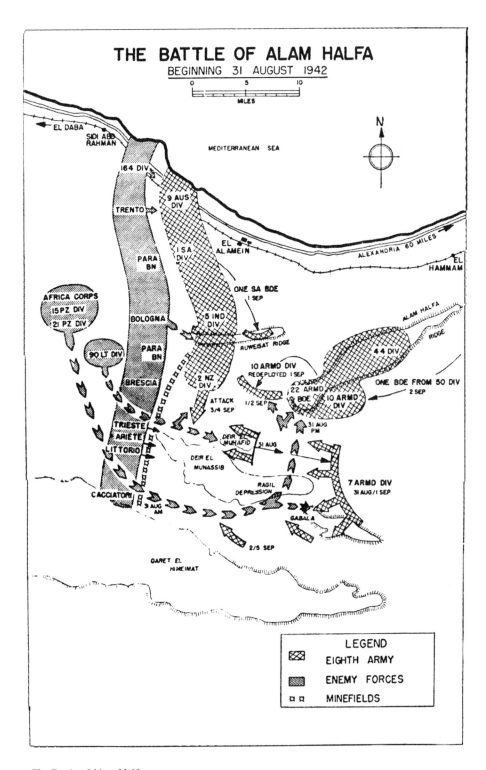

34. The Battle of Alam Halfa.

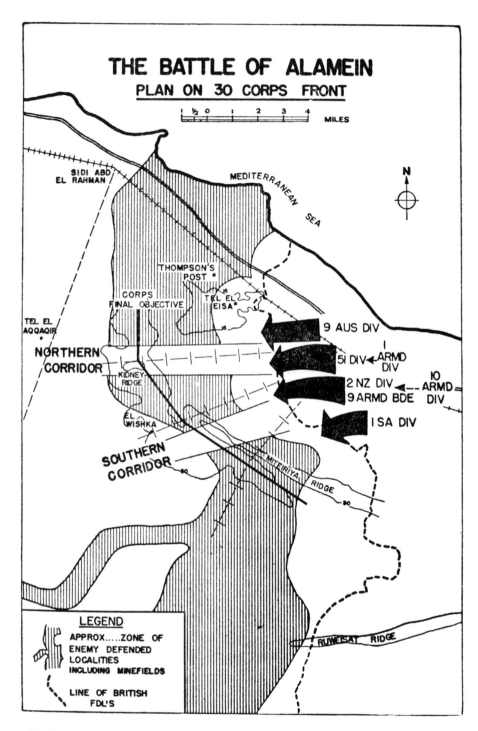

35. The Break-in – Operation 'Lightfoot'.

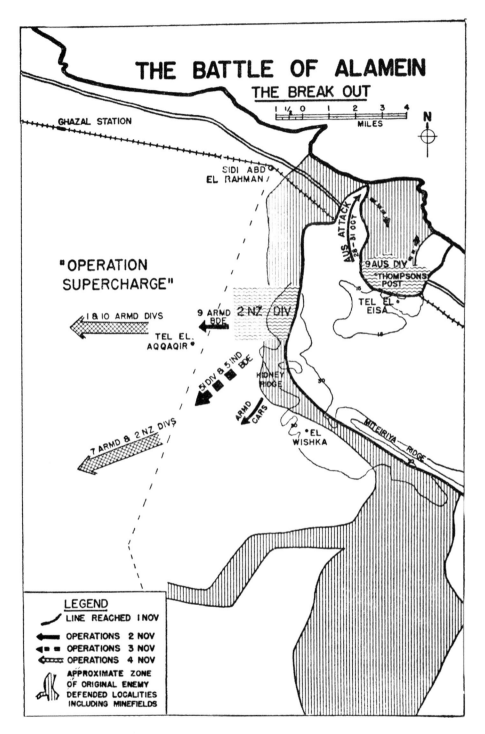

36. The Break-out – Operation 'Supercharge'.

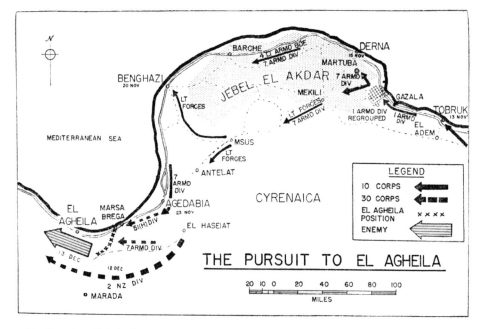

37. The Pursuit to El Agheila.

38. Rommel in his staff car.

39. British troops forty miles from Alexandria.

40. General Auchinleck.

41. British troops at El Alamein.

42. German troops captured at El Alamein.

43. British gunners manning their 6-pounder.

44. British guns firing on an enemy strongpoint. In the foreground a wounded gunner is tended by one of his comrades.

45. Vickers machine-gunners of the Middlesex Regiment firing on the German lines at El Alamein as shell bursts ahead of them.

46. British troops in a carrier take time out for a cigarette.

47. British troops taking cover behind a disabled German tank at El Alamein, a German shell bursts close to the other side of it.

48. British troops advance through the smoke of enemy shellfire at El Alamein.

49. Australian troops advancing at El Alamein.

50. British Crusader tanks move up for the tank battle at El Alamein.

51. British infantry moving forward at El Alamein in the open desert, leading men are closing in to take a German prisoner, arms raised.

52. American Sherman tanks move off into battle at El Alamein.

53. A British 6-pounder anti-tank gun at El Alamein engaging the German forces.

54. In clouds of dust raised by the blasts of their own guns a force of twenty British tanks pounds the German forces at El Alamein.

55. A British Crusader tank races through the smoke of a heavy German bomb blast.

56. A German Mark III tank lies furiously ablaze after a direct hit early in the battle of El Alamein.

57. German Mark IV Special and Mark III tanks knocked out at El Alamein.

58. Crusaders speeding along the cost road after the retreating German forces.

59. As the Eighth Army transport moved forward along the coast road, RAF Hurricane fighters race overhead in constant protective patrol.

60. British Shermans and Crusader tanks pass through Mersa Matruth.

Middle and right: 61 & 62. Symbol of the German resistance overcome: 88mm gun abandoned west of El Alamein. Nearby a tractor and 88mm gun lie wrecked by a direct hit.

63. Captured intact, this 150mm self-propelled heavy German gun is being examined by British officers.

64. The coast road is shelled by the German forces to check the British Army's advance. In the foreground an abandoned German vehicle.

Above: 65. General Alexander and General Montgomery.

Right: 66. 25-pounder gun crews launch the barrage against German forces on Friday 23 October 1942.

67. A German strongpoint captured by British infantry at El Alamein.

68. British artillerymen fire the 25-pounder guns the main instrument for the barrage.

69. British checkpoint.

70. British troops mark a newly cleared gap in a minefield at El Alamein.

while deploying his armour on the flanks to pinch out the enemy salient and surround the attackers: 'It may be necessary … for battle groups of Afrika Korps and XX [Italian] Corps to move east through our minefields to launch a concentric attack, in order to make the pincer movement as effective as possible.'[31] The *Panzerarmee Afrika* was not about to stoically accept its destruction. These men were veterans who had proved themselves many times in action. They had suffered reverses but never tasted defeat. Even if Rommel was not with them physically, the legacy and glow of his genius remained.

Deception – Operation 'Bertram'

The object of the deception plan was twofold:
1. To conceal from the enemy as long as possible our intention to take the offensive.
2. When this could no longer be concealed, to mislead him about both the date and the sector in which our main thrust was to be made.[32]

Deceit in war is as old as conflict itself, from the Trojan Horse to Operation 'Fortitude' which sought to confuse the Axis as to Allied intentions during the build-up to D-Day in the spring of 1944. In the case of Operation 'Lightfoot', as the break-in phase of the planned battle was called, deception was a significant part of overall preparation. In the north, 30 Corps sector, where the main attack was planned, a great mass of dummy vehicles, tanks and guns had been fabricated to create an impression of density. Immediately prior to the attack, under cover of darkness, these were replaced by the real thing and dummies transported to rear. Thus the static fiction was maintained. At the same time, Lieutenant-Colonel Charles Richardson, 8th Army wizard masterminding the whole show,[33] had to conceal the vast supply dumps being created. That these were satisfactorily kept hidden was a masterpiece of disguise brought into being by Lieutenant-Colonel Geoffrey Barkas,[34] director of camouflage at GHQ Middle East.

Dumps, such as that at Imayid, covered very large areas, in this case some three square miles.[35] Dummy vehicles were again employed to conceal the crates of ammunition within the timber and canvas frame, fuel cans were hidden in existing ostensibly abandoned trench lines. The distinctive 25-pounders with their equally recognisable quad tractors to be concealed in the forward areas were artfully disguised by fixing a false section to the tractor making it resemble an ordinary truck and by bunching gun and limber then placing a fake screen over.[36]

We were engaged in 'creating' a concourse of tanks and lorries and even an HQ to confuse the enemy reconnaissance planes. It was all done by hessian, some string and some very light wood, poles etc. The dummy camp and vehicle sites were erected at night with the help of moonlight and during daylight gave the appearance of busy military areas to very high-flying enemy planes. Vehicles travelled around and about creating clouds of dust and in early morning every encouragement to brewing up amongst the dummy bivouac was given, and of course, round the vehicles, or tanks, outlined in hessian, supported by thin wooden poles or 'cats' cradles of strong twine.[37]

To provide an impression that the main effort was to be directed toward the southern sector part of the overall deception involved the construction of twenty miles of dummy 'Diamond' water pipeline:

> The pipe-trench was excavated in the normal way. Five miles of dummy railway track, made from petrol cans, were used for piping. The 'piping' was strung out along the open trench. When each five-mile section of the trench was filled in, the 'piping' was collected and laid out alongside the next section. Dummy pump houses were erected at three points; water points and overhead storage reservoirs were made at two of these points.[38]

Montgomery deemed the deception plan, Operation 'Bertram' a clear success but as with most such operations this is hard to evaluate. Nonetheless, Axis intelligence remained convinced the main blow must fall in the south. One vital area, wherein 8th Army's performance improved exponentially, was that of signals and wireless communication. Ultra intercepts betrayed every Axis move and Rommel's ears had been clipped with the elimination of his elite interceptors. 'Ghost' radio traffic was added to the web of deception to mask and confuse troop movements.

> We were told that the last battle of the Alamein line – of Rommel's attack – would take place right in the sector that we were in front of – at Alam Halfa. We had something unique. We had magicians in charge of our camouflage. Large tins that had held potatoes were made to look as if they were anti tanks guns, vehicles were made with Hessian to look like tanks – tanks were made to look like vehicles. Petrol supplies were made out of any old rubbish. Water points were made where there were no water points.[39]

'Lightfoot'

'The gossip is, so I am told, that the plans for Alamein … were made by Alexander at GHQ Middle East and that I merely carried them out. This is not true.'[40] Thus Monty hastens to confirm that the planned breakthrough was all his own work. This is equally fallacious for, as we have seen, much of the concept derived from earlier appreciations penned by his predecessors, including Auchinleck, Dorman-Smith, Gott and Ramsden. He then, rather disingenuously, confirms that, 'all the plans for Alamein and afterward were made at Eighth Army HQ'. This is quite right but the intimation is that the whole scheme was Monty's alone. The General's insatiable craving for publicity was one of his least attractive characteristics.

He goes on to insist the initial plan was 'made in the first days of September; immediately after the battle of Alam Halfa was over' – Monty makes no mention of the vital conceptual work undertaken in August. Leese with 30 Corps would be responsible for the main effort in the north where infantry would 'punch' two corridors through Axis defences along which Lumsden could send 10 Corps armour. The intention was that Allied tanks would pour through the gaps and draw Rommel's panzers into a melee, where they would be irretrievably ground down.

Horrocks, in the southern sector with 13 Corps, would 'break into the enemy positions and operate with 7th Armoured Division with a view to drawing enemy armour in that direction. This would make it easier for 10 Corps to get out into the open in the north'.[41] The Desert Rats were not to get drawn into a mauling or engage in attritional 'dogfights'. They were to husband their strength for pursuit once the breakout was achieved. Monty allows himself full credit for the idea of delivering the main blow in the north and avoiding the tried tactic of the flanking attack from the south: 'I planned to attack neither on my left flank nor on my right flank, but somewhere right of centre; having broken in, I could then direct my forces to the right or to the left as seemed most profitable.'[42]

Leese was to put four divisions into the attack. Nearest the coast Morshead's 9th Australian would have the extreme right, breaking in eastwards from Tel el Eisa. Next, Wimberley's 51st Highland division, charged with assaulting towards Kidney Ridge. Then Freyberg's 2nd New Zealand Division would strike towards the western extremity of Miteiriya Ridge with, on the far left, Pienaar and 1st South African Division attacking the centre. The front stretched for four and a half miles with a depth, on the right, of five and a quarter shrinking to two and three-quarter miles on the left. Horrocks was to launch his offensive, diversions aside, on a narrower front with Harding's 7th Armoured and Hughes 44th Divisions striking out south of Ruweisat Ridge. In the main this was to convince the Axis that the main blow was indeed falling in the south and to fix 21st Panzer's full attention here. Secondary objectives included attacks on Himeimat and Taqa Plateau but these were not to be pressed home in the face of strong opposition.[43]

An intense artillery barrage, the most potent since 1918, would begin the fight at 21.40 hrs on 23 October. The guns would deluge German artillery with a weight of counter-battery fire before moving to plaster the forward defences. A rolling barrage would cosset the attacking infantry battalions, proceeding in 'lifts'. With a sufficiency of anti-tank guns in theatre, the whole weight of field artillery could be brought to bear under a centralised fire plan.[44] Early in October, Desert Air Force had taken advantage of wet weather to biff the *Luftwaffe* while much of its strength was grounded. The Axis aerodromes at Daba and Fuka were targeted and some thirty aircraft destroyed.[45] On the 18th of the month, with just five days to go till the launch of 'Lightfoot', bombing raids began in earnest. Tobruk was further damaged. Next day Daba was bombed again together with troop concentrations, road and rail traffic along the coast. Sidi Barrani, Tobruk, Daba and Fuka fields were repeatedly hit. During the night of 21/22 October Allied bombers ranged over installations on Crete. The overall strategy was for Desert Air Force to win hegemony in the air then switch to close operational support. The bombers would fly in support of the opening bombardment, seeking out those guns still able to reply. Wellingtons, suitably equipped, would jam enemy radio signals thus leaving the Axis 'blind' during those critical opening hours.

Training remained, in Monty's view and rightly, a major deficiency. His view of many of his subordinates was dismissive: 'most of the commanders had come to the fore by skill in fighting and because no better were available; many were above their ceiling'.[46] Monty had little tact and no mercy for those who came within his sights. This level of waspish tunnel vision would cause considerable difficulties with Eisenhower later on. He identifies his concerns over insufficient training as the main reason why, on 6 October, he rather radically changed tack: 'If I was not careful, divisions and units would be given tasks which might end in failure because of the inadequate standard of training.'[47] He decided to turn the key objective on its head. No longer would the intention be to draw Rommel's armour into a dogfight and leave the infantry to be mopped up at leisure. This new plan focused on a methodical destruction of the fixed defences and troops within, with enemy tanks being kept at a distance so they could not effectively intervene:

> These un-armoured divisions would be destroyed by means of a 'crumbling' process, the enemy being attacked from the flank and rear and cut off from their supplies. These operations would be carefully organised from a series of firm bases and would be within the capabilities of my troops. I did not think it likely that the enemy armour would remain inactive and watch the gradual destruction of all the un-armoured divisions; it would be launched in heavy counter-attacks. This would suit us very well, since the best way to destroy the enemy armour was to entice it to attack *our* armour in position.[48]

Monty finds the inexperience and lack of training among his formations as the perfect excuse for restricting what would have been an unsound and overly-ambitious plan. Alam Halfa had clearly shown that the way to deal with the panzers was with a wall of fire from AT guns and dug-in armour. The days of 'balaklavering' were gone.

This was a variant on the break-in battles of 1918. British armour, rather than breaking out or hurling itself into the attempt, would act as a blocking force to prevent Axis tanks coming up: 'I would then turn the enemy minefields to our advantage by using them to prevent the enemy armour from interfering with our operations; this would be done by closing the approaches to the minefields with our tanks and we would then be able to proceed relentlessly with our plans.' It was axiomatic to the success of this plan that 30 Corps could achieve the necessary break-in and open viable corridors for 10 Corps armour.

Montgomery's obsession with training was well-founded. The all important business of mine clearance and gapping had to be mastered. Without proficiency there could be no successful deployment of armour. Monty swiftly established 8th Army Minefield Clearance School (see Appendix 1). As the brunt of the break-in offensive would fall upon those four divisions from 30 Corps, training of these divisions loomed large. A major difficulty lay in the fact that two of them, the Australians and South Africans, were already in the line. Morshead's brigades were taken out one at a time for a week's intensive training while Wimberley lent one of his highland brigades from 51st Division to gain experience with the veteran Aussies. Used to the more formal regime of the British Army, the Scots found the easy ways of their new antipodean comrades something of a revelation. This did not prevent them from developing very healthy respect for these tough Aussies who had seen so much hard fighting. A series of four major dress rehearsals was held in the 51st Division's training area throughout September and October. Meanwhile, the South Africans were able to detach first the 2nd and then 3rd Brigades for training, (1st Brigade was not involved in the initial phase of the attack).

Speed was of the essence and Monty proposed the funnelling of tanks into the passages should occur before it was confirmed the breaches were fully viable. This was the tankers looming nightmare. If the tanks, bunched invitingly, were lined up and static on the morning of D+1, 24 October, they were sitting ducks. Infantrymen had been quick to castigate their armoured brethren for faint-heartedness but this was generally unfair. Tanks had severe limitations in exposed terrain and Monty's idea that, if the gaps were not cleared by dawn, the tanks should simply fight their way forwards raised hackles of alarm: 'It will be seen later how infirmity of purpose on the part of certain senior commanders in carrying out this order nearly lost us the battle.'[49]

The 'corsetting' of potentially 'unreliable' Italian units with a regular stiffening of Germans offered the possibility of employing 'crumbling' tactics primarily against the weaker partner and opening gaps in the line by destroying the Italians first; 'unreliable when it came to hard fighting'. Monty had issued general orders on morale on 14 September promising 'a real rough house'. These were followed, on 6 October, with further orders on leadership which emphasised the need to avoid mass surrendering by units simply because they were 'cut off or surrounded'. If a formation was in this invidious position they should dig in and fight it out regardless; 'by doing so they will add enormously to the enemy's difficulties'.

On 19 October, Montgomery briefed the senior officers from 13 and 30 Corps then addressed those of 10 Corps the day after. He predicted that the battle would last for twelve days (originally he proposed ten but erred, wisely on the side of caution). He reminded his officers of the task in hand and the tools they now possessed. He explained both the original and modified plans with his reasons. He pointed to the Allied superiority in guns and armour and rehearsed each element of the plan. He defined how the crumbling operation would play out and stressed the need for resolute and continued action. He cautioned against expectations of a speedy and easily won victory. This battle would produce neither.

Preparation

As early as 22 August, a major raid had been launched against Rommel's supply base at Tobruk, subsequently immortalised by Hollywood. The land based element, 'Force B', covered 1,700 miles to reach its objective, briefly rested at Kufra and was in position by 13 September. The troops were disguised as POW's under 'escort' by German speaking commandos. This ruse worked perfectly. These commandos, once the target was attained, reverted to their true, British colours. Under cover of darkness bombers pounded the port. Matters with the two seaborne detachments, Force A and Force C went less smoothly amid much confusion. The sixty or so marines who came ashore from Force A achieved nothing despite both daring and gallantry. Force B attacked and destroyed a number of coastal guns until overwhelmed. Destroyers *Sikh* & *Zulu* with the anti-aircraft cruiser *Coventry* were lost as were numerous smaller craft and eight planes. Casualties exceeded 700, (most of whom were prisoners), a very high price for such meagre gains.[50]

Similar if less ambitious attacks were put in against Benghazi and Jalo. The first, led by the legendary Colonel David Stirling,[51] failed to achieve surprise and had to fight its way clear, constantly harassed from the air. Jalo also proved too tough a nut, too heavily defended and those defenders fully alert. LRDG did however successfully attack the airfield at Barce, joyfully shooting up nearly twenty enemy aircraft. Again, however, the survivors were repeatedly blasted from the air losing nearly 50 per cent of their strength and most of their vehicles.

On 30 September the inexperienced 44th Division launched its 131st Brigade against the Deir el Munassib. The objectives were two-fold, to improve fire positions for Allied guns and also to draw the enemy's suspicions southwards. The attack was well supported both on the ground and in the air. Some ground, on the northern rim of the depression, was gained but the attack in the south stalled against stiff opposition put up by the Italian paratroopers of Folgore.[52]

For everyone, a period of waiting preceded the offensive. For senior commanders the die was effectively cast. Units were involved in moving up toward their battle positions but most found they had time on their hands. Time to rest and prepare, to play cards, to write letters home. It was an uncertain interval this period of waiting, where the worm of fear lurks in shadows, where the act of letter writing takes on a very particular significance. For those battalions of 30 Corps who would be spearheading the assault, the long daylight hours of 23 October were spent in hot, cramped and tedious anticipation, huddled in their slit trenches. Monty, as ever, breezed confidence. His tactical HQ was located on the coast north of Alamein in close proximity to those of his subordinates Lumsden and Leese. From there, on the eve of the offensive, Monty issued a 'Personal Message from the Army Commander':

1. When I assumed command of the Eighth Army I said that the mandate was to destroy ROMMEL and his Army, and that it would be done as soon as we were ready.

2. We are ready NOW. The battle which is now about to begin will be one of the decisive battles of history. It will be the turning point of the war. The eyes of the whole world will be on us, watching anxiously which way the battle will swing. We can give them their answer at once 'It will swing our way'.

3. We have first-class equipment; good tanks; good anti-tank guns; plenty of artillery and plenty of ammunition; and we are backed by the finest air-striking force in the world. All that is necessary is that each one of us, every officer and man, should enter this battle with the determination to see it through – to fight and to kill – and finally, to win. If we do all this, there can be only one result – together we will hit the enemy for 'six', right out of North Africa.

4. The sooner we win this battle, which will be the turning point of this war, the sooner we shall get back home to our families.

5. Therefore, let every officer and man enter the battle with a stout heart, and with the determination to do his duty so long as he has breath in his body. AND LET NO MAN SURRENDER SO LONG AS HE IS UNWOUNDED AND CAN FIGHT. Let us all pray that 'the Lord mighty in battle' will give us the victory.

10

Break-in:
23 October 1942 – 24 October 1942

Nothing grows in the sand-flats
Beside the salt lake at El Alamein,
The water is still and rust-pink,
And the flat sand rim is crusted with salt.

John Jarmain

El Alamein was my home for quite a while, because we were stopped. On the 23rd October, nine o'clock in the evening, that's when we heard that terrible artillery fire from the British line. I was facing the front line and suddenly the whole sky was red with gunfire. The shells were howling over you and exploding all around you – it was just horrible. We thought then that the world was coming to an end.[1]

Churchill would at last have his decisive battle:

At 22.00 hrs on 23 October three simultaneous attacks were to be made:
1. By 30th Corps, to secure before dawn on 24th October a bridgehead (objective 'Oxalic') beyond the enemy's main defended zone, and help 10th Corps to pass through it.
2. By 13th Corps, to penetrate the enemy's positions near Munassib and pass the 7th Armoured Division through towards Jebel Kalakh. This division was, however, to be kept 'in being' it was not to be exposed to serious losses in tanks.
3. Also by 13th Corps, using the French forces, to secure Quaret el Himeimat and the el Taqa plateau.[2]

Advance to Contact

Perhaps the most enduring image in the popular consciousness of the El Alamein battle is those dramatic, stabbing flames of massed artillery that presaged the attack by 30 Corps on the night of 23 October. At 21.40 hrs the guns spoke. Allied medium guns sought out the Axis batteries beyond the reach of the 25-pounders; 96 rounds were awarded to each in an intense two-minute deluge, some 1,800 shells in all;[3] an inferno of fire:

The prelude to the battle was a nightmare period of dumping ammunition at the gun position we were to occupy, on the eve of the battle … Working conditions were appalling; the
Alamein position had been fought over several times and the whole area was littered with
decomposing corpses, some unburied and others whose graves had been uncovered by the
wind. The stench of putrefaction was all-pervading and the air thick with dust and horrible
desert flies, bloated from feeding on the corpses. The fine dust stirred up by the constant
passage of vehicles during each night penetrated everywhere and a handkerchief tied over
the mouth was useless. The flies were the worst scourge … Zero hour for the battle was
some time just after dark on the night of 23rd October, and the gunners task was to start
with fire at the enemy's positions, and especially their artillery emplacements, and then go
over to a creeping barrage of fire, timed to fall just ahead of our highland infantry.[4]

As artillery boomed, leading companies in each of the four attacking divisions moved off
from their start lines. The infantry advanced, covering 100 yards every two minutes, several
yards between each individual. Most had around a mile and a half to cover to reach the
edge of the first minefield. As they moved behind the barrage, great clouds of choking dust
and cloying fumes cloaked the battlefield so men would feel they were marching literally
into the fog of war:

My most vivid memory of the battle was the opening of the barrage of over eight hundred
guns at 21.40 hours on 23rd October. I was a regular commanding my battalion – a TA
battalion of 'heavy' infantry – was in reserve but waiting to go into action and we were
therefore naturally somewhat tense. To me the sudden lighting up of half the horizon
behind us and the crash of the guns was awe-inspiring in the extreme and gave me a feeling of confidence in the Royal Regiment [Royal Artillery] that I have never forgotten.[5]

Figures loomed eerily in the shrouded night as the demonic fury of the guns split the air,
stabbing like forked lightning. The smack and thump of shells a doleful chorus as men
moved forward as though on exercise. Shock and awe of bombardment would ensure the
enemy kept their heads down in the first instance. Searchlights intended to act as beacons
punched through the murk; tracer zipped like bright and deadly fireflies. The cakewalk
would not last. Capturing this vital passage before dawn was the key objective, tanks had
to be guided through and the break-ins consolidated. For armour to be caught in the open
during daylight, strung out like a gunner's dream, was a most unattractive prospect.

It was essential that the first phase saw the enemy's outposts cleared; taking a bite
perhaps a mile beyond the forward edge of the Axis mines.[6] The gunners were assuming
infantry would be on these objectives, (collectively labelled the 'Red' Line) five minutes
before midnight. For two hours thereafter there would be a planned hiatus in the advance
while the infantry prepared to take on the main defensive positions. It was intended
these would be overrun and neutralized by 02.45 hrs and the 'Blue' Line, over two miles
distant, gained. This would leave a breathing space of three hours before dawn in which
time the attackers would dig in and consolidate; their anti-tank guns and mortars ready
to respond to the inevitable counter-attacks. Behind them, rumbling forward from 02.00

hrs, armoured formations would begin to move through gaps breached by their sappers. Operational orders stipulated tanks were never to operate at less than squadron strength, nor should they attempt un-cleared minefields, reserves should be kept in hand to meet enemy moves after dawn.[7]

Once all objectives had been gained, there would be no respite for the Axis. Fighting patrols would be sent forward to biff the enemy and spike his remaining guns. All efforts would be made to get the tanks through which was the second essential. The first was for the infantry to secure the break-in but this was incomplete if the armour did not follow. Both asked a great deal of the men involved. Battles, described in general staff terms, have a pleasing simplicity. The reality is always altogether different and the desert offered only a bare, desolate terrain unmarked by recognizable features, churned into a cloying soup. Once the ground had been taken and held, Morshead's Australians were to break out and advance further in the northern sector, Freyberg's Kiwis to burst southwards towards Deir el Shein, shadowed by the South Africans.

> What made an impression on me was not victories, large scale battles, but incidents which left an indelible impression. Such as the poor devil with his legs blown off spitting out a mouthful of sand and with it the morphia pills which had been given to ease his agony. Private Bradshaw laughing and shouting excitedly because his rifle had blown up and blown off his finger when he had fired his sand-filled weapon at a diving Messerschmitt.[8]

Close cooperation with the Desert Air Force was maintained throughout:

> Air Vice Marshal Coningham's plans for 23/24th the first night of the offensive, were to illuminate and bomb gun positions and concentrations, attack with low flying night fighters, jam the R/T communications of the enemy's armoured formations by specially equipped Wellingtons, and create confusion by dropping dummy parachutists and laying smoke. At daybreak on the 24th, day-bombers and fighter bombers would attack prearranged targets. And thereafter, with smoke-laying aircraft, were to be on call to meet the army's requests for air support.[9]

In reality, a great, massed bombardment was not entirely possible and the image of every gun along the front firing in unison, while compelling, is untrue:

> For seven minutes the enemy's forward defences received a tremendous pounding by the full weight of 30 Corps artillery. Then, at zero plus 7, the fire support began to vary with each division's needs; it consisted mainly of concentrations lifting at given times from locality to locality, except in two places where it took the form of a barrage. The whole elaborate programme lasted about 5½ hours.[10]

There was a paucity of guns in the north so the bombardment was delivered in bursts, with the main weight or fire supporting Wrigley's 20th Brigade on the left. As the brigade attacked, with two battalions 2/17th (right) and 2/15th (left) up, the Red line objectives were taken as planned. 40th RTR was then to pass through with 2/13th Battalion following.[11] The armour was held back but the infantry pushed on, not wishing to sacrifice its artillery shield. But now the going became much tougher as resistance stiffened and casualties mounted. The advance stalled. Five long hours passed till the tanks came forward, too late to prevent the curtain of night giving way to the grey of dawn and still 1,000 yards short. It was time to dig in with the exposed armour falling back to more secure, hull-down positions.

> There was a terrific explosion, and something flew past my head; it was a leg with a boot on it. A round of HE had taken Chalky White's leg off. He was looking at me with astonishment and pointing to the raw, bleeding stump with the white bone sticking through. I went towards him with the idea of helping him, I think. Just then the machine gun opened up again and poor Chalky got it full in the face.[12]

On the northern flank of the division, Godfrey's 24th Brigade was not seriously engaged, apart from mounting diversions and lending a battalion as reserve. 26th Brigade (Whiteley) was detailed to take and cover the northern shoulder. By midnight the Red Line objective had been secured by 2/24th Battalion and 2/48th passed through on schedule. Despite heavy fighting, these reached the Blue Line by the allotted time. Such precise reporting gives no true note of the horror and confusion which reigned on the field that night: 'A bullet smashed into my hand causing me to drop my rifle. I felt something boring into my shoulder and a taste of blood in my mouth. Nearly everyone seemed dead or dying, and I ran away from the senseless slaughter, unable and unwilling to stay and let myself be shot full of holes like a colander.'[13]

51st Highland Division

The highland regiments of the British Army have always enjoyed a high reputation and Wimberley, rightly, had every confidence in his men. Though new to the desert they had trained hard and were ready. Nonetheless, their task was a most formidable one. They would have to fan out from the start line to attain their final objectives with a frontage of nearly double, the whole studded with very strong defences. In recognition of this, extra halts had been added on Green, then Red, on to Black and finally the Blue lines Each of the great mass of defended areas was dubbed with a homely Scottish name. More than in any other sector this was to represent a Great War battle. The troops even had the Saltire, outlined in scrim cloth, across the rear of their packs. Each carried sufficient ammunition and rations, plus entrenching tools and materials for a full 24 hour period.[14]

It was just after ten that the rant of skirling pipes heralded the advance. Murray's 152nd Brigade was tasked to hold the front line and continue the business, begun on previous nights, of clearing and marking routes in the western openings of the three designated tracks; 'Sun', 'Moon' and 'Star'. The job facing Houldsworth's 154th Brigade was daunting; nearly three quarters of the front was their battleground.[15] Advancing on the left of the line, and on the right of the brigade frontage 1st Black Watch and 7/10th Argyll & Sutherland Highlanders would come up against 'Stirling' a very heavily fortified locality. To their left, two companies of 5th Camerons would advance to the Red Line, 7th Black Watch would leapfrog to seek out the Kiwis on Miteiriya Ridge. Into the gap between the Camerons and Argylls, 50th RTR would deploy and seize a further stronghold, 'Nairn' and then press on towards the Blue Line:

> The line had broken up into blobs of men all struggling together; my faithful batman was still trotting along beside me. I wondered if he had been with me while I was shooting. My runner had disappeared, though; and then I saw some men in a trench ahead of me. They were standing up with their hands above their heads screaming something that sounded like 'Mardray'. I remember thinking how dirty and ill-fitting their uniforms were and smiled at myself for bothering about that at this time.[16]

On the right of 154th Brigade, Graham's 153rd would attain the Red Line with 5th Black Watch who would then pass the baton to 1st Gordons tasked to assault another very strong position, 'Aberdeen'. On the left of the brigade advance, 5/7th Gordons would undertake the job of capturing yet another Axis bastion, 'Strichen'. As the pipes sounded their familiar clarion call to battle, 5th Black Watch stormed forward into an intensifying enemy fire that claimed, among others, the life of nineteen-year-old Piper MacIntyre.[17] As the dust and murk descended, lit by flashes of detonations and livened by the crack of rounds, cohesion slackened and the Green Line was mistaken for the Red. The Gordons could not immediately advance as heavy shelling was splintering the dark some 300 yards ahead; 'our guns or theirs' the not unfamiliar cry: '… when I discovered there was no on my left either, my anger turned to fear … a nauseating wave of terror went right through me'.[18]

Some minutes behind schedule the advance continued as did some confusion. 'Braemar' which was 1,000 yards west of 'Kintore' was stormed and almost overrun. This put them almost on the Black Line but losses had been severe. One company, detached in support of 'A' Squadron 50th RTR, dealt with 'Kintore' then the armour raced on to engage 'Aberdeen' only to fall foul of un-cleared mines. The other Gordon battalion had encountered similar difficulties short of the Red Line. Axis machine guns began their rapid, staccato rattle, spitting fire from 'Keith' and 'Strichen' both covered by mines. The advance was slowed. One company, attempting to flank a first minefield, became meshed in another.[19] The net result of these accumulated obstacles was that the brigade had scarcely been able to penetrate much beyond the Red Line when dawn broke.

> In front of me a terrified Italian was running round and round with his hands above his head screaming at the top of his voice. The men I had signalled started to come out. Suddenly I heard a shout of 'Watch out!' and the next moment something hard hit the toe of my boot and bounced off. There was a blinding explosion, and I staggered back holding my arm over my eyes instinctively. Was I wounded? I looked down rather expecting to see blood pouring out, but there was nothing – a tremendous feeling of relief. I was unhurt. I looked for the sergeant who had been beside me; he had come to take the place of the one who had fallen. At first I couldn't see him, and then I saw him lying sprawled out on his back groaning. His leg was just a tangled mess.[20]

1st Black Watch was on the right of Houldsworth's Brigade, hugging the fiery screen of the barrage. The Red Line was reached but moving forward from there entailed much bitter fighting. They reached and even passed their final objectives which included 'Perth', another strong bastion. Doggedly, the attacking company battled through the insidious web of anti-personnel mines, despite very heavy loss. 7/10th Argylls pressed on beyond the Red line into the teeth of furious enemy fire:

> One of the most memorable and still chilling and nightmarish things is hearing the voices of those who'd been badly wounded, their voices raised in terror and pain. I can remember one particular sergeant who's always seemed to me almost a kind of father figure … He was badly wounded and hearing his voice sort of sobbing and calling for his mother seemed to be so demeaning and humiliating and dreadful.[21]

Companies were shredded and the tanks of 'C' Squadron 50th RTR slow in coming up. 'Stirling' remained unvanquished as the survivors dug in. With dawn, chances of successfully taking the position evaporated. On the left 5th Camerons reached their Red Line without difficulty, 7th Black Watch passed through but sustained very heavy casualties before reaching Black. Captain Cathcart led a much reduced company onto Miteiriya Ridge and took 'Kircaldy' a remarkable feat of arms, though the cost was high indeed. The wounded Cathcart was able to establish a link to the Kiwis on the depleted unit's left. Even this proved difficult due to the severity of losses incurred.

> I suddenly felt furious; an absolute uncontrollable temper surged up inside me. I swore and cursed at the enemy now crouching in the corner of the trench; then I fired at them at point blank range, two, three, and then click! I had forgotten to reload. I flung my pistol away in disgust and grabbed a rifle – the sergeant's, I think, and rushed in. I believe two of the enemy were sprawled on the ground at the bottom of the square trench. I bayoneted two more and then came out again.[22]

For the tanks it was not a happy night. Gapping proved far more difficult and time consuming than had been anticipated. The flail tanks did not appear and there was a distinct dearth of detectors which forced the sappers back onto the tried if slow and dangerous business of prodding with bayonets.[23] It was 02.30 hrs before the armour moved and then only to encounter yet more un-cleared mines. As the vehicles crawled forward they were met by heavy and accurate fire which knocked out several. Wimberley's division had attacked with great élan and the highlanders had advanced upon their objectives with outstanding courage and resolution. Despite such gallantry the overall position was not satisfactory. With the exception of the extreme left, final objectives had not been secured, the main defensive line was un-breached and a number of strongpoints survived in rear: 'Kintore', 'Stirling' and 'Strichen'. The armour had not been able to punch through and the swirling chaos of dust laden darkness cast a pall of confusion over the field.

2nd New Zealand Division

Freyberg's New Zealanders were old desert hands and had learnt much from earlier fights. His front was less extensive than that allotted to Wimberley, one and a half miles widening out to twice that. Freyberg planned to husband his resources, deploying one battalion from each of his two brigades to seize the Red line objectives. When this was consolidated, a two hour pause being allowed, the other two battalions from each brigade would push on, halt briefly, then drive toward their objectives over Miteiriya Ridge. The Maoris were detailed to follow behind both and mop up as they advanced. 5th Brigade (Kippenburger) on the right would be supported by Royal Wiltshire Yeomanry, while Gentry's 6th Brigade would have the Royal Warwickshire Yeomanry.

The guns, with additional batteries from 10 Corps, delivered timed barrages against the enemy's known strongpoints with only a token fire across the front. As Kippenburger's infantry surged forward, the 23rd Battalion suffered heavy loss past Red, though ably supported by the following Maoris. 21st Battalion, passing through 23rd advanced steadily and gained their objectives, digging in on the leading edge of the ridge. Contact, as mentioned above, was established with the Scots on their right, fighting patrols probing forwards. Gapping, as ever, proved problematic and heavier weapons were slow in getting up.[24] On the brigade's left flank, 22nd Battalion suffered casualties from the same redoubt that had troubled the 23rd though the position was outflanked and dealt with. With this hurdle overcome, the Kiwis took their objectives and, despite being heavily mortared, were able to send out fighting patrols. Behind the infantry patient work of gapping went on, beset as ever by difficulties but a cleared route to the forward positions was finally opened before dawn.

Gentry's left hand battalion, the 24th, ran into heavy enemy fire and took casualties before they even reached the Red line. As 26th Battalion came forward on the right they suffered under intense shelling, possibly 'blue on blue' in the modern idiom. Nonetheless, they attained their objectives on the ridge, unlike 25th Battalion which ran into serious opposition and, though they came up to the ridge, were not able to move across the crest and dig in on the western slopes. While the New Zealanders had attained nearly all of their objectives, the line remained incomplete with a considerable gulf between 25th and 26th Battalions, nor, at this point, was their any trace of the South Africans. At length, heavier weapons were brought up and the Maoris battled their way forward to the ridge.

Behind the Kiwis, Yeomanry armour rumbled forward. The Wiltshires, who were on the right, successfully negotiated the ridge but lost nine machines to mines. Their advance was met be a stiff counter-attack from Axis tanks and the survivors withdrew behind the rise. The Warwickshires had a similar experience, gaining the ridge by 04.00 hrs but falling foul of more mines before going hull down. Initially in reserve, 3rd Hussars moved up after being heavily shelled and took station to the right of the Warwickshires. For the most part, the ridge was now in Allied hands, yet no sign of more armour passing through. The undetected mines on the crest and beyond had scuppered any chances of the Yeomanry getting forward. It was indeed a job very well done but did not offer any immediate prospect for exploitation. The late arrival of support weapons naturally left the infantry feeling vulnerable:

The inferno that was the great battle of Alamein continued unabated. The appalling din of guns firing and shells bursting, the grim sights of mangled men and twisted corpses, the nauseating smell that was a mixture of sulphur and rotting human flesh, the mental strain from sleeplessness and responsibility, the fear of breaking down in front of the men; all these became everyday things. I suppose that we grew accustomed to them, for as time went on we noticed them less.[25]

1st South African Division

In the sector allotted to Pienaar, he adopted a similar deployment to Freyberg. His 2nd Brigade was on the right, 3rd to the left. A scratch force of armoured cars and A/T guns was deployed with 1st Brigade on the extreme left to secure an open flank. Heavier armour, from RTR, with 2nd Regiment Botha was to keep pace with the advance in the centre, provide support and seize such opportunities as events might offer. The divisional guns, with extra batteries, would provide full fire support with the addition of smoke to facilitate regrouping during the pauses. The brigades attacked with one battalion 'up' and two waiting to strike beyond the Red line. It was the 1st Natal Mounted Rifles from 2nd Brigade who took Red but the Cape Town Highlanders following were badly mauled by intense enemy fire. Their difficulties led to delays in the continuing barrages. Despite this, the advance was successfully resumed and Miteiriya Ridge was gained before dawn. Left of the Highlanders, 1st/2nd Field Battalion had a stormy passage, taking many casualties and halting a mile east of their final target.

Leading 3rd Brigade's attack was 1st Rand Light Infantry, who ran into opposition barely west of their start line. Despite this they overcame the obstacle, took prisoners and reached the Red Line barely behind schedule. The delay worked to the advantage of Imperial Light Horse and Royal Durban Light Infantry, as the artillery schedule caught up and both battalions were on their objectives before first light. As ever delays in gapping slowed the divisional reserve and dawn was breaking before they approached the eastern flank of the ridge. Mercifully, they sustained no casualties. The situation overall was similar to that of the New Zealanders; most objectives had been taken but no prospect for exploitation arose. Further south of Pienaar, 4th Indian Division had performed its diversionary role admirably. Despite the very real difficulties, dust and confusion, 30 Corps had achieved a great deal, considering the plan was an extremely ambitious one. For their brethren in armoured chariots, there was no cause for celebration that night.

10 Corps

I was pretty impressed the night of Alamein, when the guns opened up. It was tremendous. All our searchlights were facing upwards in the sky to make a false daylight, to make things easier. When we went through the minefields and got to the first positions, there were dead Italians everywhere. I can remember seeing a man in his trench with his mess tin in front of him. He was dead. The barrage had opened up so suddenly, it had caught them well and truly unprepared.[26]

Montgomery had intended this formation would be his answer to DAK. Its strength was impressive containing some 434 tanks of which roughly half were Shermans. 1st Armoured Division (Briggs) was to advance on the extreme left of the Australians while 10th Armoured (Gatehouse) came on through the flank of the New Zealand Division. Each of these was responsible for gapping its individual paths. The Minefield Task Forces[27] assigned to each division would need to clear three lanes for the tanks. These would be some 500 yards separate, 1st Division had Sun, Moon and Star, 10th Division would proceed along Bottle, Boat and Hat. The monsters rumbled forth from their rearward lairs after dark. Springbok Road running south from El Alamein marked a jumping off point. Their fuel tanks replenished, these leviathans were to be on their designated lanes by 02.00 hrs. The plan was that the leading squadrons of 2nd Armoured Brigade, from 1st Armoured Division (Fisher), and 8th Brigade from 10th Division (Custance), would be in position to break out from the infantry positions astride the 30 Corps objectives. During the course of the initial move, a distance of some three miles west to 'Pierson', 24th Armoured Brigade (Kenchington), would deploy to the left of Custance.

These three brigades still, as it was hoped, operating under the cover of darkness, would be ready to meet whatever the Axis might throw at them. As the cloak of night was whipped away, Fisher and Kenchington would motor on for another mile. The tanks' northern flank would be covered by 7th Motor Brigade (Bosvile) and in the south by 133rd Lorried Infantry Brigade (Lee). The final bound, now in broad daylight, would bring Fisher as far as the Rahman track and place Custance, after a four mile dash, just south. As the tanks ground forward, armoured cars would race ahead trying to locate 15th Panzer and to give warning of any riposte by Axis armour from the south. It was thus hoped that, fog of war notwithstanding, these three brigades could engage and neutralize any enemy tanks, though Lumsden had issued a strict order against any 'balaklavering' – the days of charging full tilt onto an Axis gun line were most definitely over:[28]

> The leading armoured brigades were therefore to be prepared to deploy and if necessary fight through to open country. But General Lumsden warned them that they must on no account 'rush blindly on to the enemy's anti-tank guns or try to pass through a narrow bottleneck which is covered by a concentration of enemy tanks … There is no doubt General Lumsden was very uneasy about the role given to his Corps …[29]

This element of caution, which Montgomery was apt to decry as timorousness, would lead to friction and confirm the army commander's doubts over the corps' commander's suitability for the role.

Then there were mines. Gapping, begun generally on time, did not proceed smoothly. Sun route was not opened as far as the infantry forward positions till 05.00 hrs. On Moon track, defective detectors and enemy resistance completely disrupted the programme. The enemy strongpoint 'Kintore' was not taken till 09.00 hrs which brought the sappers only as far as the second minefield and by the time this was dealt with, the third was impossible. Star was 'loaned' to the New Zealanders for a time and they were not clear until 03.00 hrs. By 04.30 hrs, the second minefield was only partly gapped and further progress was impeded by 'Strichen' which remained in enemy hands.

For the tanks to advance, even where gapping was complete, was no easy matter. Navigating in the dark with the endless billowing clouds of dust settling a sticky pall over men and vehicles proved almost nightmarish. Signs were difficult to spot, vehicles blundered off the lanes. Some were disabled by mines. The crowding came to resemble a vast traffic jam, a driver's purgatory. Tanks struggled forwards, the Queen's Bays group astride Sun, 9th Lancers, with Brigade HQ on Moon and 10th Hussars group on Star. The Bays came to think they were a good deal further west than was in fact the case. Optimistically, they radioed they were, by 05.00 hrs, passing through the third minefield. They were not, they were barely clear of the first. The Lancers fared little better, dawn found them just clear of the first minefield, their support troops engaged in reducing 'Kintore'. 10th Hussars were similarly discommoded by 'Strichen'. In short, though enemy action had been paltry, the entire brigade was still way too far to the east; 'the achievements of 10 Corps fell a long way short of [these] expectations'.[30]

Further south, Custance and Kenchington, with more vehicles to manage, also encountered difficulties but, by 04.30 hrs a quartet of cleared lanes had opened the tank highway onto Miteiriya Ridge. Opposition had been stiffer, the mines more numerous. 8th Brigade led the way, Staffordshires on Bottle, Sherwood Rangers astride Boat and, using Hat, 3rd RTR, armoured cars following. Enemy fire and yet more mines obliged the Staffordshires to halt on the eastern flank of the ridge. A deluge of fire also greeted the Sherwood Rangers as they traversed the crest and they too were obliged to pull back, though not without loss. Delays in gapping caused 3rd RTR to lose the cover of darkness as they were still labouring through the mines. They finally managed to work forwards to positions on the left of the Sherwoods. There was no prospect of the armoured cars being able to break free. Behind Custance's Brigade, Kenchington's was stalled in the great mass of vehicles and guns attached to the Kiwis and South Africans. Another vast and apparently random scrum of vehicles began to build up.

13 Corps

As the infantry divisions of 30 Corps and the armour of 10 Corps put in their great offensive in the northern sector, 13 Corps in the south was tasked to break through 'January' and 'February' minefields and push its tanks beyond. For this, 7th Armoured Division deployed two of its brigades: Roberts' 22nd Armoured and Roddick's 4th Light Armoured. The approach was over thirteen miles and through three lines of Allied minefields. A Minefield Task Force would then clear four gaps through the Axis mines allowing 22nd Brigade to penetrate some 6,000 yards beyond[31] with 4th Light Armoured Brigade clinging to their coat tails.

This onslaught would begin at 22.00 hrs to coincide with 30 Corps attack. Four regiments of field artillery would provide a covering barrage while 131st Infantry Brigade, (from 44th Division), protected the northern shoulder with the Desert Air Force and the guns contributing dense smoke immediately south. Further south still, on the extreme flank, Koenig's 1st Fighting French Brigade Group would seek to penetrate for ten miles and seize high ground at Naqb Rala. The Minefield Task Force was led by 44th Reconnaissance Regiment with elements from 4th and 21st Field Squadron RE, a troop of Honeys from the Scots Greys with half a dozen Scorpion flails.

> We set off. Exciting, breathless. And that sort of orchestral music of the continuous guns in the background. We wondered if the Jerry saw it that way! I remember seeing a captain walking behind a Scorpion. Intent on supervising the job. This tank had a barrel fastened across its nose which revolved. Fastened by one end were chains which whirled round and thumped the ground ahead. Supposed to blow up any mines in its path. Something seemed to worry the captain and he literally screamed at the crew and someone nearby. On edge, poor devil. Some Job![32]

'January' was thought to be some 350 yards in depth, 'February' perhaps thrice that. Four lanes had to be cleared and the work progressed despite the gradual elimination of the flails and some enemy fire. By 02.30 hrs the southerly lanes were cleared of mines but Axis outposts had to be tackled by infantry from 1st Rifle Brigade. By 04.00 hrs a bridgehead had been consolidated but this now left 'February' a denser obstacle and with the task force much reduced. It was thus decided to utilise two lanes only. Even this proved too ambitious, intense enemy fire descended like the dawn chorus and the attempt could not be continued. Further north, 131st Brigade's attempts had met with equal frustration, the assault on an enemy strongpoint had resulted in heavy casualties among 1/7th Queen's Royal Regiment. Koenig's Group, after hard fighting and difficulties in bringing up heavy weapons, could do no more than win a toehold south of Naqb Rala. Gains in 13 Corps sector were modest and costly while falling far short of what was hoped for.

> So we set off late one evening, two battalions, two companies up in line abreast across a thousand yards of minefields, led by an officer on a compass bearing and Lieutenant-Colonel East using a stick as a result of a First World War wound. We were to advance behind a barrage of a thousand guns. There were casualties in the platoon on my right from one gun firing short or possibly from the enemy replying. I can still remember the shrick from one of my platoon when a booby trap on the barbed-wire literally blew him to pieces … Eventually our leading platoon and the 1st/6th Queens on our left arrived in the middle of the Italian positions and some twenty to thirty Italians cheerfully gave themselves up and remained for the next twenty-four hours, withdrawing with us at the end of that time. The remainder of the Folgore Division, however, were made of sterner stuff and proceeded to inflict heavy casualties on us, using mortars and machine guns, firing from entrenched positions. I remember young O'Connell, both legs severed by a mortar bomb, screaming for help and then for his mother before he mercifully died.[33]

24 October

The next day we moved forward through a narrow gap cleared through the enemy mine-fields and took up a new position, from which we fired another formidable box-barrage that night. During the day we came under fire for the first time from a distant ridge, on which we could just see enemy tank turrets appearing from time to time.[34]

Dawn threw the battlefield into sharp relief, though much smoke and dust lingered. Montgomery had to plan his next moves in the light of what had, and had not, been achieved. It was imperative that the northern corridor on 30 Corps front be cleared and that the Kiwis should attempt to break out southwards from the hard won ground at Miteiriya Ridge. Morshead was to prepare for a 'crumbling' operation that night. In the south, a way had to be found through the 'February' minefield. If 7th Armoured could not get tanks through then the infantry from 44th Division must undertake the task. Monty remained convinced that 10 Corps armour must penetrate as far as 'Pierson', as previously proposed. He hammered home to Lumsden, of whom he had swelling doubts, of the need to achieve this objective, even if heavy casualties were sustained. Freyberg, as he exploited southwards, would need the tanks covering his flank.

Throughout the day, Desert Air Force was heavily engaged. Axis armoured groups and aerodromes received a great deal of attention while, in the south, a squadron of British light tanks, in German hands, was destroyed by cannon-firing Hurricanes. Losses among the attacking aircraft were high and over 1,000 sorties flown.[35] Along the front, guns bickered and Wimberley's Highlanders, aided by infantry tanks from 50th RTR, eliminated Axis outposts previously bypassed. The grinding business of clearing and gapping minefields continued, enabling 2nd Armoured Brigade to inch forwards in the teeth of savage enemy fire. By evening, however, the lead units were on the 'Oxalic' line between Australians and highlanders.

Two thrusts were planned for the hours of darkness. 10th Armoured was to push on over Miteiriya Ridge with 24th Brigade to the right and 8th to the left, 'Pierson' its earlier objective, being the goal. Each brigade of tanks would be supported by a squadron of RE to deal with mines and a single battalion from the lorried infantry would remain on the ridge, acting as a 'pivot of manoeuvre'.[36] To provide further support, 9th Armoured Brigade, attached to the New Zealanders, would keep pace on the left flank of the 8th. This move would have the benefit of a full artillery programme and barrage, seeking out enemy guns and strongpoints. Axis battlegroups would again receive the very best of the Air Force's attentions.

From the very beginning the plan began to unravel. Inevitably, mines were thicker than imagined on the western slope. Axis guns were not subdued and added their chorus of destruction as the sappers laboured. Immediately after 22.00 hrs, zero-hour, the *Luftwaffe* scored a mercifully rare success when they blitzed 8th Brigade at the very worst moment, in the act of assembling. Bombs rained down havoc. The resultant flames from burning vehicles greatly assisted the Axis gunners. In such circumstances, it made excellent sense for all vehicles to disperse but this destroyed the timetable. The artillery barrage disappeared, rolling westwards. By midnight, Custance felt the advance could not proceed and accordingly reported to Gatehouse who, sharing his subordinate's fears, alerted Lumsden, who concurred.

> As we topped the crest the enemy opened up. The covering party rushed the post. Half of them were hit before they got there, but they captured the chaps causing us all the trouble. While they were doing this we probed for mines. Yes, there they were, our own, captured in June and re-laid by the Boche. That was a good start. I found the far end of the field and placed my light. I went over to the infantry and told the dazed corporal to get back. The prisoners carried their officer – shot in the stomach. They told he'd led the charge waving an empty pistol. A Boche prisoner told me in French there were no more mines and that the next field was a dummy. I believed him, he was in such a state. The enemy machine gun fire grew worse, the tracer appearing to fill the air and make an impenetrable wall.[37]

Montgomery's doubts in his 10 Corps commander stuck deep. Lumsden was not one of his nominees and was, if nothing else, a handy scapegoat should one be needed.

> In accordance with my orders I expected the armoured divisions to fight their way out into the open. But there was some reluctance to do so and I gained the impression during the morning they were pursuing a policy of inactivity. There was not that eagerness on the part of senior commanders to push on and there was a fear of tank casualties ... The 10 Corps commander [Lumsden] was not displaying the drive and determination so necessary when things begin to go wrong and there was a general lack of offensive eagerness in the armoured divisions of the corps.[38]

This was, of course, grossly unfair and reflects more upon the Army commander's antipathy to his subordinate than upon tactical realities. De Guingand, on hearing from Lumsden, had summoned both him and Leese to 8th Army Tactical HQ for a meeting at 03.30 hrs. Monty, on being awakened, agreed:

> Leese and Lumsden arrived on time and I asked each to explain his situation ... I discovered that in the 10th Armoured Division, one of the armoured regiments was already out in the open and that it was hoped more would be out by dawn. The divisional commander [Gatehouse] wanted to withdraw it *all* back behind the minefields and give up the advantages he had gained; his reason was that the situation out in the open would be very unpleasant and his division might suffer heavy casualties. Lumsden agreed with him; he asked if I would personally speak to the divisional commander on the telephone. I did so at once and discovered to my horror that he himself was some 16,000 yards (nearly ten miles) behind his leading armoured brigades. I spoke to him in no uncertain voice, and ordered him to go forward at once and take charge of his battle; he was to fight his way out and lead his division from in front and not from behind.[39]

Admirable firmness but the real problem was that Monty's plan was not, at this stage working. Both Custance and Gatehouse were correct in not wishing to see their formations decimated to no purpose. They were not faint-hearted merely pragmatic. Of course, this would simply not do for the Army Commander:

> … there would be no departure from the plan. I kept Lumsden behind when the others had left and spoke very plainly to him. I said I was determined that the armoured divisions would get out of the minefield area and into the open where they could manoeuvre; any wavering or lack of firmness now would be fatal. If he himself, or the commander 10th Armoured Division, was not 'for it', then I would appoint others who were.[40]

By 04.20 hrs Lumsden, doubtless still smarting, instructed that 24th Armoured Brigade must attain its goal and that the 8th had to have one of its regiments moving forwards to maintain contact with 9th Armoured on its left. Initially, it appeared that two regiments from 24th Armoured were on 'Pierson' by the time dawn broke on the 25th though this was probably inspired more by optimism than reality but all three regiments of 8th Armoured had filtered through the single cleared lane past the mines. 9th Brigade and the New Zealand Divisional Cavalry, in the teeth of fierce bombardment, had moved perhaps half way to their objectives. Here they were stalled by a hail of rounds from dug in tanks and guns perhaps 1,000 yards distant. Currie now sought permission from Freyberg to retire and replenish before attacking but his request was denied. Custance, as he moved west, was coming under an intensive and increasing enemy fire. The bare ground offered no suitable features for taking hull-down positions so he fell back to the eastern slope of the ridge. By now, with the New Zealanders' 5th Brigade in situ and the fresh battalions of lorried infantry crowding in, the locality was becoming rather congested:

> One of my recollections is about our divisional coppers. The Military Police manned the entrances to the gaps in the enemy minefields throughout the early days of our attack. It was a lonely job, not without its dangers from odd shells and mines going up. I was most impressed by their fortitude and I passed up and down to have a word.[41]

In 13 Corps sector to the south, renewed efforts to force the passage of the dense 'February' minefield, despite the immense courage of both sappers and infantry to clear the lanes, were not ultimately successful. The soldiers of 131st Brigade succeeded in passing through but could get no further such was the weight of enemy fire. Despite the storm of fire, sappers mostly with the patient prodding of bayonets, cleared two lanes. The tanks, from 22nd Armoured Brigade, rumbled forward under bright moonlight and a deluge of iron, losing thirty-one vehicles.[42] Neither they nor the infantry could do any more.

Relentlessly, Desert Air Force kept up pressure from the night skies. Over 135 tons of bombs fell[43] directed mainly onto support vehicles for 15th Panzer grouped near the Rahman Track. Several convoys were strafed. Since the commencement of operations there had been activity at sea. A dummy task force put out to sea from Alexandria and MTBs loosed some lead and flares. Planes flew in support and dummy paratroops were dropped.

After over 24 hours fighting, Montgomery had to take stock and consider his next move. The opening phase had gone partly according to plan, though at no inconsiderable cost.

This accomplished, 26th Brigade (Whitehead) was to secure a not inconsiderable area between the extreme northern tip of the penetration and an expanse of barren salt marsh, east of the road, itself east of the railway tracks. A major obstacle lay in the strongpoint known as Thompson's Post. 2/23rd Battalion was to secure the main road some way north-east of 2/13th Battalion. Thompson Post remained the objective of 2/24th. The third battalion, 2/23rd was to dash forward in carriers and riding on the hulls of their supporting Valentines from 46th RTR. Just attaining the start line proved both difficult and hazardous, due to complex manoeuvring and omnipresent dust clouds. It was 23.40 hrs before they moved forward and immediately encountered difficulties in locating gaps in the Allied minefield. Barely 600 yards beyond this they ran into Axis mines and sustained fire. Men leapt from tanks as tracer zipped through the moonless night. Confusion swiftly ensued as the battalion commander led forward those men he could collect and, though some may have penetrated as far as the railway line, they were pushed back. The Valentines did attempt to provide support but they themselves suffered heavy loss. 24th Brigade (Godfrey) was already placed east of the railway and was tasked to advance to the north-west and effect a junction with 26th Brigade. The prevailing chaos led Morshead to the inevitable decision, taken at 04.50 hrs, that the attack could not proceed further.

Morshead's assault had not achieved its final objectives, though the butcher's bill had been relatively light. It had inflicted losses on II/125th Panzer Grenadier Regiment and eliminated an Italian *Bersaglieri* Regiment. A half-hearted counter-attack towards Point 29 next morning failed to develop. For Rommel, there was no good news. He heard, on the 29th that another tanker, the *Luisiano* had been sunk. With the Axis fuel crisis biting deep, Rommel was considering how he might break off and withdraw. This would be a most difficult extrication, given how his forces were so fully committed and getting his infantry away intact seemed nigh on impossible. He now decided that it would be prudent to consider establishing a fall back position at Fuka and withdrew 21st Panzer, though the division had no more than sixty 'runners' at this juncture.[34] The depleted panzers would go into reserve north of Tel el Aqqaquir while the gap was filled by Trieste. Kampfgruppe 155 of 90th Light Division with the remnant of II/125th Panzer Grenadier was to pull out towards Sidi abd el Rahman. The remaining Panzer grenadiers were to hang on for another full day in their present positions. With 90th Light covering the coast, it appeared the Fox had divined his opponent's next move in the north. Montgomery, knowing the Axis to be desperately stretched, decided to shift the direction of his next blow further south.

Now, Freyberg was to attack on the night of 31 October/1 November, with Point 29 as his right pivot and across a frontage of some 4,000 yards. During the preceding night, Morshead's weary Australians were to seek to finish that which they had earlier begun and achieve all final objectives. 26th Brigade would thrust north-east to seize ground thus straddling both road and railway. Phase two of their attack would involve advancing along the line of the tracks, eliminating Axis outposts and reaching the rear of the enemy in the tip of the Salient. The reduction of Thompson's Post was to constitute a final objective, though a single battalion would attempt to strike directly for the coast. Desert Air Force would carry out raids in the target zones and a complex artillery programme was devised. This was a tribute to the gunner's art, to deliver counter-battery fire, barrages and timed concentrations in support of separate attacks all with different start times. Armour would not be placed in close support but 40th RTR would be deployed so as to weigh in whenever and wherever the need arose.

Repeated and sustained sorties pounded Axis positions during daylight hours. Rising to the attack at 22.00 hrs, 2/32nd Battalion gained its objectives. At 01.00 hrs on 1 November, 2/24th and 2/48th Battalions rose for the next bound. Initially both made progress down the length of the track but cohesion was lost and casualties were sustained. Both then fell back towards the ground won by the first wave. This reverse denied any chance of success for the proposed third wave but the fourth was not dependent. At 04.25 hrs 2/3rd Pioneer Battalion moved into the attack but met with no more success and withdrew behind the man-made shelter of the line. Again, there was no final success though some 500 prisoners had been bagged.[35]

Even though the Australians had failed to reach all of their objectives the tactical situation was critical from Rommel's perspective. A remnant of 125th Panzer Grenadiers was cut off but initial moves by 361st Panzer Grenadiers were seen off by Allied artillery. Rommel now had to draw on his slender reserves to form an armoured battlegroup from 21st Panzer which put in an attack along the railway line at 13.00 hrs. 2/32nd Battalion with 40th RTR fought a savage fight which was renewed around 16.00 hrs. The slow and under-gunned Valentines suffered badly in the exchanges of fire and twenty-one were knocked out before the survivors were permitted to withdraw. Next morning battle was again joined with much hard fighting. Both sides took and gave ground but the Australians clung to their hard-won gains. Rommel was at least successful in reaching 125th Panzer Grenadiers.

There was still no sign of break-through. Rommel was stretched but not bursting. It is impossible, however, to overstate the advantages which accrued to the Allies through control of the skies and havoc wrought by Desert Air Force. Though armoured formations might be relatively safe, movement of soft-skinned and supply vehicles behind Axis lines during this critical 'dogfight' phase was continually interdicted by attack from the air. Nor should the corrosive effect on morale be overlooked, as Montgomery himself observed: 'The moral effect of air action is very great and out of all proportion to the material damage inflicted. In reverse direction, the sight and sound of our own air forces operating against the enemy have an equally satisfactory effect on our own troops.'[36] The damage inflicted upon Axis shipping was steadily increasing the pressure on Rommel's jugular. On 1 November two more Italian ships, *Tripolino* and *Ostia*, laden with fuel and ammunition were sunk. As Kesselring was trying to fly in fuel stocks from Crete, Maleme airfield, site of the Axis landings in May 1941, was also bombed.

Planning 'Supercharge'

That there was progress and that, in a battle of attrition, the Allies were winning, could not be denied, but there was no breakthrough, no great victory that could set the church bells, so long silent, ringing out. Moreover, as 8 November, the date fixed for the 'Torch' landings approached, Churchill needed a decision in the western desert. Much has been said about the 'long screwdriver' applied by Whitehall to the desert campaigns, usually to detrimental effect. Tradition in the British army is for the local commander, while he receives his general

orders from his superiors, to be permitted discretion as to how he puts these into effect. This
convention was not one which appealed to the Prime Minister. Gott had, after all, been his
choice for 8th Army command and, when frustrated by Montgomery's brusque intransigence,
he was apt to remind Brooke of the shortcomings of 'Your Monty'. In Montgomery,
Churchill had finally discovered a will and egotism to match his own. Churchill found
Monty's bland briefing from 28 October, detailing his proposed re-grouping disquieting. His
week of battle was five days old and now he talked of re-grouping. Whatever had happened
to crushing and overwhelming victory? Brooke was able to add assurances, despite his own
disquiet and a frank assessment he received from 8th Army commander shortly after which
appeared not augur altogether well but Monty, as ever, was brimful of confidence:

> It was fairly clear to me that there had been consternation in Whitehall when I began to
> draw divisions into reserve on the 27th and 28th October, when I was getting ready for
> the final blow. Casey had been sent up to find out what was going on: Whitehall thought
> I was giving up, when in point of fact I was just about to win … I told him all about my
> plans and that I was certain of success; and de Guingand spoke to him very bluntly and
> told him to tell Whitehall not to bellyache. I never heard what signal was sent to London
> after the visit and was too busy with SUPERCHARGE to bother about it. Anyway I was
> certain the CIGS would know what I was up to.[37]

Montgomery was indeed busy drafting the final orders for what he intended as the knock-
out blow. He fully understood the strategic requirements:

> I knew that Operation TORCH, mounted from England, was to land in the Casablanca-
> Oran area on the 8th November. We must defeat the enemy, and break up his army, in time
> to be of real help to TORCH. Quite apart from wanting to get to Tripoli first! But more
> immediately, the timing was affected by the need to get the Martuba airfields so as to assist
> by giving air cover to the last possible convoy to Malta, which was short of food and almost
> out of aviation fuel. The convoy was to leave Alexandria about the middle of November.[38]

He then went on to assess the tactical position at El Alamein and the manner in which he
intended to deliver his next major assault:

> I decided on the night of 30th/31st October the 9th Australian Division would attack
> strongly northwards to reach the sea; this would keep the enemy looking northwards.
> Then on the next night, 31st October/1st November, I would blow a deep hole in the
> enemy front just to the north of the original corridor; this hole would be made by 2nd
> New Zealand Division which would be reinforced by the 9th Armoured Brigade and two
> infantry brigades; the operation would be under the command of 30 Corps. Through the
> gap I would pass 10 Corps with its armoured divisions … We already had the necessary
> divisions in reserve and they had been resting and refitting … What in fact, I proposed to
> do was to deliver a hard blow with the right, and follow it the next night with a knock-out
> blow with the left. The operation was christened SUPERCHARGE.[39]

12

'Supercharge':
29 October 1942 – 3 November 1942

Behind his lolling head the sky
Glares like a fiery cataract
Red with the murders of two thousand years
Committed in His name and by
Crusaders, Christian warriors
Defending faith and property.

David Gascoyne

Were you there when the desert lay silent
And they counted the cost that was paid
To ransom a world and its freedom
Mid the sand dunes and the graves?
Well, this was the arras of battle.
The weft and warp of our strife.
With bonds that were forged forever
From the broken threads of life.

El Alamein Tapestry

I spent the morning [30th October] writing out my directive for SUPERCHARGE. I always wrote such orders myself, and never let the staff do it. This was the master plan and only the master could write it. The staff of course has much detailed work to do after such a directive is issued. This procedure was well understood in the Eighth Army (and later because of experience in the Mediterranean, in 21 Army Group).

1. Operation SUPERCHARGE will take place on night of 31 Oct – 1 Nov. The operation is designed to:

(a) Destroy the enemy armoured forces.

(b) Force the enemy to fight in the open, and thus make him use petrol by constant and continuous movement.

(c) Get astride the enemy supply route, and prevent movement of supply services.

(d) Force the enemy from his forward landing grounds and aerodromes.

4. His A/T guns had been significantly reduced in number.

5. He had no reserves.

6. It was therefore inevitable the 8th Army should at some point, and soon, break-through.

7. It was therefore time to withdraw.

Rommel concurred, British attacks were, as he felt, both ponderous and predictable, therefore a planned withdrawal, at this juncture, was feasible and might yet be carried through without further and fatal losses. New positions at Fuka had already been scouted and Ariete Division would now move to Tel el Aqqaqir to bolster Italian XX Corps while XXI Corps retreated on their right flank. Under cover of night Italian X Corps would disengage and slip around behind sheltering 'mine marshes' between El Taqa and west of Bab el Qattara. From there to Quatani minefield would be held by Ramcke's *Fallschirmjager*. As the amount of ground to be covered was nowhere greater than ten miles, it was proposed to execute these manoeuvres on the night of 3 November while the mobile units, Italian XX Corps, the panzers of both armoured divisions, 90th Light and 19th Flak Divisions would form a rearguard screen.

Axis objectives were to maintain a line north/south through Ghazal Station. The armour would pull back south of the railway line while the infantry would utilize every vehicle that could be got to move, soldiers of 164th Division riding on 15th Panzer's tanks. Light reconnaissance units would form a flexible reserve. On paper this was sound but Rommel was painfully aware of how difficult in reality and that marching infantry formations without motor transport would be heavily exposed. His reports to OKW were gloomy.[20]

Antennae quivering with finesse and informed of enemy intentions via Ultra; the shift was already understood: 'There were indications the enemy was about to withdraw; he was almost finished.'[21] Montgomery saw the decisive moment as being at hand. What remained of 9th Armoured Brigade clung to the northern shoulder as 1st Armoured Division's two brigades deployed to attempt to hold on around Tel el Aqqaqir (8th) and ground to the north-west (2nd). The north flank of the salient was held by 151st Brigade (Durhams) while the Highlanders occupied the southern 'wall', armour facing west. The Allies had not yet taken all of their original objectives – the ridge of el Aqqaqir was not completely secured nor had the full 'Skinflint' bound been achieved. Nonetheless, a decisive armoured clash was underway. As the days of 'balaklavering' were now distant, British tanks, dug in, awaited the panzers. When these failed to make headway Axis guns took up the gauntlet flinging down a fearful curtain of fire. For British infantry this was a most unpleasant time:

> We were up the sharp end with a vengeance. I'd never seen any shelling like that before … the worst I'd seen, and every time it died down the tanks would roll forward again to our slit trench line and fire their guns. Then they would pull back and Jerry would send some stuff back, all of which fell in our area. The battalion's anti-tank guns had it very bad. For a long time they were out in the open and unprotected.[22]

Monty could sense the very fulcrum of battle had been reached. He was well supplied with intelligence via Ultra decrypts and his superiority both on the ground and in the air was substantial. On the evening of 2 November, 152nd Brigade with 2nd Seaforths and 50th RTR was to capture 'Skinflint' while, a little later, 5th Royal Sussex from 133rd Lorried Infantry Brigade was to assault 'Snipe'. Both attacks would go in under cover of a heavy barrage. In each instance the infantry secured their objectives and a respectable haul of Italian prisoners from Trieste. With these strongpoints eliminated, the prime obstacle to a westerly break out was the Axis gun line along Rahman Track. Lumsden now, in the late evening, proposed to deploy his infantry (7th Motor Brigade) in a bid to seize a two mile stretch of ground north-east of Tel el Aqqaqir. Once they were on their objectives, 2nd and 8th Armoured Brigades would advance for three and a half miles westwards. This would enable 7th Armoured Division, early on 3 November, to leapfrog 1st Armoured and drive toward Ghazal Station.

This attack by 7th Motor Brigade was an expensive failure, born from a catalogue of errors. Orders arrived late, intelligence was lacking and gathering dusk frustrated any recce. Guns were ready and plentiful but devoid of a meaningful programme. Zero hour was fixed for 01.15 hrs but the three battalions seem to have got off badly from the start, running into an alert, well-prepared enemy and could achieve little. Further muddles arose as 10 Corps HQ became convinced 2nd KRRC was on Point 44 at Tel el Aqqaqir. Acting on this incorrect and rather pious assessment, 4/6th South African Armoured Car Regiment dashed forward and came to grief. During the hours of darkness, Desert Air Force continued with business as usual. Enemy transport clustered around Ghazal Station was pounded and Maleme airfield on Crete received a further pasting.

For the British tanks, tasks were for 2nd Armoured Brigade to bolster 2nd KRRC, allowing 8th Armoured Brigade to exploit south-west. Axis guns and tanks dug in along the Rahman track frustrated efforts by the former brigade while more guns, mainly 88s held up the latter.[23] During the course of that afternoon the Notts Yeomanry attempted charge the line 'balaklavering' with no more success then previously. Though some vehicles may have reached the line of the track, net result was more losses. However, 3 November brought intimations from the Australians in the north and 13 Corps to the south that the enemy was or appeared to be withdrawing. As the morning wore on, 1st Armoured Division also appeared to be pushing forward against weakening resistance: 'On 3rd November one of the troop commanders and No 1 of the battery working with the armoured brigade had the satisfaction of capturing an Italian tank. They walked up to it with revolvers, knocked on the front door, and the crew came out and surrendered.'[24]

When writing to his 'Dearest Lu' the same day, Rommel was singularly pessimistic:

> The battle is going very heavily against us. We're simply being crushed by the enemy weight. I've made an attempt to salvage part of the army. I wonder if it will succeed. At night I lie open eyed, racking my brains for a way out of this plight for my poor troops … We are facing very difficult days, perhaps the most difficult that a man can undergo. The dead are lucky, it's all over for them. I think of you constantly with heartfelt love and gratitude. Perhaps all will be well and we shall see each other again.[25]

Sensing that the dam was about to burst, Montgomery imposed two further operational tasks upon the infantry of 51st Division. That afternoon, at 16.45 hrs, they would attempt to seize a span of the Rahman track west of 'Skinflint'. Later, under cover of darkness, they would strike south, aiming at Tel el Aqqaqir and a portion of track lying south.[26] These moves would, it was hoped, finally allowed the South Africans to get their cars out into the open and join in the merry havoc Royal Dragoons were enthusiastically creating. Monty had already deduced that Rommel might attempt to form a fresh line on suitable ground either at Fuka or perhaps Matruh. Once these attacks achieved their objectives 10 Corps would seek to break out north towards the coast. Freyberg, his division beefed up accordingly, would march west in a move to flank the Fuka position from the southern approaches. He might then have to prepare for a further advance towards Matruh, 10 Corps detaching one division to hold ground gained at Fuka.

Rommel was indeed seeking to disengage. By mid-afternoon on the 3rd his planned withdrawal was progressing; 90th Light Division with both Italian Corps was falling back south of DAK, though his 164th Division was immured for lack of serviceable vehicles.[27] The Axis commander might yet hope the ponderous pace of 8th Army advances could work in his favour. He next ordered Italian 10 Corps to begin stepping back towards Deir el Harra; Ramcke's paratroopers to head twenty miles and more south and Italian XXI Corps to occupy ground at Fuka. So far so good and final disaster might yet be averted. At this crucial juncture, Montgomery found he had an unexpected ally in the person of the Führer himself. Adolf Hitler ordered Rommel to hold his ground 'not to yield a step'.[28] Mussolini, in the unlikely event Rommel would take notice, sent a similar order through Cavallero. Sick at heart, Rommel read the order out over the telephone to von Thoma, who was understandably outraged. Both he and his army commander understood that such an order spelt nothing but destruction. Though phrased in suitably flowery terms the Führer's direct order was crystal clear:

> To Field-Marshal Rommel … It is with trusting confidence in your leadership and the courage of the German-Italian troops under your command that the German people and I are following the heroic struggle in Egypt. In the situation in which you find yourself there can be no other thought but to stand fast, yield not a yard of ground and throw every gun and every man into the battle. Considerable air force reinforcements are being sent to C in C south [Kesselring]. The Duce and the Comando Supremo are also making the utmost efforts to send you the means to continue the fight. Your enemy, despite his superiority, must also be at the end of his strength. It would not be the first time in history that a strong will has triumphed over the bigger battalions. As to your troops, you can show them no other road than that to victory or death.[29]

This was, for Rommel a bitter blow, to have his carefully prepared but fragile chance to save the bulk of his forces dashed, not by the enemy, but by his own higher command. For him, this must have been the absolute nadir. He knew the orders to be tantamount to suicide and yet, who would dare defy Hitler? Such heroic prose which ignored every tactical and strategic reality, promising reinforcements that did not exist, amounted to little more than insult. The only remedy was in compromise which might give the appearance of compliance yet also provide a means of partial escape. 90th Light, Italian X and XXI

Corps must hold their ground but von Thoma was permitted to withdraw the remnants of his panzers six miles west of Tel el Aqqaqir with Italian XX Corps. Ariete, coming up from the south, would deploy on von Thoma's right flank. Darkness would provide the cloak and Rommel's reply to the Führer stressed the crippling losses already sustained. Having let that sink in, he requested, early on 4 November, permission for a withdrawal as far as Fuka. He might yet salvage something in spite of Hitler's best efforts. 'At 2 a.m. I directed two hard punches at the "hinges" of the final break out area where the enemy was trying to stop us widening the gap which we had blown. That finished the battle.[30]

Montgomery, on the evening of 3 November, was firmly and rightly convinced Rommel was seeking to break off. The Australians had penetrated further along the coast in the north and found Thompson's Post abandoned. Throughout the hours of daylight Desert Air Force maintained its relentless harrying. Aqqaqir was deluged, coastal routes and desert tracks were pounded. Both bombers and strafing fighters maintained the Allies total dominance in the skies. Though the *Luftwaffe* effort was continually declining, Ju87s and Me109s did attempt, in two instances, to make their residual presence felt over the battlefield. None of the Stukas succeeded in dumping their payloads on any other than their own side, though Allied fighters paid a heavy price in the searing dogfights. In total, over 1,000 sorties were flown and nearly 200 tons of bombs dropped.[31]

Monty now ordered Wimberley's Highlanders to mount three lunges. At 17.45 hrs 5/7th Gordon Highlanders, supported by tanks from 8th RTR would aim to size a section of the track some two miles south of Point 44. Some hours later, beneath the cloak of night, 5th Indian Brigade was to make a further bound of two miles. Early on the morning of 4 November at 06.15 hrs, 7th Argylls would attempt to seize the elusive prize of Point 44 itself. The Gordons' attack began with a misapprehension and concluded in tragedy. 1st Armoured Division, quite wrongly, assumed 8th Brigade had passed to the west of the current objective and that mere mopping up remained. Thus it was deemed that air and artillery support were, in such an instance, redundant. Nothing more than a blanket of smoke would be needed and the infantry *schwerpunkt* could ride comfortably on RTR tanks. The tankers had doubts but these were brushed aside. In fact, as the attackers soon discovered, the enemy were still in possession and in no mood to be easily dispossessed. Tanks were destroyed and efforts to re-direct the bombardment became confused, a confusion assisted by breakdown in radio contact. Men were lost and Valentines knocked out with the infantry forced to dig in, under fire from a presumed non-existent enemy, well short of their objective.

Brigadier Russell, commanding 5th Indian Brigade, experienced frustrations of a different nature. His difficulties in forming up meant he had to seek an hour's delay in igniting the barrage, now back to 02.30 hrs. He also decided to switch operational roles for two of his battalions. Despite these significant glitches the overall attack, once launched, proved entirely successful, Axis withdrawal having commenced leaving only stragglers for the net. The story of the Argyll's attack was similar; opposition melted, though some shells were still falling. Soon, as dawn's lightening finger illuminated the ground, the armoured cars were away, racing like hounds over open desert:

It was full daylight and, getting among the soft transport vehicles, our work of destruction began. In the first quarter of an hour the two squadrons destroyed 40 lorries, simply by putting a bullet through the petrol tank and setting a match to the leak. The crews of lorries which had got bogged in the breakthrough, transferred themselves to German vehicles holding petrol. Spare men climbed aboard Italian vehicles mounted with Breda guns, and on we pushed Germans panicked from their lorries into slit trenches. We had no time to take prisoners. We just took their weapons and told them to start walking east. Only those who refused were shot. Few refused …[32]

More sedate, the tanks of 22nd Armoured Brigade were also moving forward, at last in open ground. The infantry were still unimpressed at the sight: 'They flew pennants. I did not know these little flags had any meaning. I thought they were typical of the bullshit bravado of tank mobs.'[33] Some, however, witnessing the beginnings of the developing tank battle between 7th Armoured Division and Italian XX Corps, were caught by the imagery of warships, majestic on the ocean of the sands:

The tanks – there seemed thousands of them – looked like a whole fleet of little boats on the sea. Miles away, to the left of me, there was a great dark cloud where there was a great 'stonk'[34] going on. There were little shiny specks dodging about. I could see flashes where there were guns firing.[35]

This action heralded the demise of Ariete Division. In the north, as the Australians probed along the coast, it was a very similar story. Desert Air Force had already picked up the scent and had chased retreating columns throughout the dark, Wellingtons pouncing between El Daba and the sea where targets clustered invitingly. Telltale columns of smoke and bright flaring bursts of explosions offered resonant witness to the enemy's flight as stores were abandoned and burnt.

For Rommel, the scale of this defeat was enormous. Assessments differ, but the Axis had lost something in the order of 30,000 prisoners, two thirds Italian and perhaps as many as 20,000 dead and wounded.[36] Most of his Italian formations had been decimated and such transport as could be found reserved for German survivors. Out of nearly 250 tanks DAK could barely field thirty-six and though the Italians had more runners these were inferior and no match for Shermans: 'The Italian divisions in the south, in front of 13 Corps, had nothing to do except surrender; they could not escape as the Germans had taken all their transport. I directed Horrocks to collect them in, and devoted my attention to the pursuit of Rommel's forces which were streaming westwards.'[37] Well might the marching soldiers have lamented, those who would never see Rome or Naples, Milan or Bologna again:

Captain, captain of the guard
Summon the buglers all,
Make them stand in the barrack square
And sound the demob call.

Driver, driver of the truck,
Start your engine off,
We're in a hurry to get home;
Of war we've had enough.

Oh driver, driver of the bus,
Run through the streets of Rome;
Make her go like a racing car,
We're hurrying to get home.

Italian marching song

'One remark from my diary at the time is significant: "We are throwing stones at the Italians and they are running away". There was no doubt that the enemy, at last, was in retreat.'[38] 'Can you wonder that, the battle having lasted some twelve days and ended in complete victory, I keep saying that he [Montgomery] was in a class by himself as an army commander.'[39]

Such a victory, resounding as it was, had been dearly bought. Allied losses were heavy in all arms: 2,350 officers and men killed, 8,950 wounded and 2,260 missing. Some 500 tanks were damaged, say half of which could be repaired, 111 guns of all types were destroyed and 97 aircraft of all types lost (as against say 84 Axis), though the Allies had flown a vastly greater number of sorties at nearly 12,000, six times the Axis total.

After Alamein

Montgomery subsequently divided the fighting at El Alamein into three distinct phases. First, the break in, which he defines as a struggle for tactical advantage. He felt that this was successful, though the record might tend to question. Secondly, the crumbling or dogfight phase, aimed at 'crippling the enemy's strength'. This did succeed; a nasty, vicious attrition that told heavily in favour of the Allies. This was as much due to the fact Rommel squandered his precious resources in set piece counter-attacks in unfavourable conditions. Allied success was mainly due to Axis inability to learn from past mistakes and a propensity to fling men and vehicles into a maelstrom where the Allied held vital trumps in air and artillery superiority. Finally, the break-out which Monty saw as successful as it was aimed at the weakest link in the crumbling Axis chain, the juncture between Italian and German units. Rommel had taken the gamble of drawing his remaining strength into the northern sector where he was misled into thinking the final blow would be directed.[40]

If your enemy stands to fight and is decisively defeated in the ensuing battle, everything is added unto you. Rommel's doom was sounded at Alam Halfa; as Von Mellenthin said, it was the turning point of the desert war. After that, he was smashed in battle at El Alamein. He had never been beaten before though he had often had to 'nip back to get more petrol'. Now he had been decisively defeated. The doom of the Axis forces in Africa was certain – provided we made no more mistakes.[41]

Monty was not shy in attributing the victory to his own all-consuming genius. In this he may have been prone to overlook that much of the strategic planning had been done previously by others such as Auchinleck, Dorman-Smith, Gott and Ramsden. These are not mentioned. Nonetheless, even his most constant critics must concede that Montgomery brought to 8th Army cohesion, a simplicity and directness of approach that had been lacking. He restored confidence:

> Generals who become depressed when things are not going well, who lack the 'drive' to get things done, and who lack the resolution, the robust mentality and the moral courage to see their plan through to the end – are useless. They are, in fact, worse than useless – they are a menace – since any sign of wavering or hesitation has immediate repercussions down the scale when the issue hangs in the balance.[42]

General Carver puts it rather more succinctly:

> It may have been expensive and unromantic but it made certain of victory, and the certainty of victory at that time was all important. 8th Army had the resources to stand such a battle, while the *Panzerarmee* had not and Montgomery had the determination, will power and ruthlessness to see such a battle through.[43]

Subsequent writers, most notably perhaps, Niall Barr, have offered a more objective assessment, though the critical development in the fighting skills of British arms during the period before and during the El Alamein offensive is acknowledged by all. A key component in final victory is perceived as the re-concentration of artillery which 'dominated the Alamein battle'. Too often the guns had been distributed in penny packets without the impact and delivery of a detailed programme which brought a telling weight of firepower to bear. The Royal Engineers too, had broken the stalemate of the minefields by perfecting gapping techniques. While the clearing of mines had remained hazardous it had been accomplished, with loss and confusion in some cases but generally the clearance work had been a superlative example of planning, technique, courage and resourcefulness in action.

Infantry had honed their offensive skills demonstrating a clear ability to attack at night, under difficult conditions and yet still overcome major obstacles and defended locations. Liaison between commanders on the ground and Allied planes in the air had been both crucial and effective. Desert Air Force had pulverized the Axis, relentlessly and without respite. To the physical damage inflicted, especially on supply lines must be added the vast attrition imposed upon morale. What lessons were learnt over the deployment of armour are perhaps less clear. During the course of the Desert War the Allies had, for a very long period, been at a significant technological disadvantage; neither tanks nor anti-tank guns were as effective as those of the Axis. By the time of Alam Halfa this gap had been significantly narrowed. The arrival of Sherman tanks and the 6-pounder anti-tank gun had significant impacts. The action at 'Snipe' clearly showed how effective these new guns could be.

John Strawson is of the opinion that the last word on the battle should be left to General Carver, a most distinguished student of the campaign. I believe him to be entirely correct:

> To the infantryman in the attack or sitting it out day after day in his slit trench in the front line; to the tank crew grinding forward in the dark and dust among the mines, or trying to edge forward by day towards the ridge from which the anti-tank guns were firing; to the sapper clearing the mines, the anti-tank gunners and, to a lesser extent, the other gunners, it frequently seemed a chaotic and ghastly muddle. The area of the salient east of Kidney Ridge was the worst of all. The whole place was knee deep in dust. Nobody knew where anybody or anything was, where minefields started or ended. There was always somebody firing at something and usually somebody being fired at, but who and what it was and why was generally a mystery. To try and find out led from one false clue to another. The information one gleaned would probably be wrong anyway.[44]

The battle was won but could the rout be transformed into *Gotterdammerung*?

13

Break-out:
4 November 1942 – 23 January 1943

Flood tides returning may bring with them blood and fire,
Blenching with wet panic spirit that must be rock.
May bring a future tossed and torn, as slippery as wrack.
All time drifts in torrents of blind war.

J. F. Hendry

O, Lord, our only Master
Our victories were Yours,
Pray keep us now and after
May peace be assured.
Look up you sons of Glory,
The Crusader flags unfurled;
Remember our true story;
'We fought to free the world'.
So hoist our Banner highly,
Our cause shall not be lost;
For we were the proud Eighth Army,
Our emblem was the cross.

Eighth Army Hymn

The Battle of El Alamein may be said to have ended at dawn on 4th November, with the enemy breaking away and the British setting out to catch him … Seldom can a communiqué have been more welcome to the Allies, nor, indeed, to the free world at large, than the announcement from Cairo on 4th November that the Axis forces were in full retreat … Mr. Churchill has praised the whole achievement as one which will always make a glorious page in British military annals, and observes that 'It marked in fact the turning of the "Hinge of Fate".'[1]

The Hinge of Fate

My ultimate objective was Tripoli; this had always been considered the objective of Eighth Army. But unfortunately the operations to get there had become known as the 'Benghazi Handicap'. As one officer expressed it to me: 'We used to go up to Benghazi for Christmas and return to Egypt early in the New Year'.

I was determined to have done with that sort of thing. Egypt must be made secure for the duration of the war. I had long considered the problem, and when the pursuit began I was clear that the way to achieve this task was as follows:

(a) to capture the Agheila position, and hold securely the approaches to it from the west.

(b) to locate a corps strong in armour in the Jebel about Mekili, trained to operate southwards against any enemy force that managed to break through the Agheila position and make towards Egypt.

(c) to get the A.O.C. to establish the Desert Air Force on the Martuba group of airfields, and to the south of Benghazi.[2]

On the 12th November, when we had driven the enemy forces out of Egypt, I issued the following message to the Eighth Army:

1. When we began the Battle of Egypt on 23rd October I said that together we would hit the Germans and Italians for six right out of Africa. We have made a very good start and today, 12th November, there are no German and Italian soldiers on Egyptian territory except prisoners. In three weeks we have completely smashed the German and Italian Army, and pushed the fleeing remnants out of Egypt, having advanced ourselves nearly 300 miles up to and beyond the frontier.

2. The following enemy formations have ceased to exist as effective fighting formations: 15th Panzer Div., 21st Panzer Div., 90th Light Div., 164th Light Div., 10th Italian Corps, (Brescia, Pavia & Folgore Divs.), 20th Italian Corps (Ariete & Littorio Armoured Divs, Trieste Div.), 21st Italian Corps (Trento & Bologna Divs.). The prisoners captured number 30,000 including nine generals. The amount of tanks, artillery, anti-tank guns, transport, aircraft etc., destroyed or captured is so great that the enemy is completely crippled.

3. This is a very fine performance and I want first, to thank you all for the way you responded to my call and rallied to the task. I feel that our great victory was brought about by good fighting qualities of the soldiers of the Empire rather than by anything I may have been able to do myself.

4. Secondly, I know you will all realize how greatly we were helped in our task by the R.A.F. We could not have done it without their splendid help and cooperation. I have thanked the R.A.F. warmly on your behalf.

5. Our task is not finished yet; the Germans are out of Egypt but there are still some left in North Africa. There is some good hunting to be had further to the West, in Libya and our leading troops are now in Libya ready to begin. And this time, having reached Benghazi and beyond, we shall not come back.

6. On with the task, and good hunting to you all. As in all our pursuits some have to remain behind to start with; but we shall all be in it before the finish.[3]

Breaking-out

A great deal has been written about the pursuit after Alamein, much of it critical. Prominent among critics was Rommel himself: 'The British command continued to observe its usual caution and showed little evidence of ability to make resolute decisions.'[OH p.96] In part this is unfair. The victory at El Alamein represented a further, and this time final, swing of the pendulum. Montgomery was determined there should not be another and, if he was cautious, he was also successful. Pursuit meant that the British were now operating at the end of a lengthening supply line and, from time to time, pursuit would be interrupted by chronic fuel shortage (see below). Those factors which had hamstrung the Axis began, once again, to haunt the Allies. Furthermore, the Allies had fought and won a titanic struggle. Men and machines were exhausted and worn out, tanks and other vehicles badly in need of overhaul.[4]

One trump which continued to deal a winning hand to the Allies was Egypt herself. The patient and complex work of creating a vast supply base in the Delta was still providing dividends. Since July 1942, the whole gigantic undertaking had been managed by Lieutenant-General Sir Wilfrid Lindsell.[5] As previously described, transport and manufacturing capacity within the Delta had increased exponentially, out of all previous recognition with a significant and sustained investment in road and rail links, water supply, transport and delivery services, manufacturing and repair capacity. Great caravanserais of stores had been built up, mountains of every commodity necessary to sustain a modern army continuously in the field. No such equivalent was created by the Axis; the Allies had a clear lead in logistics which they never subsequently relinquished.

Moreover, as the problems engendered by the 'pendulum' effect were well understood, there had been close and detailed planning previously undertaken between 8th Army and GHQ. Given the importance and sensitivities inevitably occurring, a single designated staff section from GHQ under Brigadier Surtees, the DQMG, was allocated for liaison and proved highly effective. Victory in the North African Campaign was to be won as much by patient staff work and logistical capacity as offensives in the field. Indeed without this, no such triumphs could possibly have been achieved. The desert railway was a key element in the overall strategy of supply. A series of railheads would be developed along the north flank of the advance. The distance from Alamein to Tobruk was some 335 miles.[6] Water was key to running the railroad and an order for US built diesel locomotives which ran on comparatively little was providentially delivered in October 1942.

Road repairs were an obvious priority as the need to commission ports would have to keep pace with the advance. Initially the smaller harbours of Matruh, Sollum and Bardia would be pressed into early service. Tobruk, despite the terrible damage wrought by continuous bombing was able, within a week of its capture (19 November), to receive a daily tonnage of supply which was nearly double that of initial estimates. Benghazi, which fell a day later, represented a great technical problem as, having no natural harbour, man made works were easily slighted. Work began immediately and in earnest with supply commencing as early as 26 November. Impressive as this was, the speed of the advance was such that progress could only be sustained by impressive labours of the transport companies. These largely unsung and outwardly unglamorous formations provided the arteries through which supply and replenishment could pass. Without this circulatory system, the body that was 8th Army would have quickly ground to a dead halt.

Any enemy airfield was a keenly sought prize. Some were degraded by vehicles, other slighted by the foe but Desert Air Force had a set drill to meet such challenges. After an initial recce, engineers, sappers and a construction would crew would move in to assess the damage and commence necessary repairs. The RAF Regiment would provide ground troops to secure the perimeter. Following on was the initial technical team from the squadron assigned, then fliers and their machines. This process was slick and efficient but, until equipment and supplies could be flown in, the transport required added to the existing congestion on the over-taxed roads.

When, on 4 November, it became clear, as Monty had predicted, that the long awaited and hard won breakthrough had been achieved, the tempo shifted from grinding attrition to fluid warfare spread across a vast canvas, not unlike the late summer and early autumn of 1914 on the western front in reverse. Freyberg had, under his hand, two additional lorry-borne infantry brigades: 9th Armoured and 6th Light Armoured Brigades. His instructions were to push steadily westwards, over the desert tracks for sixty miles, passing through Sidi Ibeid, which would place him on the Fuka Escarpment. 10 Corps was to swing around west of Sidi Abd el Rahman to scoop up Axis forces trapped in the pocket thereby created.

All Allied forces now committed to the chase were themselves, battered and depleted by the hard-fought battle and no obvious reserves remained. One plan had been to breathe life and substance into shadow 8th Armoured Division (Gairdner) and create a fresh, independent striking force. To bring this up to strength, however, could only have been achieved by denuding other formations and Monty swiftly discounted the notion. The task of completing the destruction of DAK and 90th Light would be left to 10 Corps and the Kiwis. It was here in the north that the final maelstrom would be orchestrated, in the south Axis infantry, deprived of means of escape 'would wither away or be captured'.[7] Monty's message to 8th Army, timed at 08.15 hrs 4 November was, as ever, upbeat. He reminded his troops of the hard fighting they had endured and that the hour of final victory was at hand: '… The enemy is in our power and he is just about to crack'.[8]

Desert Air Force was already straining at the leash, as tensed as hawks for the kill. That the Allies continued to enjoy near total air superiority was providential for progress on the ground was severely hampered by a vast build up of traffic, congesting the minefield gaps. This giant, motley scrum of vehicles would have presented a perfect target has the Axis been able to take advantage. Freyberg was hamstrung in his efforts due to the wide dispersion of his formations. 4th Light Armoured all the way back on Springbok track did not commence its advance until daybreak on the 4th. By mid morning they were no further west than Tel el Aqqaqir, so thick was the press with 10 Corps units also struggling westwards. It was 14.00 hrs before 9th Armoured, following on, began to move, 6th New Zealand Infantry Brigade were at a similar pass. By the fading of the light lead elements of the division were some fourteen miles south of El Daba. Freyberg entertained hopes he could kick-start the advance at 23.00 hrs. As the authors of the OH rather drily observe: 'this hope was not realised'.

Congestion hampered the efforts of 10 Corps, the diversion of guns to support the attack by 5th Indian Brigade and a cloying skein of early morning mist had exacerbated these difficulties. By around 09.30 hrs lead elements of 2nd Armoured Brigade were sparring with 21st Panzer. 7th Armoured Division got underway about the same time and took on the remnant of Ariete which, high odds notwithstanding, fought gallantly until almost completely destroyed.[9] Lumsden ordered Gatehouse to lead 8th Armoured Brigade around to the south-west, avoid the melee and pass round behind the enemy formations. Rommel was aware that, to save his army, he must be permitted to fall back to Fuka. He telegraphed Hitler at 11.15 hrs, stating the situation was now critical: 'We cannot expect any new German forces. Added to this the Italian troops have no more fighting value because of the enemy's great superiority on the ground and in the air …' Hitler replied tersely later that evening: '… I have caused the Duce to be informed of my views. In the circumstances … I consent to your decision.'[10]

Again the Führer obliged Montgomery with his truculence. By the time consent was received the Axis position had deteriorated rapidly. The panzers, already depleted were ripe for shaking, and von Thoma, leading with his forward units, was captured. Trooper Lindsay of 10th Hussars was present:

Heat haze in the desert, even in November, was enough to distort vision, and this is per-haps the reason why the captain and I did not see a large, immobile shape about 200 yards in front of us. For all I know it may have been camouflaged as well. Anyway, neither of us saw that it was a Panzer III until there was a sudden flash, followed immediately by a crashing explosion. A 50mm armour-piercing shell had torn through one side of our Dingo[11] and had passed out through the other side. The solid shot had passed between Captain Singer's head and mine, without injuring either of us. I reversed the Dingo very quickly …'[12]

Having alerted British armour, the Hussars had the satisfaction of seeing the enemy tank 'brew up'. There appeared to be only one survivor who was waving a white flag:

We drove towards the upright figure, and I could see that he was holding his pistol upside down, that is by the barrel and he had a white handkerchief in his left hand … I could see that there were rank badges on his lapels and on his shoulder straps. He had a very large pair of binoculars round his neck. The German walked forward, then stopped, saluted Captain Singer and handed over his pistol. Both officers then shook hands.[13]

For Trooper Lindsay, spoils included the General's fine binoculars.

The inevitable hiatus caused by the loss of so dynamic a field commander caused further difficulties.[14] Nonetheless, the retreat got underway, formations in the south, Italian X and XXI Corps with Ramcke's *fallschirmjager* would move immediately while forces remaining in the north fell back in good order, 90th Light on the coast road, DAK in the centre and Italian XX Corps on the right, further south. Unhampered by the rampant congestion which had delayed the Allied pursuit, these mobile formations gained the level, high ground atop Fuka escarpment. This feature stands east of the main coastal escarpment, running north/south before, some miles south of the coast road, it bends eastwards and eventually merges into the flat. In his approach march Freyberg was aiming not to ascend by the road but across the desert, keeping south of Alam el Qassim.

Due to the prevailing confusion and spread of his forces the 23.00 hrs deadline proved unfeasible and he delayed zero hour till 05.30 hrs. At this point DAK was retreating along a similar axis to that of the New Zealanders pursuit, experiencing similar difficulties. There was a gap of seven or eight miles between the main bodies and both were aiming to reach the higher ground. Meanwhile 8th Armoured Brigade, attempting their wide, flanking sweep, could make little headway in the enveloping darkness and paused to await any fitful moonlight. Between El Daba and Fuka a solid mass of Axis transport crowded the road, a most inviting prospect but Freyberg could not promise to attain his objectives before 10.00 hrs. 1st Armoured Division was ordered to converge on El Daba, 7th Armoured Division was to interdict the highway between there and Galal. The latter was also the objective for 10th Armoured. Desert Air Force continued their nightly ministrations without respite, inflicting considerable damage on Axis soft-skinned transport.[15] The Royal Navy too was active, ensuring the sea offered no alternative escape.

Making up for lack of progress during the night 8th Armoured Brigade dashed the thirty miles to Galal in four hours.[16] This involved some brisk rearguard skirmishing. An Italian column was met and dealt with and the charge continued for a further nine miles, driving along both highway and railways towards Fuka. Freyberg had a less fulfilling morning. His advance was slower than anticipated. Lead units, though they covered some thirty miles of ground, ran into both panzer rearguards and un-gapped mines. Shells now began falling and the laborious task of clearance consumed a full three hours. By dusk only two formations, 4th Light Armoured and 5th NZ Infantry brigades had crossed the mine-marsh. DAK thus reached the plateau ahead of the hounds, but their situation remained serious, disorganised and thinly spread. As a stand was deemed reckless, Rommel gave the orders for a further withdrawal under cover of night.

The Pursuit Proper

> [5 November] moving forward rapidly, sitting on top of the ACV and greatly elated. Some distant dust-clouds were said to be the Germans getting away. There was the cheering sight of the 'Air Umbrella' – Bostons in formations of eighteen. The Colonel said it's the end of the Germans in Africa; I did not believe him.[17]

Montgomery too, sensed the need for haste. Victory had been won but this could still turn to ashes if Rommel escaped annihilation. The Desert Fox was never more dangerous or brilliant than when his back was against the wall. His soldiers were defeated but were far from beaten. Monty urged more haste upon Lumsden, setting as the armour's objective the area of Derna-Tmimi-El Mechili. November 5th had netted rather meagre gains, stragglers had been rounded up but the bulk of the fleeing enemy had got clear. As preliminary moves 7th Armoured was to divert towards aerodromes at Sidi Haneish and Quasaba while 1st Armoured Division whose lead units (2nd Armoured Brigade) were already some miles west of El Daba, was to embark upon a wide flanking movement which would place it in position to then advance upon Matruh. In executing these orders 7th Armoured Division was constrained to turn south-west to avoid entanglement with the New Zealanders but ran into further mines and finally halted twenty miles short of its objective. 1st Armoured Division fared little better: supply vehicles became lost, lack of fuel caused some elements literally to run dry and overworked tank engines swallowed vast quantities of gasoline.[18] Those who had fuel pressed on at a lively pace but increasingly progress stalled as tanks ran dry, 'everyone fuming'.[19]

For the transport companies it was not only the speed of the advance but difficulties of ground and movement which impeded replenishment. As dusk was falling on 5 November a supply convoy moved west wards to make contact with the divisional 'B' echelon. By now the tracks were horribly churned and deeply rutted, soft sand and a maze of old trenches added further pitfalls, unseen until encountered in the inky darkness. Rain, sluicing down in monsoon like torrents, added further miseries. Net result was that the going became increasingly difficult for wheeled transport. Tanks could move relatively unimpeded but only if they had fuel in their tanks – no fuel, no pursuit. November 5th had also been a disappointing day for Desert Air Force as the very speed of pursuit made close coordination increasingly difficult. That degree of intimate liaison which had obtained during the battle could not therefore be as easily sustained.

For Rommel this was fortuitous. *Luftwaffe* squadrons were in exceedingly poor shape and promised reinforcements were still nowhere in sight. The Field Marshal by this time was doubtless rather cynical over such bland assurances. Allied difficulties gave the Desert Fox his opening for a further planned withdrawal westwards. During the hours of darkness on 5/6 November he pulled 90th Light back towards Matruh, 21st Panzer to Quasaba and the remainder into the vicinity of 'Charing Cross'.[20] Desert Air Force was by no means idle. These moves were harassed by both fighters and bombers but deteriorating weather conditions and the inevitable confusion over retreating foe and advancing friend limited sorties. Despite these difficulties of supply, Freyberg's division resumed its advance on the morning of 6 November pushing on towards Sidi Haneish, 9th Armoured Brigade leading. Fuka itself, the escarpment and several Axis airfields fell to 8th Armoured Brigade. Rain, in great muddied torrents, was becoming a real problem and soaked and exhausted prisoners were rounded up in penny packets, though 133rd Lorried Infantry Brigade at Galal captured 1,000 more.

With the creeping light of grey, rain-lashed dawn 22nd Armoured Brigade ground on towards Quasaba. Its advance was blocked by elements of Voss Reconnaissance Group[21] and tanks of 21st Panzer, and was also afflicted by chronic fuel shortage. As the waves of rain lashed the battlefield with biblical fury, the leviathans clashed with the crash and flame of gunfire stabbing through the gloom. Before the remnants broke off, German losses steadily mounted and sixteen tanks and a quantity of guns were claimed.[22] Though activity in the air was muted, US bombers hammered Tobruk and then Benghazi, sinking more vital tankers.[23] So rapid was the pace of the advance that 8th Army was outpacing some of its air support.

Dawn on 7 November found 90th Light and 21st Panzer at Matruh with the remainder of the Axis forces centred on 'Charing Cross'. Rain had lashed the sodden ground into a churned frenzy of cloying mud to the extent that even tracked vehicles, those which had fuel, could move only on the road. 10 Corps was still tasked to reach Matruh, the New Zealanders Sidi Barrani and 7th Armoured Division, Sollum. Despite poor flying conditions there was some action in the air. *Luftwaffe* transports attempted to fly fuel up to the front line, Ju87s attempted to bomb 1st Armoured while Allied fighters shot up Axis vehicles along the coast road. 10th Armoured Division, with fuel to move dispatched 8th Armoured Brigade to seize that portion of highway lying between Fuka and Matruh resulting in contact with German stop lines just east of the objective. Anti-tank guns from 90th Light halted the British tanks and conducted a skilful rearguard action, breaking off after dark so that cautious patrols sent out at first light on 8 November found the ground bare.

Rommel was still intent upon a further withdrawal. His tactics were to form a fresh block at Sidi Barrani permitting the rump of his forces to filter through the narrow passes at Halafya ('Hellfire Pass') and Sollum. Desert Air Force, during the night of 7/8 November, was already bombing and strafing up the passes. November 8 was also significant in that Anglo-American landings in the west Operation 'Torch' took place, adding immensely to the Axis burden. Il Duce wanted a stand to be taken in the immediate area to allow firstly, a defensive position to be established at El Agheila and secondly, to allow marching Italian formations to escape the net. Rommel was loathe to commit himself, advising he lacked the resources to stand and must retreat, by bounds, as far as Sirte; the pace of such a withdrawal being largely dependent upon the zeal of the pursuers.

Without reference to Rommel, Cavallero and Bastico decided that a stand should be made on the axis of Mersa Brega–El Agheila–Marada and that substantial reinforcements would be fed in. These would comprise two infantry divisions, the Spezia and Young Fascists with an armoured division (Centauro). *Panzerarmee* could be further replenished with German tanks and guns from Italy. To facilitate this process of rebuilding, Rommel would need to hold current ground for at least a week.²⁴ The German Field Marshal was understandably furious at being sidelined in a war that he was conducting, remaining adamant in his dealings with *Comando Supremo* that his army was in no state to fight a major engagement. The Duce was not listening and Cavallero remained convinced the Axis could hold a line at El Agheila for the time it took (he estimated about a month) the Allies to prepare a full scale assault. Hitler, on 22 November, finally weighed in on his ally's side and issued another order to hold the El Agheila position to the last man. Rommel who privately and correctly concluded 'they [*Comando Supremo* & *OKW*] did not see things as they were, indeed they did not want to'. It would, even with the inestimable blessing of hindsight, be very hard to disagree.

In the south, Allied 13 Corps had begun its advance against sporadic opposition. A rearguard offered spirited resistance south of Jebel Kalakh but slipped away under cover of darkness. Some 6,000 prisoners were eventually mopped up but Ramcke's paratroopers with the rump of Folgore showed their mettle in a sharp fight and, though they lost some prisoners, withdrew in good order. These *fallschirmjager* were still very much an elite and undefeated. Ramcke and his survivors, roughly battalion strength rejoined the main Axis forces on the 7th.[25] By 14 November the total 'bag' of captured Axis prisoners, the bulk of whom were Italian, had topped 17,000.

It was not Montgomery's intention to allow his enemy respite. Before dark on 9 November, Rommel's forces had been cleared from Sidi Barrani and Freyberg was marching on Sollum as 7th Armoured Division, in another wide, flanking arc pivoted upon Fort Capuzzo and Sidi Azeiz. Twenty-four hours later and 4th Light Armoured was at the approaches to Halfaya Pass. Kippenburger's infantry scaled the heights with commendable élan taking some 600 Italian defenders prisoner. Now replenished 22nd Armoured, also on 10 November, reached El Beida. Egyptian soil would soon be clear and the fall of Hellfire Pass spurred the Axis retreat. Montgomery had already ordered a temporary halt on the line of Bardia–Capuzzo–Sidi Azeiz, to allow for supply to catch up. The pursuit in the interim would be continued by armoured cars.

In spite of the Allies and his own commanders' best efforts, Rommel had executed a brilliant strategic withdrawal. To bring off the bulk of his forces from under the very muzzles of Allied guns, despite lack of supply, notwithstanding relentless pounding from the air, was a masterpiece which clearly indicates the Desert Fox was as adept at countering defeat as he was in capitalizing on success. His very legend was a potent tool in saving *Panzerarmee*. No Allied commander would take any excess risk knowing Erwin Rommel was in the field. Difficulties which the British had encountered: the congestion through and behind minefields, the adverse weather, the supply limitations, had all imposed checks but the extent of Rommel's achievement should not be understated. Had it not been for Hitler and his ludicrous posturing, yet more might have been salvaged. Though Montgomery could have been, and was, criticized for the apparently ponderous nature of the pursuit, he was well aware of the mettle of his opponent and did not intend to hand him the opportunity for a counter-stroke. The pendulum had swung too often before and, if Monty was systematic, even cautious in his advance to El Agheila, it remained his steadfast intention to deal the Axis so severe a blow that their ruin in North Africa would be assured. By 12 November the hounds were coursing west of Tobruk, scene of such great heights and profound depths of Allied hopes, which was entered the day after. On the 14th Lumsden detailed four flying columns, each with specific tactical objectives:

1. Column (a) 12th Lancers was to seize the vital airfields at Martuba, which it accomplished next day (finding the aerodrome flooded and unserviceable), then press on to take the aerodrome at Derna. The former Monty had identified as a key objective to provide air cover for Malta bound convoys.
2. Column (b) HQ 4th Light Armoured Brigade, to assist in the capture of Martuba then press on towards Benghazi. The main component of each of the columns was armoured cars though this one had a troop of Grants with it. All possessed units of field, anti-tank and flak guns.
3. Columns (c) (The 11th Hussars) and (d) (The Royal Dragoons) were to take Msus airfield, then beat up any enemy still standing between Benghazi and Antelat. Talking enemy airfields enabled fighter squadrons to begin operating from new forward bases but neither day bombers nor fighter bombers were able to operate as effectively partly from a dearth of targets and partly from difficulties in getting supplies of bombs so far up.

Renewed worries over fuel supply hampered the Axis and 90th Light and Italian XX Corps came to a forced halt outside Barce, the former's rearguard just avoiding 4th Light Armoured. Next day, 16 November, the rains returned, water-laden winds whipping the dust to a consistency of glue, no one moved, no one could. On 17 November, as the tempest ameliorated, Monty, realizing the *Panzerarmee* was hamstrung by want of fuel, again urged Lumsden to sweep in from the south and force the enemy into a pocket. Bad weather and supply problems severely hampered 10 Corps and Rommel came to regard 18 November as the most critical day of the retreat. The flying columns heading west were constantly sparring with Axis rearguards. By the 20th the British again entered Benghazi, another dot on the map 8th Army had cause to recall. Finally, during the night of 23/24 November Rommel was able to deploy his survivors in the Mersa Brega–El Agheila. He had not escaped unscathed, far from it, but the *Panzerarmee* was still in the field and still capable.

Despite problems of exploiting and supplying newly captured forward air bases, Desert Air Force maintained the upper hand, beating up remaining Axis fields and preventing the diminishing power of the fuel-starved *Luftwaffe* from interfering with 8th Army ground operations. By a bold initiative Coningham succeeded in establishing 'Landing ground 125' a hundred miles or so north-west of Jarabub. Essential equipment, personnel and stores were flown in and the place made operational in exemplary time. By 13 November, Hurricanes from the strip were shooting up Axis traffic on the road between Benghazi and El Agheila. This impudent hideaway sprang more surprises over the next few days, even though it was largely devoid of any anti-aircraft cover. After several satisfying and productive days during which time much useful harm had been done, the planes withdrew. This was the flyer's equivalent of a deep commando raid and remarkably successful. During the latter stages of the Axis retreat to El Agheila Desert Air Force sorties continued to exact a toll on enemy shipping. Within a week three more tankers and large supply vessels were sunk or destroyed.[26]

At Rastenburg on 28 November, Rommel attempted to reason with Hitler. In this he was singularly unsuccessful and was subjected to a near-hysterical diatribe which ignored all of the uncomfortable realities the Field-Marshal had vainly attempted to introduce. The Führer was not minded to countenance a further withdrawal – the El Agheila position must be held at all costs. That Rommel lacked the means to do so and, in the attempt would invite the total disaster he'd so skilfully avoided thus far, did not feature in the discussion. Monty could not possibly have asked for more.

El Agheila, nonetheless, had bad memories from 8th Army as too much blood and materiel had been expended there. Montgomery could sense British units were not looking forward to more desperate fighting with the bloodshed of Alamein still fresh. He had fixed upon Tripoli as his immediate strategic goal and its attainment would require the reduction of the El Agheila line and the secondary, rearward position at Buerat. Rommel had determined upon a policy of nominal acquiescence to Hitler's raving, masking a series of further staged withdrawals. In the circumstances, as might be expected, he was quite right and, as early as 6 December, had begun to dispatch his marching formations further west.

Montgomery had, in his usual careful manner, made detailed preparations for a renewed offensive on 15 December but, sensing the hare was poised for flight, sent in the hounds on the 11th instead. His intention was to engage the enemy frontally, on the coast, with 51st Highland Division while Freyberg executed a wide flanking move to the south which would strike home against the Axis on 14 December. But the Desert Fox was too canny. The initial Allied probing confirmed his suspicion that a major assault was imminent and he pulled back forthwith. The New Zealanders made a desperate dash to close the jaws of the trap but, hamstrung by supply difficulties, failed to net more than some 450 prisoners. The bulk of Rommel's forces with his guns and armour slipped clear.

As ever the *Panzerarmee* conducted its retreat with skill and some panache. A series of rearguard actions were fought as the Axis forces set up a number of temporary stop lines, employing mines, booby-traps, anti-tank guns and ditches. On 15 December the lead elements of 8th Armoured Brigade fought a brisk engagement and inflicted some loss but like a will o'the wisp Rommel avoided encirclement. The New Zealanders battled bravely on, nearly trapping a rearguard unit at Wadi Matratin, some sixty miles west of El Agheila. Confusion and onset of darkness allowed the Germans to escape, dynamiting bridges and culverts as they went, sowing a liberal, lethal crop of mines to mark their passage, a bitter harvest for the pursuing Allies. The chase continued with a further clash at Nofilia on the evening of 16 December. Here the Kiwis, with 4th Light Armoured Brigade, came up against elements of 15th Panzer. The redoubtable Kippenberger deployed his brigade for a mad and daring dash, charging forward in their vehicles till obliged by bad ground and the weight of enemy fire to dismount. A brave attempt but again frustrated by a strong defence which slipped away in darkness.

This was hard fighting, deadly and relentless but Montgomery's longer game was working; the road to Tripoli stretched invitingly ahead. Almost the Msus Stakes in reverse as 8th Army charged westwards, great columns of men and vehicles moving under clouds of dust and churned sand. Presently, the nature of the terrain began to shift as the Allies entered the fertile coastal belt Il Duce was trying so hard to deny them, as his North African empire was coming rapidly unstuck. On 23 January 1943, 11th Hussars, one of the formations which had first 'bounced' the Italians in 1940, entered the deserted streets of Tripoli. The place was as silent as the grave, defeat closing in like a mantle of despair. The funereal atmosphere was shattered when one begrimed wag stuck his head from the turret and shouted 'Taxi!'[27]

The pendulum had swung for the final time.

14

'Torch' to Tunis:
November 1942 – May 1943

Things may be the same again; and we must fight
Not in the hope of winning but rather of keeping
Something alive: so that when we meet our end,
It may be said that we tackled wherever we could,
That battle-fit we lived, and though defeated,
Not without glory fought

Henry Reed

From Alamein to Tunis,
Forward did we go;
The proudest of all armies –
Thro' Italy and o'er the Po.
O'er Desert sands and mountains,
The sea and in the air,
Ever onward marching,
Thrusting everywhere.
So hoist our Banner highly,
Our cause shall not be lost;
For we were the proud Eighth Army,
Our emblem was the cross.

Eighth Army Hymn

Churchill, at last, after seemingly endless frustration and heartache had what he desired, a major strategic breakthrough. Rommel was not finally beaten, nor was the Axis presence in North Africa immediately expunged for much hard fighting remained. For the Desert Fox nothing but the bitter dregs of defeat and all his restless brilliance could not now stem the rot and none knew this better than he. During the course of Rommel's unsatisfying interview with Hitler he had been advised, in florid terms, that: 'The Afrika Korps no longer matters'.[1]

Operation 'Torch'

Nearly three weeks earlier, on 8 November, a joint Anglo-American fleet had made several landings on the coast of French North Africa; the long heralded liberation of Vichy provinces had begun. The Allies came ashore at Algiers, Oran and Casablanca. If Eisenhower, as C in C, was expecting a rapturous welcome he was sadly deluded. The French in fact resisted, treating the landings more as a hostile invasion than liberation. Memories of the sinking of French ships and the fight for Syria rankled. Even the presence of the Americans, who might be expected to be less tainted than the British, did not prevent stiff fighting. Admiral Darlan, who commanded all Vichy forces was a rabid Anglophobe and had to be bribed with residual power as 'supreme civil authority'. This angered supporters of De Gaulle and the Free French who regarded the Admiral with loathing.[2] Compromises were needed as speed was of the essence. The Axis had to be caught and crushed between a swift advance from the west with Montgomery closing in from the east.

Despite the mounting odds, Axis reinforcements were arriving in Tunisia and an active defence was underway. The country was mountainous and winter rains barely a month away. General Anderson, commanding British 1st Army, made good progress, despite renewed activity from the *Luftwaffe*. Rommel continued to fall back, ignoring all and any pleas to make a stand. By the end of November Anderson's forces appeared to be closing in upon Tunis but deteriorating weather imposed its own check. Anderson's planned swoop down from the hills was met with determined resistance, the formidable Tigers (PzKw VI) making their first appearance.[3] Fighting hard and utilising interior lines the German defenders could not be budged. Allied losses were mounting steadily and the Axis able to mount a series of sharp, local counter-attacks. Then the rains began to fall in earnest turning ground into quagmire, bogging men and vehicles in a viscous sea of impotent misery. Tunis was not about to fall and Eisenhower wisely decided to suspend further major operations.

An End to the Pendulum

On 15 February, 1943, 8th Army moved against Rommel's positions at Beurat. Hopelessly outnumbered and outgunned, *Panzerarmee* could only continue with a further withdrawal. A major conference was held at Casablanca where Eisenhower revealed his intentions for a major offensive in Tunisia, though Brooke felt such a move unwise. The potentially contentious question of who should exercise overall command once 1st and 8th armies were united was settled in favour of Eisenhower, with Alexander as his subordinate and Tedder having direction of all Allied aircraft. De Gaulle had been persuaded or browbeaten into a makeshift accommodation with General Giraud. Rommel had retired behind the relative security of the Mareth Line which afforded him a respite and the opportunity of striking a fresh blow in the west.

As ever, the Desert Fox chose an ambitious and risky strategy while his fellow officers, Von Arnim, commanding 5th *Panzerarmee* in North Tunisia and, equally predictably,

Kesselring favoured a less perilous course. The result was an inevitable compromise. The Germans made initial gains. The Americans, facing these battle-hardened desert veterans, were caught off-guard and suffered losses but the offensive soon began to run out of steam. Von Arnim had severe doubts and these translated into lukewarm support. Rommel's assault on the Kasserine Pass, spectacular and rapid, ran into a thin screen of Allied guns and stalled. With resources depleted and the Allies recovering, the attack was abandoned.

Alexander was frankly appalled by the unprepared state of his American allies but the crisis in the western sector had passed. Rommel was ordered to launch a blow in the east, despite his misgivings, exacerbated by failing health. This attack, hurled at 8th Army positions at Medenine in early March, ran into a well prepared and concealed gun line. Both tanks and infantry were badly shot up as they struggled to come to grips. Rommel's last attack was a total failure. He left North Africa for a final attempt to talk sense into Hitler but the Führer still was not listening. The Desert Fox had seen the last of North Africa, placed on mandatory sick leave and Von Arnim was left to oversee the final *Gotterdammerung*.

Despite heavy losses incurred at Medenine, von Arnim felt he could continue to hold the Mareth Line, still formidable and with both flanks secure. The line was, however, less solid than the Germans might have hoped. Indefatigable as ever, LRDG had found practicable gaps through which Montgomery proposed to send a powerful force comprising Freyberg's Kiwis, bolstered by armour. As the New Zealanders executed their dashing left hook, 30 Corps would batter down the front door and break through from east to north. This frontal attack ran into stiff opposition and a series of difficulties and the bridgehead, so dearly won, was nearly lost when adverse weather intervened on the Axis' side. The DLI hung on fiercely as the *panzers* stormed their makeshift positions calling on the Durham men to surrender. The Durhams declined the offer and clung on grimly till finally relieved. As more British tanks appeared the Germans sought to disengage and retreat westwards. Again DAK managed, by dint of resilient rearguard actions and rapid manoeuvre, to escape the closing net but 8th Army had still notched up another important victory.

Relentlessly, the Allies tightened the vice. General Patton, with the US 2nd Corps, displayed his customary bullish energy. Von Arnim was threatened with encirclement. The Italian General Messe commanded a strongly posted Axis line which was to be assaulted using both 1st and 8th Armies. Montgomery was to punch through at Gabes Gap to break out onto the coastal plain where his superior armour would deploy to best advantage. Ghurkas led the assault in a classic night attack to secure vital high ground but 51st Division ran into heavy fire, losing many casualties and the Germans again avoided encirclement. Finally, Indian soldiers from 8th Army shook hands with Americans from Patton's 2nd Corps. By 10 April Sfax had fallen, Sousse two days later.

Despite these expanding triumphs, Alexander had decided the final blow must fall further north and thus be delivered by 1st Army, though 8th Army was to assault the remaining Axis bastion at Enfidaville. This was essentially a sideshow. In part this was due to recognition that the Enfidaville position was an extremely strong one. Nonetheless, the orders were subsequently modified, perhaps in consequence of matters in the north proving more strenuous than anticipated. Several army commanders had grave doubts over the attack on the Enfidaville defences, fearing the price paid in casualties would be exorbitant. Montgomery, as ever, was aggressive and fully confident.

In the third week of April, fighting in this sector reached an intensity and fury easily the equal of the worst which had gone before. Men scrambled, fought and died on scarred and rock strewn slopes, pounded by artillery and small arms; a soldier's battle of rifle and bayonet. As this attack stalled, similar difficulties were experienced in the north, where Axis formations bitterly contested each foot of mountainous ground. Montgomery, not to be denied a victor's crown, renewed his attack on 25 April. Both sides fought with great skill and valour, losses again were high, every inch of ground contested. The result was a temporary stalemate.

On 6 May, Alexander planned a final, overwhelming blow in the north. To add irresistible weight to Anderson's assault, two veteran 8th Army units, 4th Indian and 7th Armoured Divisions, would be detached in support, together with 201st Guards Brigade.[4] Thus, two units which had endured the whole gruelling campaigns in the Western Desert, including the original 'Desert Rats' would take part in what promised to be the last battle. Von Arnim knew the plight of his exhausted survivors, some 135,000 Germans and nearer 200,000 Italians, was desperate. Despite the odds, Axis defenders continued to fight long and hard as the onslaught began. After intensive bombardment and a successful break-in, dusk found the leading British units some fifteen miles from Tunis. Next morning British armour and armoured cars rolled into the city. On 12 May von Armin and General Messe each formally surrendered their commands.

At 14.15 hrs on 13 May Churchill finally received the telegram from Alexander he had waited so long to read: 'Sir, it is my duty to report that the Tunisian campaign is over. All enemy resistance has ceased. We are masters of the North African shores.'

The War in the Desert was over but the bones of some 22,000 British and Imperial soldiers would remain: 'For most of them there is a grave in the sand … only a mound of sand that the wind will soon soften and gently erase.'[5] Though the Desert Campaign had been won the wider global conflict still raged. Many of the hard and bitter tactical lessons had to be learnt over again on very different battlefields.[6] British armies toiled through the endless mud and sleet of the Italian campaign, battling the seemingly endless stop lines thrown up by Kesselring's troops in a country seemingly created for defence. Others landed in north-west Europe on D-Day and after to finally liberate the continent. Victory was still a long way distant in the spring of 1943 but the era of continuous defeat was over and the men of 8th Army became the stuff of legend. El Alamein was indeed the final swing of the pendulum.

If you can keep your kit, when all around you
Are losing theirs and blaming it on you;
If you can scrounge a gag when all refuse you,
But make allowance for their doubtful view;
If you can wait, and not be tired of waiting,
Or, being pushed, let no man push you back,
Or, being detailed, waste no time debating

But force a British grin and hump your pack;
If you can drink, and not make drink your master,
And leave the thinking to your N.C.O.,
If you can meet with dear old Lady Astor
And treat her just as though you didn't know –
If you can bear to see your rations twisted
Into the weird concoction known as stew;
If neither knees nor face are ever blistered,
And neither flies nor fleas can worry you;
If you can face the other fellow's chinnings
And turn deaf ears to their unleashed abuse;
If you can force your heart and nerve and sinew
To serve on guard when you should be relieved,
And swear like hell with all the breath that's in you,
With all the curses ever man conceived;
If you can walk with blondes and keep your virtue,
Or ride in trams and keep your pay book safe;
If needle stabs and castor oil don't hurt you,
And rough angora shirts don't even chafe;
If you can fill a sandbag every minute,
Dream that your trench is Lana Turner's flat –
Yours is the blue my son, and all that's in it.
And what is more, you are a DESERT RAT.

R. F. Marriott (Crusader no. 37 11 January, 1943)

Appendix 1:
Desert Tactics

Armoured Warfare

The Western desert appeared to open up a vast canvas over which tanks, leviathans of the battlefield, could race, sleek as frigates or potent as ships of the line. Pure warfare where the featureless desert formed an inland sea, unencumbered by towns, rivers, forest or marsh and with a tiny, nomadic and largely unconsidered civilian population. Reality inevitably proved to be somewhat different. In 1939 numerous British armoured units had only recently converted from cavalry, either regular or yeomanry[1] regiments with proud traditions and social cachet. These tended to rather look down upon the rude mechanicals of the RTR who, in turn, resented the amateurs' condescension. Infantry disliked all alike. Relationships between infantry, armour and artillery were frequently based on ignorance, disdain and suspicion. Infantry in the desert felt exposed without armoured support and resented the ability of their mechanized comrades to withdraw from the front of an evening and their ability to stock up on luxuries. They did not understand the need for tanks to re-fuel and replenish and the intricacies of maintenance in trying desert conditions, dust and harsh surfaces taking a fearful toll on moving parts.

British armour proved often to be inferior to its German opponents and the reasons for these deficiencies were partly tactical and partly technological (see below). The inter-war years had seen a rivalry between the 'tank' school, led by Fuller and Liddell Hart and the 'cavalry' school, who chose to ignore telling lessons from the Great War. General Sir Percy Hobart[2] was a passionate advocate of the former and advocated to the full the Fuller/Liddell Hart concept of armoured warfare. This envisaged tanks as an independent, striking arm not dependent on a tail of infantry and guns but playing a cavalry role in firstly pinning enemy forces by a frontal feint then executing a series of flanking movements, not unlike the mounted caracole on previous centuries, to strike the foes from side and rear. To exactly what extent these theories contributed to *Blitzkrieg* is not our present concern but Guderian's exploits in Poland, though not strategically decisive, and the crushing blow delivered in France in 1940 served to reinforce this view. Thus British doctrine was based essentially on a cavalry charge 'Balaklavering' – where tank fought tank. What was not fully considered was the crucial role to be played by anti-tank guns.

Hobart, in 1938, had been appointed to lead what would become 7th Armoured Division.[3] He lasted only a year before being dismissed and disappearing into temporary obscurity.[4] His theory influenced his successors and the success of Operation 'Compass' appeared to fully vindicate the 'all-tank' approach. How a tank might best deliver fire was also a subject of debate. Cautious counsel preferred static fire from a 'hull-down' position, where the vehicle takes advantage of natural cover or folds in the ground to expose only the turret. Such fire will be, by definition, more accurate than where the tank fires on the move. RTR were great exponents of the latter school and trained hard but movement must inhibit accuracy and the tank, if it manoeuvres to deliver fire side on, akin to the naval broadside, is consequentially more exposed to AT guns.

Within British concepts of armoured warfare lay a dichotomy as to the role of the tank and thus the creation of two distinct types. First of these was the 'I' or Infantry Tank whose role, as its name implies, was to advance in support of the footsloggers. The early versions, during the Great War had lumbered over desolate trenchscapes, at ponderously slow speed, unable to exploit a breakthrough when one occurred. That role was better accomplished by light or 'Cruiser' tanks. Both the recently converted cavalry formations with their long traditions and RTR itself preferred the notion of speed and dash. Passing through the front line to wreak havoc in the enemy rear echelons, a function performed in the First war by light Whippet tanks and armoured cars which, though not decisive, had filled the role more spectacularly than cavalry. In the armoured regiment some three or four tanks would form a troop, four of these plus an HQ component of three formed a squadron and three squadrons a regiment. Behind the AFVs was an 'A' or logistics echelon with the 'B' echelon of those who for whatever reason comprised the LOBs relegated to base camp.

Protection, mobility and firepower are the three principal concerns of the tank designer and every variant thus embodies elements of compromise. A tank which moves fast cannot carry a greater weight of armour while a heavier tank is likely to be slower. Attempts were made to improve the armament on the Crusader Mark II and Valentine Mark II by replacing the obsolete 2-pounder with a 6-pounder but this conferred limited benefits. The Crusader III suffered from the same lack of adequate armour and mechanical reliability. Valentine IX, while gaining a 6-pounder, lost its 7.92mm machine gun, a significant omission. It was not until the introduction of Sherman marks II and III, (fitted with twin diesel motors), that the Allies acquired a tank that could match its Axis opponents.

Shermans boasted strong tracks, heavier and deflective, sloping armour. The 75mm M3 main armament was a distinct improvement on its predecessors, including the 75mm M2 mounted in the sponson of the Grant tank. A further crucial disadvantage of Lee/Grants[5] was the severe restriction imposed on the tanks seeking a hull-down position. Mounting its main gun in the sponson inevitably meant the turret remained fully exposed. Better M48 HE shells gave the Sherman more effective killing power against German armour.[6] British Churchill tanks were other welcome newcomers to the Desert War. The Mark I was still lumbered with the 2-pounder, though the Mark III was up-gunned with a 6-pounder. The Churchill proved rugged and reliable in service and its cross-country capability was remarkable. Its armour was effective against the German 5cm Pak anti-tank weapon but ineffective against the dreaded 8.8cm.

If German armour was initially superior in design then German tactics were equally superior in execution. The élan of the cavalry was not an element in German tactical thinking. Rommel did not expect his *panzers* to engage in Homeric duels with their enemies. Killing Allied tanks was primarily the function of anti-tank guns leaving the armour free to punch through and wreak havoc. When the *panzers* did take on Allied tanks, their superior armour and armament told. British cruisers might sweep forward in a gallant but doomed charge but well sited anti-tank weapons exacted a fearful toll. The issue decided before the *panzers* discharged their first round. Indeed the German armour might be nothing more than bait to tempt British opponents into pelting towards a well concealed gun line.

Bltizkrieg as a concept had always depended not primarily upon tanks but on an all arms offensive, avoiding dispersal and concentrating armoured forces in a decisive fist, avoiding any tendency to spread tanks around in penny packets. In such dispositions speed was not the first imperative and tank commanders' urges to rush ahead should be curtailed to maintain cohesion. To retain this high level of overall mobility the ability to recover and repair damaged vehicles was paramount. Thus, there was an incentive to seek to hold ground won at the end of the day rather than retire to base camp. Radio communication was an essential tool. There could be no victory without constant keeping in touch. With an all arms concept, firepower and aerial bombardment could and should properly be employed to unleash a hail of destruction, pulverising enemy positions prior to any advance. Towed anti-tank guns accompanied armoured columns to be used in the offensive as well as purely defensive role. Reconnaissance was another vital ingredient. Enemy positions had to be located and then, after softening-up, assessed to identify if the bombardment had produced sufficient cracks to allow an advance to proceed. If the commander could not be satisfied that the targets were sufficiently reduced or damage then he should not hazard his tanks.

DAK employed two main workhorses in its *Panzer* divisions. The first was the *PzKwIII*, designed in the mid thirties, with a five man crew, and armed initially with a 3.7cm gun. This relatively light tank (around fifteen tons) underwent a constant series of improvements and modifications mainly involving more and better armour and heavier armament. By the time of the Desert War many were armed with the vastly better long 5cm KwK L/60 (model J); models N & O were fitted with the low-velocity 7.5cm KwK L/24.[7] Second was the *PzKwIV* a heavier vehicle weighing some twenty tons. It was originally intended as a support tank with the *PzKwIII* being the main workhorse. Gradually the Mark IV grew into this role and continued in use throughout the war and after production of the Mark III was abandoned in 1943. Early models were armed with the short-barrelled 7.5cm KwK L/24 till this was replaced by the long-barrelled 7.5cm KwK L/43. Like the Mark III successive variants had increasingly improved armour.[8] The long-barrelled 7.5cm became the preferred gun for all *panzers* during 1942. HE rounds were becoming more common than AP and hollow-charge ammunition for this gun was issued from the summer of 1942.[9]

Infantry Tactics

Since the time of Homer's bronze clad Achaeans the job of the infantry was to take enemy ground and hold it. By and large this was a thankless and invariably dangerous task. During the previous war of 1914–1918, lines of largely static trenches had scarred a swathe of Europe that extended from the North Sea to the Swiss Frontier. The opposing lines at El Alamein had taken on the fortress-like quality which had fuelled the fearful attrition of the Western Front. Most senior commanders on both sides had fought in that conflict and it was not an experience they were keen to repeat. In dress and equipment the 8th Army soldier resembled to an extent the previous generation. He still marched in hob-nailed leather ammunition boots and his uniform was made of rough wool serge with heavy woollen overcoat, cap comforters and the ubiquitous 'tin hat' instantly recognisable to veterans of the Great War or even a medieval archer. Greatcoats may seem anomalous in a desert war but were much needed in plummeting night-time temperatures and soaking, wind laden winters.

The infantryman's canvas webbing was the 1937 pattern comprising ammunition pouches, water bottle cradle, entrenching tool and pack which contained mess gear and personal items. The webbing also had a frog that supported the bayonet. This could be the eighteen-inch sword for the Mark III Enfield or the utilitarian spike fitting the Mark IV. Both rifles were bolt action designs with a ten-round box magazine and .303 ball cartridge; effective, accurate and rugged. American Thompson .45 calibre sub-machine guns 'Tommy guns' were carried as was the British 9mm Sten, a rather crude wartime expedient that possessed some alarming characteristics.[10] The soldier's pouches each held three spare magazines for the Bren gun[11] and he carried a brace of linen bandoliers with 100 rounds for his rifle.

War for the footslogger was never an affair of strategy or grand tactics. It was a daily grind of discomfort and tedium, poor and monotonous rations, dirt, squalor and the odd burst of sheer terror. His basic tactical unit was the infantry section of ten men, led by an NCO. Second and third men in the file were jointly responsible for the Bren. Three riflemen followed, two bombers and a lance corporal completed the section file. This composition would have been recognisable to veterans of the later battles of the Great War. Three sections with the Lieutenant's three man HQ function formed a platoon. Three of these constituted a rifle company, led by a major with a captain as 2/ic and his HQ group including CSM, medics, signallers and company runners. Four rifle companies with a specialist HQ company completed the infantry battalion. The battalion HQ Company included the tactical support units, mortar platoon, the carrier platoon, equipped with Bren carriers, an MT platoon and, latterly some anti-tank weapons. The transport platoon had a single three-ton truck per company. The battalion could be a self-contained unit with its medical, signals and pioneer complement.

Three battalions would form a brigade and three brigades a division. In attacking, each battalion would normally leave one company in reserve together with specialists and those key personnel who were deliberately left out of the attack, the LOBs, whose skills would be required to rebuild the unit if it was thinned by heavy losses. The company would normally leave a platoon in reserve so the proportion of men actually engaging with the enemy would be relatively small, perhaps 300 out of the nominal battalion strength of 1,000. Second Alamein would be a battle of attrition, akin to those of the previous war though casualties, while heavy, would not be as severe. Men would rise up with fixed bayonets, emerging like armed wraiths from their trenches, following the initial bombardment, then advance towards their fixed objectives. Inevitably the battle, at some point, would become a savage hand to hand between opposing infantry, fought with rifle, grenade, boot, butt and bayonet, till one side fled or was overrun.

Influenced by the dire experience of the Battle for France in 1940 and subsequent experience in the Desert, infantry rightly dreaded the onslaught of German *panzers*. Hence the constant cry for armoured support. Infantry officers were aware of the shortcomings of the 2-pounder anti-tank gun and the Boys AT rifle.[12] A company or battalion strongpoint would be constructed for defence against the enemy's infantry and guns, with the ability to call down supporting fire. Platoons would deploy in slit trenches with pits for the Bren guns which, with rifles and grenades, would supply the immediate firepower. Separate positions for the heavier Vickers MGs would be dug behind the infantry line and sited so as to provide interlocking fields of fire. It was customary, as the war progressed, to gird defensive positions or 'boxes' with minefields and wire, forming mini-fortresses or redoubts. An obvious weakness, amply demonstrated during the Gazala battles in the spring of 1942, was the vulnerability of widely dispersed brigade boxes. These could be eliminated in turn and were not so placed as to provide mutual support. In the featureless terrain, vehicles could not easily be accommodated within the box so were parked, as a rule, well to the rear. This protected the valuable transport but meant that the infantry were denied a quick means of escape if the box was overrun.

In 1918 the British Army had demonstrated a mastery of combining sustained and accurate gunnery with well coordinated infantry attacks aimed at securing limited tactical objectives, a function of 'bite and hold'.[13] Attacks were best put in under cover of darkness with support from tanks – 'I tanks'. Usually an armoured brigade with some 150 tanks was attached to the infantry division and, as Paddy Griffiths points out, the ratio of arms here was not dissimilar to that found in a German *panzer* division, potentially a highly efficient instrument of war.[14]

Digging slit trenches might, depending on the composition of the desert floor, be relatively easy but in areas where the relentless wind had scoured down to the unyielding bedrock. In such circumstances, pick and shovel would not avail and trenches had to be bludgeoned or blasted through by sappers. 'Real' mines would be interspaced with fields of dummies and safe paths through defined. Platoon trenches would be sited in approximate oval patterns with the HQ element located centrally. Company HQ would be slightly to the rear to give the CO on overview of the fight as it unfolded.

The Gunner's War

In some ways the deadly German 8.8cm gun is that most associated with the Desert War yet the RA achieved considerable successes. Chief among its arsenal was the 25-pounder gun/howitzer. This inspired a similar degree of terror in DAK as their 8.8cm did for 8th Army. Such was the gun's rate of fire that the Germans came to suspect the weapon was belt fed![15] The 25-pounder could throw a shell 13,400 yards on a low trajectory or rather less for higher. It weighed only 1.75 tons which made it both light and easily manoeuvrable. It could fire both HE and AP so it possessed a tank-killing capacity. If its range was less than that of the 8.8cm it had a far lower profile and worn out barrels could be changed with relative ease.

British gunners also fielded the 4.5-inch gun and 5.5-inch gun/howitzer and the RA constantly displayed magnificent skill in gunnery. One deficiency which was not remedied by the time of 2nd Alamein was for greater range and increased weight of shot. It would not be until the campaign in Tunisia that the 7.2-inch howitzer partially satisfied this need and the fearsome US 155mm howitzer would not be provided to UK forces until after the end of the North African campaigns. Air burst HE shells were increasingly perceived as having both a deadly and morale-shaking effect. Problems with suitable fuzes were not, however, resolved until later in 1943. A direct competitor for the 8.8cm was the British 3.7-inch anti-aircraft gun, this was a first class weapon though one which was not generally deployed in an anti-tank role. There were several reasons for this: correct sights for the job proved problematic, the gun was heavier, slower to deploy and had a dangerously high profile by comparison. There may have been some reluctance to deploy these weapons for an offensive role when it was felt they were more needed to defend base areas and fixed installations.[16] With suitable air burst HE fuzes for most artillery unavailable or unsuitable the 3.7-inch gun was increasingly used as a stop gap.

A limitation affecting all of the British ordnance discussed above was their dependence on a towing vehicle or tractor. Gunners constantly sought a form of gun that was self-transporting, the self-propelled or SP gun. One expedient on which opinions differ was the US 'Priest'. This mounted the potent 105mm gun on a Grant chassis. The gun was formidable but not as effective or durable as was hoped and the Grant was not entirely suitable, nor outstandingly reliable. The requirement was for a suitably modified 25-pounder mounted on a compatible tank chassis but no such variant was available for the period under consideration.[17]

Much has been said of the failings of the British 2-pounder anti-tank gun. The weapon was still one of the best in its class, superior to the German 37cm Pak 36, stable and with a full 360 degree traverse. It was simply not powerful enough to dent Axis tanks and was never used with an HE round. Towing, over rough desert conditions, was apt to damage the weapon, thus many were mounted on trucks 'en portee'. Gunners often fired their weapon from the truck bed for greater mobility though the higher profile was dangerous. Habitually the trucks were thus reversed towards the enemy to utilise the protection afforded by the gun shield. The more powerful 6-pounder destined to be the main British anti-tank weapon for 2nd Alamein (the formidable 17-pounder did not enter service till February 1943), was a significant improvement with greatly enhanced tank-killing potential. Work on a more powerful gun had begun as far back as 1938 but the catastrophic losses in materiel, occasioned by the defeat at Dunkirk, severely delayed the process. The 6-pounder was thus not seen in the Desert until April 1942, fitted with a conventional split trail carriage. The guns did good service in the battles of 1st Alamein, Alam Halfa and 2nd Alamein.

The German 8.8cm FlaK 18, 36 or 37 (the 'eighty-eight') began life as an anti-aircraft role. It's usefulness as an anti-tank gun was handy improvisation but one which proved devastatingly effective. This was an exceptionally fine weapon with extremely high muzzle velocity. It could punch through 150mm of armour at 2,000 metres and, with excellent sights, was in its element deployed over the flat terrain of the desert. An obvious weakness of the original AA model was an alarmingly high profile, potentially fatal to crew. Later variants were developed more suited to the specialist anti-tank role. The FlaK 41 version had a lower profile, a superior gun-shield and improved muzzle velocity. The standard purpose-built German anti-tank gun was the 5cm Pak 38. In response to the introduction of better armoured Allied tanks, Lee/Grant and then Shermans, a more powerful weapon was required and, consequently the first class 7.5cm Pak 40 came in, with the 7.62cm Pak 36. Throughout the North African campaigns the main field artillery gun deployed by DAK was the 10.5cm lfH 18. Rommel, from his early days as a field commander in the battle for France, was an advocate of massive and ruthless firepower, believing that a first and decisive strike by artillery was a key component of tactical success.

Mortars are the infantryman's artillery and, if inferior in range and accuracy to their large siblings in the gun line, are highly effective at closer quarters. In general terms the British 3-inch mortar was a useful weapon, capable, at least in theory of dropping some 200 lb of bombs in a mad minute of rapid fire. Its principal failing was its short range. In this it was thus markedly inferior to the Axis equivalents. The German 8cm (7.7 lb bomb) and Italian 81mm (7.25 lb or 15 lb bomb) outranged the British weapon, in the former case, by 1,000 yards and, in the latter, by nearly three times that distance. Added to this both had a higher rate of fire and the fragmentation or spread of the bombs was excellent.[18]

The Sappers

World War Two, like all major and most minor conflicts, provided a range of challenges to military engineers. In the desert these focused around the use of mines. Operations such a bridging swift flowing rivers under enemy fire did not occur in the bare amphitheatre of empty desert. The complexity and depth of minefields grew exponentially as the campaign unfolded. Initially it was the British who made use of defensive belts at Gazala, 1st Alamein and Alam el Halfa but, as the advantage in materiel strength swung toward 8th Army, the Axis began to sow mines in earnest. Mine clearing operations on the British side were directed by Brigadier Frederick Kisch[19] who significantly improved on existing techniques hitherto both laborious and hazardous. The tally of mines laid across the front ran to hundreds of thousands and dense belts were sown as far eastwards as the shadow of the Pyramids, should the Axis advance penetrate that far.[20]

Mines were attractive for dense fields created a kind of Great War defensive system enabling a commander to exercise sway of great tracts of landscape, channelling attacks into gaps covered by his guns. The British found themselves, at the outset, desperately short of effective tactical mines which produced an unexpected windfall for local engineering companies called upon to produce large numbers of what became known as the Egyptian Pattern Mark 1 mine ('EP1'). These were crude and unstable, dangerous both in the laying and in the lifting. Gelignite, the explosive compound used had a nasty habit of 'sweating' in the intense heat and this deadly perspiration was raw nitro-glycerine!

Montgomery established a training school, initially for sappers but then extended to draw in all arms. Though techniques might vary from army corps to army corps, the formation of specialised minefield task forces was common. The Axis forces were both thorough and ingenious. One of the principal DAK devices was the Tellermine, (model T.Mi.35), about the circumference of a dinner plate and packed with several pounds of explosive. Intended primarily to disable vehicles, the fuze could be fitted so the foot passage of an unwary infantryman would not dissipate the blast on an unworthy target. Mines could be linked in tandem by attaching wire to the fuze-ring. The devices could be laid one on top of the other so the lifting over the uppermost triggered the detonation of the second. Mine clearance was nerve-wracking and immensely dangerous; it demanded knowledge, skill, dexterity, thoroughness, nerve and judgement. Latterly the more specifically anti-personnel or 'S' mine (model S.Mi.35) appeared and these were laid in vast quantities in the German defences before 2nd Alamein. A very nasty 'jack in the box:

> … the whole thing looked like a tin of baked beans with a nozzle on top, but of course all that were visible were the three prongs of the detonator. When a foot trod on the deto-nator there were two distinct explosions. The first flung the mine up into the air and the second explosion was at waist height and it spewed out hundreds of ball bearings horizon-tally. You can guess how we felt about those things.[21]

Obviously an added peril was the likelihood of de-lousing being carried on under enemy fire. The sapper cannot concentrate upon his specialised task and fight as infantry at the same time. Engineers therefore had to be protected by a screen of infantry and, if necessary armour, a bridgehead into enemy territory. Obviously it was not necessary to lift the entire enemy minefield. What was required was a systematic clearance of roads or lanes which would enable the attacking troops and AFVs to pass through unharmed. The infantry vanguard advanced ahead of the sappers, through the live mines: 'Speaking from personal experience, it was a horrible feeling.' This nerve-wrenching chore was accomplished by sappers crawling crablike across the ground, feeling for the tell-tale trip wires. Behind them a further dispersed group prodding with bayonets, moving foot by foot, dreading the feeling of contact as the point of the Lee-Enfield sword bayonet glanced from a solid object. The mine had to be painstakingly exposed and checked for booby traps after which it was lifted, stacked and possibly defused.

Despite the weight of the challenge the RE rose heroically to the occasion and the products of the training schools became, in due course, consolidated into training manuals. 'Gapping' was the essential precursor to any successful attack, beginning with the relatively easy job of clearing lanes through the British defensive belt. Then the attackers advanced into the uncharted and heavily infested areas of Axis minefields, many of which were consolidated on old British positions. DAK lines of defence, all girded by aprons of mines, were formidable, thorough in concept and construction. In the most accessible areas, in the north of the intended battlefield, a second line ran behind the first, linked by transverse fields that would funnel an attacker towards the waiting gunners. This pattern of defence in depth obtained from the Mediterranean in the north to Deir el Meirar, a shallow basin lying south-west of the Axis controlled extremity of Ruweisat Ridge. This was not all, behind these two dense fields ran a third line which stretched from just east of Sidi Abd el Rahman eight miles south, this too was liberally garnished with mines.

Obviously, traditional mine clearing techniques were far too slow to facilitate a fast moving advance yet the sappers were the vanguard of the army and unless the defender's fields were gapped there could be no offensive. At 2nd Alamein, the forlorn hope[22] would not comprise purely infantry but of engineers with infantry supports. Polish officers had devised an electronic mine detector which worked through electrical impulses and was operated like a vacuum cleaner sweeping the ground. This was quicker and easier but by no means safer, for the operator was obliged to remain standing, wielding his cumbersome equipment and thus presenting a most attractive target. Detectors worked in pairs with the second man marking the mines located by the first, sowing a trail of improvised cones. The detector teams were literally at the front, either with or even in front of the supporting infantry and with certain knowledge enemy artillerymen knew the ranges most exactly.

One device which could ensure the process was both quicker and, for the sappers, safer was the 'Scorpion' or flail tank. This was a standard chassis and tracks with projecting arms or boom fitted to the front which supported a revolving drum fitted with chains which literally flailed the ground to detonate mines. These could be effective but were of course very noisy and created a vast khamsin of tell-tale dust in their wake. In the vanguard of the Scorpions was a lead or pathfinder lorry, fortified by sandbags, which drove forward till it struck a mine, thus indicating a further belt. Behind these flail tanks came the 'snails' – more transport spewing out a trail of diesel to leave a trammelled track-way in the desert sand.

When the sappers and their escorts had accomplished their task there would be three clearly marked lanes cleared through the British minefields with a fourth, reserve track provided for contingency use. Attacking units would queue in orderly columns at each passage, ranked in order of their deployment in the coming action. Clearing the lanes was a vital curtain raiser but the job was not done yet for traffic had to be controlled. No reckless 'balaklavering' but a disciplined, controlled and steady progress.

This was a highly skilled business. Liaison officers travelling in armoured cars would set up at key points and progress would be directed by the provosts. Military police were the unsung heroes of the battle, their calmness, steadiness and efficiency proved exemplary. They stood at the start lines, halfway points and established a controlled zone a few hundred yards short of the mouth. Ingenious lamp signals marking the end of the British minefields and the gateways to the Axis forces were set up, shining one way only so as not to alert enemy gunners. With such ingenuity, calmness, professionalism, dedication and sublime courage sappers, provosts and vanguards opened up the axes of advance.

Transport & Rear Echelons

In the Desert War, transport and logistics were absolutely vital to the ability of combatants to maintain their effort. Without the vast trail of second and third echelons neither side could even maintain the defensive, far less mount an offensive. Transport thus was the key. Throughout the course of the war, Germany suffered a chronic lack of motor vehicles. She looted and requisitioned all available stocks from the subject nations but was chronically deficient. Thus an attack on Rommel's soft-skinned supply vehicles constituted a potent threat, more damaging than a head-on assault on his armour.

It was also axiomatic that, as the campaign see-sawed back and forth across the open expanses, the side that was nearest its base areas had a significant logistical advantage. For 8th Army therefore retreat to El Alamein, a bare sixty miles west of Alexandria, helped rather than hindered supplies. Rommel was continually at odds with his nominal Italian superiors who faced his considerable wrath when they repeatedly fell short of promised targets. This was not entirely a consequence of their incompetence. Ultra and the broken Italian naval code (see below) provided the RN and RAF with good intelligence which resulted in many sinkings. The failure of the Axis forces to conquer Malta was a significant defeat.

Alarums in the Desert could, in the worst cases, produce a form of mass-panic in exposed transport columns. Such incidents of 'scarpering' were variously dubbed 'the Gold Rush', 'Gazala Gallup', 'Msus Stakes'. They were more decorously described in official communiqués as 'an unnecessarily rapid movement of transport'. Where the featureless terrain, largely devoid of cover, exposed soft-skinned transport of both sides to the hostile attentions of enemy armour, drivers and other rear echelon 'wallahs' could be excused for feeling apprehensive. In such circumstances a rapid relocation elsewhere, taking shelter in the vast natural dust cloud thrown up, seemed a sensible tactic. Preserving the precious vehicles was also important. The British army had suffered massive haemorrhages of soft-skinned vehicles in the withdrawal from France, the debacle in Greece and defeat on Crete.

Transport was the function of the RASC, which could trace its origins back to the Corps of Waggoners formed in 1794.[23] When initially deployed in France as part of the BEF in 1939, every division, each corps, had an element of logistics transport. The entire supply was now mechanised, even if some 14,000 vehicles had been requisitioned from civilian supply. The whole lot were lost at Dunkirk of course, and rapid re-equipping became an instant priority. Some 21,000 additional privately owned vehicles were impressed to part remedy the deficiency. An influx of US imports helped and the ATS supplied drivers for home service to allow MT drivers to be sent to North Africa. RASC was responsible for the storage, transport and distribution of supplies and operated first, second and third line functions. These included, foodstuffs, ammunition, POL and hospital supplies. It was in the Desert War that the ubiquitous 'Diamond T' Tank Transporter[24] made its first appearance. These moved AFVs up to the line and assisted in the recovery of those broken down or damaged in fighting. In 1942 the REME was formed and though the RASC kept control of the actual vehicle workshops the repairs were undertaken by REME personnel.

War in the Air

The DAF variously known as Air HQ Western Desert, the Western Desert Air Force and First Tactical Air Force performed a vital role during the Desert War. Formed in 1941 to provide close air support to 8th Army, DAF comprised squadrons drawn from the Royal Air Force, its South African and Australian counterparts and latterly the USAAF. Prior to the formation of a united air arm, RAF Middle East Command, then under Air Chief Marshal Sir William Mitchell, was responsible for a quartet of different regional functions: Egypt, Malta, Iraq and Aden. When war broke out in the Mediterranean theatre the RAF, now under Air Vice-Marshal Sir Arthur Longmore had some twenty-nine squadrons with no more than 300 machines spread over this vast canvas.

In Egypt, Air Commodore Raymond Collishaw could deploy nine squadrons and the primary tasks revolved mostly around support and aerial reconnaissance with the odd dogfight against planes of Mussolini's *Regia Aeronautica*.[25] Three squadrons were equipped with Gladiators,[26] largely outdated, one with Lysanders[27] and several squadrons of medium bombers Blenheims[28] and Bombays.[29] Despite the disparity in numbers the RAF, soon augmented by Hawker Hurricanes,[30] began to gain an ascendancy through aggressive tactics and a certain sleight of hand to convince the Italians they were facing rather more squadrons than was the case.

Re-supply of aircraft was a major difficulty and this spurred the long flight via Takoradi on West Africa's Gold Coast. By the end of November 1941 the RAF had received two Hurricane and two Wellington bomber squadrons. Consequently air support for Operation 'Compass', if stretched was adequate. However urgent the demands of the Desert War, the RAF here tended to be the poor relation and usually received those machines not required for or suited to defence of Britain. At the end of July 1941 Collishaw handed over to Air Vice-Marshal Coningham. But, by the end of the year, the whole of Middle East Air Command came under the aegis of Air Marshal Arthur Tedder, destined to be one of Montgomery's most bitter opponents. Three wings were deployed in the skies over North Africa: 258 and 269 Wings covered the front with 262 Wing held in reserve over the Nile Delta. As the direct threat to the homeland receded, more and newer machines were sent to the Mediterranean, more Hurricanes and the Douglas Boston medium bomber.[31] A further, useful addition was the P-40 Tomahawk/Kittyhawk.[32]

Throughout 1942, DAF provided long-range interdiction and tactical support to 8th Army though its fighters were significantly outclassed by the German Messerschmitt 109E & F variants[33] which inflicted heavy losses, even if their Italian counterparts were outdated and outclassed. It was not until August, with the arrival of Spitfires, that the strategic balance in air to air combat shifted in the Allies' favour. In part, this was due to a shift in tactical doctrines, utilising the *Luftwaffe* concept of close army cooperation through the deployment of forward air controllers, the DAF's answer to the gunners' FOO. DAF then began to deploy 'cab-ranks' of fighter-bombers, waiting to be directed onto specific targets. By this means DAF won control of the desert skies and provided significant and highly effective tactical support to 8th Army during 2nd Alamein, the pursuit and Tunisian campaign.

DAF contained many pilots from German occupied territories; 112 Squadron mainly comprised Polish airmen. The Polish Fighting Team ('Skalski's Circus') was attached to 145 Squadron. From July 1942, the US Army Middle East Air Force, under Major-General Lewis H. Brereton, attached USAAF fliers from 57th Fighter Group and 12th Bombardment Group to DAF formations. Initially these personnel were classified as 'observers' as technically US servicemen were only permitted to serve in American units.[34] Nonetheless, from mid-September, squadrons of US P-40 Warhawks and B-25[35] bombers were officially attached to DAF formations. By the end of 2nd Alamein USAMEAF was re-constituted as 9th Air Force.

Unquestionably the most famous and successful Axis air formation engaged in the Desert War was *Jagdgeschwader 27 'Afrika'. I Gruppe* was first deployed to support Rommel in the Gazala battle in April 1941, led by *Hauptmann* 'Edu' Neumann. On 19 April, JG 27 claimed its first four combat 'kills'; more would soon follow. German fighter formations, prizing the 'Red Baron' spirit of competitive aces, flew their superior Me109Es ('Emils') and latterly the F or 'Friedrich' types with great skill, technically and often qualitatively superior. *II Gruppe* arrived in theatre in September and then *III Gruppe* was sent from the Eastern Front in November. Now synonymous with DAK on 24 March 1942 JG 27 claimed its thousandth victim – a Boston bomber. The Bombay carrying General Gott was a 'celebrity' kill on 7 August. Though highly effective against inferior Allied fighters, JG 27 did not score many successes against bombers. There is a suggestion the fighter aces were more concerned with adding to their tally than strategic intervention. By the time of 2nd Alamein more and better Allied fighters, Spitfires, were beginning to have an effect. A trio of German aces swiftly fell and, in December 1942, the remnants of JG 27 were withdrawn from theatre, the tide had irrevocably turned.

Appendix 2(a):
Orders of Battle

Allied Forces

GOC Middle East – General the Honourable Sir Harold R. L. G. Alexander

British 8th Army – Lieutenant-General Bernard L. Montgomery
BGS: Brigadier P. W. de Guingand

Army formations

1st Anti-Tank Brigade
1st Armoured Brigade (42nd and 44th RTR)
2nd Anti-Aircraft Brigade
12th Anti-Aircraft Brigade
21st Independent Infantry Brigade
Tank Delivery Regiment
1st Camouflage Company RE
566th & 588th Army Troops Company RE
Eighth Army Signals
4th Light Field Ambulance
200th Field Ambulance

10 Corps; Lieutenant-General Herbert Lumsden
BGS: Brigadier R. Cooney

1st Armoured Division (Major-General R. Briggs)
2nd Armoured Brigade: (Fisher) The Queen's Bays, 9th Lancers, 10th Hussars, Yorkshire Dragoons, (motor battalion)
7th Motorised Brigade (Bosvile) 2nd & 7th Battalions The Rifle Brigade, 2nd KRRC
'Hammerforce' (from 8th Armoured Division)

Divisional Troops:
10th Lancers;
RA, (Fowler) 2nd & 4th RHA, 11th RHA (HAC) 78th Field Regiment, 76th Anti-Tank Regiment, 42 LAA Regiment;
RE, 1st & 7th Field Squadrons, 1st Field Park Squadron, attached 9th Field Squadron & 572 Field Park Company
1st Armoured Divisional Signals
Two companies RNF
1s & 2nd Light Field Ambulances

8th Armoured Division (Major-General C. H. Gairdner)
24th Armoured Brigade (to 10th Armoured Division)
'Hammerforce' (to 1st Armoured Division)

10th Armoured Division (Major-General A. H. Gatehouse)
8th Armoured Brigade (Custance)
24th Armoured Brigade (from 8th Armoured Division – Kenchington)
133rd Lorried Infantry Brigade (from 4th Division – Lee)

13 Corps – Lieutenant-General Brian G. Horrocks

7th Armoured Division (Major-General A. F. Harding)
4th Light Armoured Brigade (Roddick)
22nd Armoured Brigade (Roberts)
1st Free French Brigade Group

44th Division (Major-General I. T. P. Hughes)
131st Brigade (Stamer)
132nd Brigade (Whistler)
133rd Lorried Infantry Brigade – see under 10th Armoured Division

50th Division (Major-General J. S. Nichols)
69th Infantry Brigade (Cooke-Collis)
151st Infantry Brigade (Percy)
1st Greek Brigade (Katsotas)
2nd Free French Brigade Group

30 Corps – Lieutenant-General Oliver W. H. Leese

23rd Armoured Brigade Group (Corps Reserve)

Indian 4th Division (Major-General F. I. S. Tuker)
5th Indian Brigade (Russell)
7th Indian Brigade (Holworthy)
161st Indian Brigade (Hughes)

51st Highland Division (Major-General D. N. Wimberley)
152nd Brigade (Murray)
153rd Brigade (Graham)
154th Brigade (Houldsworth)

Australian 9th Division (Lieutenant-General Sir L. Morshead)
20th Australian Brigade (Windeyer)
24th Australian Brigade (Godfrey)
26th Australian Brigade (Whithead)

New Zealand 2nd Division (Lieutenant-General Sir B. Freyberg VC)
5th New Zealand Brigade (Kippenburger)
6th New Zealand Brigade (Gentry)
9th Armoured Brigade (Currie)

South African 1st Division (Major-General D. H. Pienaar)
1st South African Brigade (du Toit)
2nd South African Brigade (Poole)
3rd South African Brigade (Palmer)

Axis Forces

Italian Commando Supremo – Benito Mussolini; Chief of Staff – Marshal Count Ugo Cavallero

German C in C South – Field Marshal Albert Kesselring

Italian Commando Supremo Africa – Marshal Ettore Bastico

Panzerarmee Afrika – Field Marshal Erwin Rommel

ITALIAN FORMATIONS

X Corps – General Enrico Frattini (acting)

9th Regiment Bersaglieri

17th Infantry Division 'Pavia' (General Nazareno Scattaglia)
27th Infantry Regiment
28th Infantry Regiment

27th Infantry Division 'Brescia' (General Brunetto Brunetti)
19th Infantry Regiment
20th Infantry Regiment

185th Parachute Division 'Folgore' (General Enrico Frattini)
186th Parachute Regiment
187th Parachute Regiment
Battle Group 'Ruspoli'

XX Corps – General Guiseppe De Stefanis

101st Motorised Division 'Trieste' (General Francesco La Ferla)
65th Motorised Infantry Regiment
66th Motorised Infantry Regiment
VIII Bersaglieri Battalion
XI Bersaglieri Battalion

132nd Division Corazzata 'Ariete' (General Francesco Arena)
132nd Corazzato Regiment
8th Bersaglieri Regiment
III Gruppo Squadrini 'Nizza Cavalleria'

133rd Division Corazzata 'Littorio' (General Gervasio Bitossi)
133rd Corazzato Regiment
12th Bersaglieri Regiment
III Gruppo Squadrini 'Lanceri de Novaria'

XXI Corps – General Alessandro Gloria (acting)

7th Bersaglieri Regiment

25th Infantry Division 'Bologna' (General Alessandro Gloria)
39th Infantry Regiment
40th Infantry Regiment

102nd Infantry Division 'Trento' (General Giorgio Masina)
61st Infantry Regiment
62nd Infantry Regiment

Reserve (not fully formed)

136 Division Corazzata 'Giovani Fascisti' (General Ismaele di Nislo)
Regiment Fanteria 'Giovani Fascisti'
III Gruppo Squadrini 'Cavalleggeri di Monferrato'

GERMAN FORMATIONS

90th Light Division (Lieutenant-General Theodor Graf von Sponek)
155th Regiment
200th Regiment
361st Motorised Regiment

164th Light Division 'Afrika' (Major-General Carl-Hans Lungerhausen)
125th Panzergrenadier Regiment
382nd Panzergrenadier Regiment
433rd Panzergrenadier Regiment

Ramcke Parachute Brigade (Major-General Hermann-Bernhard Ramcke)

Deutsches Afrika Korps – Lieutenant-General Wilhelm Ritter von Thoma

15th Panzer Division (Major-General Gustav von Vaerst)
8th Panzer Regiment
115th Panzergrenadier Regiment

21st Panzer Division (Major-General Heinz von Randow)
5th Panzer Regiment
104th Panzergrenadier Regiment

Appendix 2(b):
Extract From a Tactical Appreciation 27 July 1942

27th July 1942 An Appreciation of the Situation in the Western Desert: EL AMAMEIN

Factors

Strength

The Axis is unlikely to secure a decisive victory over Eighth Army, since the Germans would have an inferiority of infantry of about three brigade groups and a superiority in armour of possibly 40 per cent. It would seem, therefore, that … they are hardly strong enough to attempt the conquest of the Delta except as a gamble and under very strong air cover … any offensive action would have to be 80 per cent German.

Training

None of the formations in Eighth Army is now sufficiently well trained for offensive operations. The Army badly needs either a reinforcement of well trained formations or a quiet period in which to train.

Time & Space

Had the enemy the available resources, Italy and Germany are both nearer to El Alamein than is anywhere in the United Kingdom. The enemy should, therefore, be able to reinforce quicker than we. On the other hand, apart from distant Benghazi, he has only two serviceable sea ports, Tobruk and … Matruh. He is faced with long road hauls and a sea passage vulnerable to air-raid and submarine attack. This affects the build up of reserves for an offensive. We are nearer to our bases. Our limitation is the rate that men and materials can reach Egypt from overseas. His limit is the rate at which it can reach his troops when it arrives. This indicates the necessity of blocking Tobruk and Matruh and attacking his road communications and shipping.

Russian Front

The operations of Eighth Army are linked to the fate of Russia. Should the Axis penetrate the Caucasus, Eighth Army might be reduced to the lowest margin to provide reinforcements for the new front. Moreover, an Axis success in Russia would release air and land forces and equipment for the reinforcement of the Western Desert.

Tactical Techniques & Future Organisation

We have to prepare to fight a modern defensive battle in the area of El Alamein–Hamman. The troops detailed for this must be trained and exercised so as to get the maximum value from the ground and from the prepared positions. Eventually we will have to renew the offensive, and this will probably mean a break through the enemy positions about El Alamein. The newly trained infantry and armoured divisions must be trained for this battle and for the pursuit …

Reproduced in Lucas, op. cit. p.39

Appendix 3:
The Ultra War

Ultra, Britain's best kept secret in 1941, was born of Enigma and this was the brainchild of a German inventor Arthur Scherbius whose objective had been to design a machine that could both encipher and decipher automatically. The concept was not a novel one. The machines all worked on a rotating disc principle and Scherbius was not the first to attempt a mass produced version. His design came onto the market in 1923 and was adopted by the German army five years later. Its capabilities were sufficient to also enthuse the Navy and, latterly *Luftwaffe*. Its value was for usage in all secret messaging that was vulnerable to interception, primarily radio traffic. What, in modern business parlance, would rank as the Enigma's unique selling point 'USP' was its reflector disc which empowered the machine to both crypt and decrypt. Powered by dry cell batteries, it was also lightweight and easily portable. In appearance it seemed as innocuous as a contemporary portable typewriter. Its potential in the field of modern warfare was immense.

Because of its ability to multiply possible encryptions to such an infinite degree, it was thought utterly impregnable to 'cracking' by even the most gifted of cryptanalysts. The Germans believed that hundreds or even thousands of mathematicians could labour for generations without success. This belief persisted even once the codes had been thoroughly penetrated. It was not in fact the 'boffins' at the British Government's Code and Cipher School (GCCS) at Bletchley Park who first began to fracture the Enigma but the cryptanalysts of the Polish army who achieved miracles by means of pure applied mathematics with some 'mechanical aids'. The latter, which were to assume increasing importance at Bletchley, were electro-mechanical devices that tested the solutions of encrypts much faster than could be achieved by pure manpower, 'bombes' as they were known.

In July 1939 as the threat of war loomed, British and French Intelligence officers attended their Polish counterparts in Warsaw where they were presented with a facsimile of the Enigma the ingenious Poles had constructed. However, they had been beaten by the Enigma designers who had now added two additional discs thus multiplying the complexity. Room 40 at Bletchley continued on the Polish model with the recruitment of civilian academics, an eccentric and eclectic mix of genius whose existence became the stuff of legend. The most outstanding of these was Alan Turing, whose Olympian intellect stood out even in such gifted company. He could be described as the originator of the computer and it was he who designed the bombes at Bletchley.

An element of operator laziness and, in the case of *Luftwaffe* personnel, inexperience, greatly facilitated the cryptanalysts work as did the use of some partial guessing or 'cribs' as they were known. The great intellectual powerhouse that was Hut 40, where operators put in thousands of hours of painstaking work, saw them achieve miracles. Firstly the *Luftwaffe* codes were broken and then others. Some of the naval codes and that used by the Gestapo were never cracked. 'Shark' the Atlantic U-Boat key remained inviolate all through the murderous months of 1941–1942, when the Battle of the Atlantic hung in the balance and thousands of seaman with hundreds of thousands of tons of merchant shipping succumbed to U-Boat attacks. One of the limitations with Ultra, as the Enigma intelligence was designated, was that officers in the field never saw the original decrypts. These were frequently unintelligible and needed to be translated and, effectively, interpreted, so that which was passed on was in an edited form. In the early days this fine art of interpretation was left to linguists rather than IOs with the risk that a competent IO might have read the decrypt in a subtly different way. Ultra was Britain's most closely guarded secret and was perceived as the trump that could tip the finely wrought scales between survival and defeat. Entry to the circle of initiates was restricted. The source of the intelligence had to be concealed so that the Germans would not come to suspect Enigma had been broken. Field commanders were generally told that information had been gleaned from well-placed agents or detailed reconnaissance.

For this reason Bernard Freyberg, when he commanded on Crete was not within this charmed circle. Ultra intelligence was thus filtered through Cairo and, as early as 1 May 1941 there was an intimation of the intended attack on Crete. Four days later further intercepts revealed the main targets and set a date of the 17th when the assault would begin. This signals traffic, crucially, mentioned seaborne elements and made reference to 5th Mountain Division. Creforce HQ had been set up in a disused quarry above Souda Bay, utilising a network of caves that offered good protection from aerial bombardment. Freyberg's staff was somewhat makeshift, with a chronic shortage of signallers and reliable wireless sets. His predecessor Weston, huffed at his removal from overall command, retained a separate and well equipped HQ. Freyberg was too punctilious to 'pull rank'. In the troglodyte world of Creforce HQ Captain Sandover was the IO responsible for decrypting the ULTRA intercepts.

It must, therefore, be borne in mind that Freyberg was not in the 'know' where this marvellous intelligence was coming from. The signals were codenamed 'OL' for 'Orange Leonard' the usual fiction about agents in place being employed. The key Enigma decrypt, (OL 2/302), was passed to Creforce at 17.45 hrs on 13 May and, on the surface, was pure gold. This confirmed that the date of the attack was to be the 17th as previously understood, (this was moved to the 20th subsequently). It specified the first day's targets for the paratroops as Maleme, Chania, Rethymnon and Heraklion. It revealed the extent of the air support that would be thrown into the fight, that additional troops would be brought in by glider and, latterly, once an airstrip was secured, by transports. It finally confirmed that elements of the projected invasion force would arrive by sea, together with AA batteries.

Although the units to be employed in the assault were listed, there was no specific mention of which units would appear where or how, precisely, they were to be landed.

Ultra, despite the very precision of the intelligence actually misinformed Freyberg or allowed him to form a wrong assessment – that a substantial element of the attacking force would be amphibious. Given that Crete was an island and that, as mentioned, the concept of vertical envelopment was untried this was not an unreasonable conclusion. Had the fine detail shown that only relatively minor elements of the force would be coming in ships then the General might have re-considered his defensive strategy. The decisions made during the critical period of 21/22 May need to be considered in the light of this. Freyberg was convinced that the initial airborne landings were merely an overture and that the more solid threat would come over the water. This assessment was fatally flawed and the Ultra intelligence in fact created a fatal obfuscation despite the accuracy of the material.

The arrival of Rommel in the North African Theatre coincided with the establishment of a Special Signals Link to Wavell and Middle East Command in Cairo. Hut 3 at Bletchley could now transmit reports directly to the GOC. Ultra intelligence was not able to identify Rommel's immediate counter-offensive but Hut 6 had broken the *Luftwaffe* key now designated 'Light Blue'. Early decrypts revealed the concern felt by OKH at Rommel's maverick strategy and indicated the extent of his supply problems. Though the intercepts were a major tactical gain in principle, the process was new and subject to delay to the extent that they rarely arrived in time to influence the events in the field during a highly mobile campaign.[1] Equally, Light Blue was able to provide some details of Rommel's seaborne supplies but again in insufficient detail and with inadequate speed to permit a suitable response from either the RN or RAF.

Then, in July 1941 a major breakthrough – an Italian navy cipher, 'C38m', was also broken and the flood of detail this provided greatly amplified that gleaned from Light Blue. Information was now passed not just to Cairo but to the RN at Alexandria and the RAF on Malta. Every care, as ever, had to be taken to ensure the integrity of Ultra was preserved:

> Ultra was very important in cutting Rommel's supplies. He was fighting with one hand behind his back because we were getting information about all the convoys from Italy. The RAF were not allowed to attack them unless they sent out reconnaissance and if there was fog of course they couldn't attack them because it would have jeopardised the security of Ultra, but in fact most of them were attacked.[2]

Ultra thus contributed significantly to Rommel's supply problem. On land a number of army keys were also broken; these were designated by names of birds. Thus it was 'Chaffinch' which provided Auchinleck with detailed information on DAK supply shortages and weight of materiel including tanks. Since mid-1941 a Special Signals Unit (latterly Special Liaison Unit) had been deployed in theatre. The unit had to ensure information was disseminated only among those properly 'in the know' and that, vitally, identifiable secondary intelligence was always available to mask the true source. Experience during the Crusader offensive indicated that the best use of Ultra was to provide detail of the enemy's strength and pre-battle dispositions. The material could not be decrypted fast enough nor sent on to cope with a fast changing tactical situation. At the front, information could be relayed far more quickly by the Royal Signals mobile Y-Special Wireless Sections and battalion intelligence officers, one of whom, Bill Williams, recalled:

> Despite the amazing speed with which we received Ultra, it was of course usually out of date. This did not mean we were not glad of its arrival for at best it showed that we were wrong, usually it enabled us to tidy up loose ends, and at least we tumbled into bed with a smug confirmation. In a planning period between battles its value was more obvious and one had the opportunity to study it in relation to context so much better than during a fast moving battle such as desert warfare produced.[3]

Wireless in the vastness of the desert was the only effective mode of communication but wireless messages are always subject to intercept. Jews from Palestine, who had temporarily buried the hatchet in the face of a greater foe, provided specialist skills. Many were German in origin and understood only too well the real nature of the enemy they faced. The Germans had their own *Y Dienst* and the formidable Captain Seebohm, whose unit proved highly successful. The extent of Seebohm's effectiveness was only realised after his unit had been overrun during the attack by 26th Australian Brigade at Te-el-Eisa in July `1942. The captain was a casualty and the raiders discovered how extensive the slackness of Allied procedures actually was. As a consequence the drills were significantly tightened. If the Axis effort was thereby dented Rommel still had a significant source from the US diplomatic codes which had been broken and regularly included data on Allied plans and dispositions, the 'Black Code'.

Reverses following on from the apparent success of Crusader were exacerbated by 'a serious misreading of a decrypt from the Italian C38m cipher'. Hut 3 could not really assist the British in mitigating the defeat at Gazala or, perhaps worse, the surrender of Tobruk. This was one which Churchill felt most keenly: '… a bitter moment. Defeat is one thing; disgrace is another'. Until this time it had taken Bletchley about a week to crack 'Chaffinch' but, from the end of May, the ace code-breakers were now able to cut this to a day. Other key codes, Phoenix' and 'Thrush' were also broken. Similar inroads were made against the *Luftwaffe*. 'Primrose' that employed by the supply formation and 'Scorpion' the ground/air link were both broken. Scorpion was a literal Godsend. As close and constant touch with units in the field was necessary for supply German signallers unwittingly provided a blueprint for any unfolding battle.

On the ground 8th Army was increasing the total of mobile Y formations while the Intelligence Corps and RAF code-breakers were getting fully into their stride.[4] None of these developments could combine to save the 'Auk' but Montgomery was the beneficiary of high level traffic between Rommel and Hitler, sent via Kesselring – as the latter was *Luftwaffe*. The Red cipher, long mastered by Bletchley, was employed. Monty had already predicted the likely genesis of the Alam Halfa battle but the intercepts clearly underscored his analysis. By now the array of air force, navy and army codes penetrated by Bletchley was providing a regular assessment of supply, of available AFVs and the dialogue of senior officers. The relationship between Rommel and Kesselring was evidently strained. Even the most cynical of old sweats had cause to be impressed: '… he [Montgomery] told them with remarkable assurance how the enemy was going to be defeated. The enemy attack was delayed and the usual jokes were made about the 'crystal-gazers'. A day or two later everything happened according to plan.'[5] Ultra was dispelling the fog of war.

In some ways the Desert War provided the coming of age for the Bletchley Park code-breakers:

> … Until Alam Halfa, we had always been hoping for proper recognition of our product … Now the recognition was a fact and we had to go on deserving it. I had left as one of a group of enthusiastic amateurs. I returned to a professional organisation with standards and an acknowledged reputation to maintain.[6]

Appendix 4:
The Battlefield Today

It would not be trite to assert that the desert is eternal, and hostile. Sixty years on and the ground has really changed very little. Any description must now come with the obligatory 'health and safety' warning, the arid but, in this case, apposite mantra of our bureaucracy-obsessed society. The Western Desert is no place for the uninformed and under-equipped sightseer. The land is harsh and unyielding as ever, trackless and unforgiving. The visitor needs expert guides or to participate in an organised battlefield tour with one of the numerous reputable providers. An additional hazard is the vast quantity of unexploded ordnance, particularly mines which still litter the former battlefields and which fickle winds may suddenly choose to expose, potentially as lethal as ever.

The former hamlet of Alamein is now a township and the tide of development spreading westwards from Alexandria has changed the face of the coastal strip. The famous station exists only as an abandoned shell, replaced by a more modern structure. There is an excellent municipal museum which hosts a first rate array of AFVs in the grounds and a series of galleries covering all aspects of the conflict with dioramas, maps, uniform, small arms and general kit. It was opened in 1956 but substantially refurbished in 1992, a 'must-see' for the visitor.

The CWGC cemetery is located on the line of the old coast road which runs parallel to the modern highway. A turning is marked just past the Alamein police checkpoint. The graves are placed beyond a low ridge and the entrance is well-signposted. Inside are the remains of some 7,240 Commonwealth servicemen, of whom 815 are unidentified 'known unto God'. Some 102 dead of other nations are also interred here. The Land Forces Panels name 8,500 casualties from the War in the Western Desert, up to 19 February 1943 who have no known grave, together with the names of those who died in the subsidiary campaigns in Syria, Lebanon, Iraq and Persia. The Air Forces panels record some 3,000 and more personnel from all Commonwealth nations who perished across the entire theatre of operations, including East Africa and who also have no known grave. The Italian and German graveyards lie outside the town on the hill of Tel el-Eisa. The former features a high monument opened in 1959. This consists of a mausoleum with galleries of tombs for the remains of 4,634 soldiers and the German memorial is a fortress styled ossuary housing commemorating 4,200 dead.

Notes

Introduction: 'Up the Blue'

1. Warner, P., *Alamein, Recollections of the Heroes* (London, 1979) p.39.
2. The largest is in fact Antarctica.
3. The Bedouin are an Arab nomadic, pastoralist people divided into related tribes.
4. The trigh had previously only been trodden by travellers and camels.
5. Crawford, R. J., *I was an Eighth Army Soldier* (London, 1944) p.21.
6. Obviously not affected by the presence of metals, may have been a Viking invention.
7. Crawford op. cit. p.21.
8. Ralph Algernon Bagnold (1896–1990) a noted desert explorer in the 1930s, he later founded LRDG.
9. Patrick Andrew Clayon (d.1962) another inter-war desert surveyor, served with Bagnold in LRDG.
10. Count Lazlo Almasy (1895–1951), real life version of the fictional character immortalised in *The English Patient* whose life was, if anything more colourful.
11. de Manny, E., 'Silver Fern Leaf up the Blue' in *Return to Oasis* (1980).
12. Executed at Benghazi 1931.
13. Lucas, J., *War in the Desert* (London, 1982) p.9.
14. Crawford, op. cit., p.86.
15. Sangar – from the Northwest Frontier denoting any small temporary fortification made up of stone and perhaps sandbagged wall.
16. Lucas, op. cit. p.74.
17. Ibid. p.74.
18. AL63 – anti-louse powder.
19. Crawford, op. cit. p.20.
20. Manning, O., *The Danger Tree* (London, 1977) p.10 – though this is fiction the descriptive passages are both accurate and evocative.
21. Crawford, op. cit., p.p.19–21.
22. Ibid. p.19.
23. Ibid. p.22.
24. Ibid. p.22.
25. Strawson, J., *The Battle for North Africa* (London, 1969) p.8.
26. Crawford, op. cit. p.27.
27. Literally 'war without hate'.
28. See dramatis personae.
29. Strawson, op. cit., p.10.
30. Warner, op. cit., p.30.
31. Alan McRae Moorehead (1910–1983) Australian born war correspondent and author of popular histories.

32. Bowen, R., *Many Histories Deep – The Personal Landscape Poets in Egypt 1940–1945* (London, 1995) p.25.
33. Hermione, Countess of Ranfurly (d.2001) – her wartime diaries were published as *To War with Whittaker* (London, 1994).
34. Ranfurly, op. cit., p.135.
35. Cited in Lucas, op. cit., p.31.
36. Carver.
37. Ibid.
38. *Kesselschlact* = Cauldron Battle.

1. Prelude

1. Clark, A., *The Fall of Crete* (London, 1962) p.1.
2. Ibid. p.2.
3. Ibid. p.p.2–3.
4. Quoted in Simpson, A., *Operation mercury – the Battle for Crete* (London, 1981) p.22.
5. Ibid. p.24.
6. See Appendix 3 – the Germans preferred to blame Italian incompetence than contemplate the penetration of Enigma.
7. Simpson, op. cit., p.28.
8. Ibid. p.29.
9. Clark, op. cit., p.6.

2. 'Compass': June 1940 – March 1941

1. Barr, N., *Pendulum of War – the Three Battles of El Alamein* (London, 2005) p.4.
2. Ibid. p.4.
3. Pitt, B., *The Crucible of War – Western Desert 1941*(London, 1980) p.p.22–23.
4. Strawson, op. cit., p.18.
5. Ibid. p.18.
6. Ibid. p.17.
7. Ibid. p.16.
8. This was accomplished by spring, 1941.
9. Barr, op. cit., p.7.
10. Pitt, op cit., p.p.22–23.
11. Ibid. p.27.
12. Balbo's aircraft was shot down by alleged 'friendly fire' on 28 June while attempting to land at Tobruk, in the wake of a British raid. There were some suspicions he was deliberately assassinated on Il Duce's orders.
13. Pitt, op. cit., p.49.
14. Bierman, J. & S. Smith, *Alamein – War Without Hate* (London, 2002) p.p.46–47.
15. Strawson, op. cit., p.p.26–27.
16. OH vol. 1 p.p.259–260.
17. Ibid. p.260.
18. Ibid. p.260.
19. Bierman & Smith, op. cit., p.46.
20. Ibid. p.47.
21. The General earned this sobriquet on account of his spiky white beard, parted centrally!
22. Strawson, op. cit., p.39.
23. The 4th Indian Division had been withdrawn for service in Abyssinia and its place taken by the Australians.

24. Bierman & Smith, op. cit., p.p.48–49.
25. Ibid. p.49.
26. Strawson, op. cit., p.39.
27. Ibid. p.39.
28. OH vol. 1 p.272.
29. Ibid. p.277.
30. Strawson op. cit., p.47.
31. Ibid. p.47.
32. OH vol. 1 p.315.

3. A New Thermopylae: March 1941 – May 1941

1. Garret, D., *The Campaign in Greece and Crete* (HMSO, 1942), p.p.5–6.
2. Major-General R. F. K. Belchem, quoted in Simpson, op. cit., p.49.
3. *Oberkommando des Heeres* – German Army High command.
4. *Oberkommando des Wehrmacht* – overall command of all German armed forces.
5. Quoted in MacDonald, C., *The Lost Battle: Crete 1941* (London, 1993) p.51.
6. Simpson, op. cit., p.50.
7. Quoted in Clark, op. cit., p.9.
8. See Chapter Two for details of Operation Compass.
9. OKW's original estimate for the successful conclusion of Operation Barbarossa, the attack on Soviet Russia, had suggested a total of ten weeks fighting would be needed. In the event this proved something of an under-estimate.
10. MNBDO was a self-contained force intended for the defence of harbour and coastal installations.
11. Simpson, op. cit., p.52.
12. Clark, op. cit., p.16.
13. Simpson, op. cit., p. 63.
14. Ibid. p. 75.
15. MacDonald, op. cit., p. 57.
16. Ibid. p. 57.
17. George Orwell writing in *Partisan Review* July, 1941.
18. ANZAC doggerel.
19. Simpson, op. cit., p. 86.
20. Ibid. p. 91.
21. It may be certain elements within the Greek armed forces had already begun tentative negotiations with the Axis.
22. Clark, op. cit., p. 20.
23. 'Aerial Envelopment' was General Student's theory of invasion by parachutists – Crete his nemesis.
24. See Appendix 3.
25. The Germans dealt ruthlessly with those Cretans, and there were many, who took up arms.

4. 'Brevity' & 'Battleaxe': May 1941 – July 1941

1. Parkinson, R., *The War in the Desert* (London, 1976) p. 40; Pitt op. cit., p.241.
2. Pitt op. cit., p.243.
3. Barr, op. cit., p.65 – Rommel found his trucks with double rear wheels were not as useful as the single wheeled British vehicles.
4. Ibid. p. 65.
5. Ibid. p. 65.

6. Ibid. p.p.66–67; each Panzer Division was made up of a reconnaissance unit, a Panzer regiment of two battalion strength, a rifle regiment of three battalions with a supporting artillery regiment.

7. Ibid. p.67, the motorised Light Division was formed with four infantry battalions, each having a full array of weapons, two anti-tank and one artillery battalion.

8. The *Panzerwaffe* = 'Armoured Force', or 'Armoured Arm' – the element of the *Wehrmacht* which controlled tank and motorised formations. These were very much of an elite body. The mass of German infantry and guns relied upon horses as had their fathers in the previous war.

9. OH vol. 2 p. 153.

10. The fall of Crete had eased Axis supply difficulties but the losses in airborne troops sustained in such a pyrrhic victory saved Malta from a similar experiment.

11. OH vol. 2 p.24.

12. Leslie Morshead KCB KBE CMG DSO ED, (1889–1959) vies with Monash for the honour of being considered his country's finest general. He was commonly dubbed 'Ming the Merciless' from *Flash Gordon* on account of his facial characteristics.

13. Pitt, op. cit., p.250.

14. Parkinson, op. cit., p.41.

15. OH vol. 2 p.p.31–32.

16. *To War With Whittaker* The wartime Diaries of the Countess of Ranfurly 1939–1945 (London, 1994) p.84.

17. Parkinson, op. cit., p.44.

18. OH vol. 2 p.p.31–32.

19. Strawson, op. cit., p.33.

20. OH vol. 2 p.41.

21. Strawson, op. cit., p.57.

22. OH vol. 2 p.p.31–32.

23. Ibid. p. 41.

24. Pitt, op. cit., p.288.

25. Ibid. p.280.

26. Ibid. p.281.

27. Strawson op. cit., p.68.

28. OH vol. 2 p.159.

29. Ibid. p.161.

30. Rommel's forces at Halfaya were commanded by a militant cleric Major the Reverend Wilhelm Bach.

31. Strawson, op. cit., p.63.

32. Parkinson, op. cit., p.55.

33. Ibid. p.55.

34. Ibid. p.56.

35. Strawson op. cit., p.67.

36. For a more detailed note on intelligence intercepts please refer to appendix 3. Rommel's 'ace' Captain Seebohm became, with his company, a casualty of the fighting on 10 July 1942 when 26th Australian Brigade attacked at Tel-el-Eisa and his unit was overrun by 1/24th Battalion.

5. 'Crusader': August 1941 – January 1942

1. Force K comprised two light cruisers and two destroyers, lost to mines off Tripoli on 18 December.

2. East African Command was formed in September 1941.

3. Pitt, op. cit., p.354.

4. Parkinson, op. cit., p.59.

5. Ibid. p. 61.

6. Ibid. p. 61.
7. The rate of attrition among senior DAK officers was considerable. Neuman-Sylkow died of his wounds on 10 December.
8. 5th Light Division became 21st Panzer.
9. Von Ravenstein was captured on 29 November and was replaced by Bottcher.
10. The 90th Light Division was created in August 1941 as Division *zbV Afrika*. Summermann also died of wounds on 10 December.
11. Parkinson, op. cit., p.63.
12. Ranfurly, op. cit., p.113.
13. Pitt, op. cit., p.355.
14. Ibid. p.355.
15. Ranfurly, op. cit., for a fuller entry on the abortive raid see p.p.118–120, see also Pitt, op. cit., p.p.349–352.
16. OH vol. 3 p.40.
17. Strawson, op. cit., p.p.79–80.
18. There was a continual tendency to overstate the level of Axis losses which were generally far lower than broadcast, plus many of the damaged vehicles were recovered.
19. OH vol. 3 p.p.45–46.
20. Pitt, op. cit., p.387.
21. Parkinson, op. cit., p.82.
22. OH vol. 3 p.44.
23. Strawson, op. cit., p.80.
24. Keith Douglas, war poet and author or of, inter alia, *Alamein to Zem Zem*.
25. Bowen, R., *Many Histories Deep – the Personal Landscape; Poets in Egypt 1940–1945* (London, 1995) p.81.
26. OH vol. 3 p.59.
27. Quoted in Parkinson, op. cit., p.79.
28. OH vol. 3 p.57.
29. Robert Crisp was a troop commander in 3rd RTR and later wrote a superb memoir of the 'Crusader' battles, see bibliography.
30. Strawson, op. cit., p.83.
31. OH vol. 3 p.53.
32. Parkinson, op. cit., p.67.
33. Ranfurly, op. cit., p.114.
34. OH vol. 3 p.70.
35. Ibid. p.96.
36. Crawford op. cit., p.34.
37. OH vol. 3 p.96.
38. Ibid. p.71.
39. Ibid. p.71.
40. Parkinson, op. cit., p.85.

6. 'Msus Stakes' & 'Gazala Gallop': January 1942 – June 1942

1. OH vol. 3 p.136.
2. Ibid. p.139.
3. An expression used by C. R. M. F. Cruttwell in his outstanding single volume history of the Great War (1934).
4. Strawson, op. cit., p.96.
5. Parkinson, op. cit., p.89.
6. Ibid. p.91.
7. Strawson, op. cit., p.96.

8. OH vol. 3 p.145.
9. Strawson, op. cit., p.97.
10. OH vol. 3 p.151.
11. Ibid. p.152.
12. Ibid. p.p.153–154.
13. Ibid. p.154.
14. Parkinson, op. cit., p.92.
15. Ibid. p.93.
16. OH vol. 3 p.153.
17. Ibid. p.153.
18. Strawson, op. cit., p.100.
19. Ibid. p.101.
20. Parkinson, op. cit., p.95.
21. Ibid. p.94.
22. Ibid. p.95.
23. Ibid. p.95.
24. Ibid. p.96.
25. Field-Marshal Walther von Brauchitsch (1881–1948).
26. OH vol. 3 p.215.
27. Ibid. p.213.
28. Ibid. p.213.
29. Ibid. p.214.
30. Ibid. p.214.
31. Parkinson, op. cit., p.103.
32. Ibid. p.p.103–104.
33. Ibid. p.104.
34. Strawson, op. cit., p.104; Parkinson op. cit., p.105.
35. OH vol. 3 p.229.
36. Ibid. p.233.
37. Ibid. p.237.
38. Ibid. p.243.
39. Ibid. p.243.
40. Ibid. p.243.
41. Parkinson op. cit., p.110.
42. Ibid. p.110.
43. OH vol. 3 p.246.
44. Barr, op. cit., p.16.
45. Ibid. p.17.

7. Mersa Matruh & First El Alamein: June 1942 – August 1942

1. OH vol. 3 p.285.
2. Barr, op. cit., p.17.
3. OH vol. 3 p. p.281–283.
4. Barr, op. cit., p.18.
5. Ibid. p.19.
6. Ibid. p.19.
7. Ibid. p.24.
8. Ibid. p.27.
9. 'Leathercol' drawn from 29th Brigade, 5th Indian Division.
10. 'Gleecol' also from 29th Brigade, see OH vol. 3 p.p.288–289.
11. OH vol. 3 p.289.

12. Crawford, op. cit., p.79.
13. Ibid. p.41.
14. The Consolidated B-24 Liberator bomber had the capacity to transport a large bomb load over great distance. Those that came to North Africa had been part of 'Halpro' Force originally destined to China. The plane's admirable performance was somewhat offset by its unfortunate propensity for catching fire.
15. Sir Arthur ('Mary') Coningham 1895–1948; he was responsible for the development of the concept of tactical air power during his time with Desert Air Force and put these ideas to good use in Normandy. He was lost at sea when the liner *Star Tiger* went down in mysterious circumstances.
16. OH vol. 3 p.332.
17. Barr, op. cit., p.31.
18. Ibid. p.32.
19. Ibid. p.33.
20. Ibid. p.41.
21. The expression 'Desert Rats' became the universal description for all who served in 8th Army though the emblem of the Jerboa was the symbol adopted by 7th Armoured Division.
22. Crawford, op. cit., p.48.
23. OH vol. 3 p.296.
24. 'Robcol' comprised part 11th (HAC) Regt. RHA., 11th Field Regiment R.A., two companies of 1/4th Essex regiment, three platoons 1st Royal Northumberland Fusiliers and a detachment of Guides Cavalry, see OH vol. 3 p.342 (n).
25. OH vol. 3 p.243.
26. Ibid. p.244.
27. Strawson, op. cit., p.p.115–116.
28. Lt Upham won a bar to his VC in this action, see OH vol. 3 p.350.
29. OH vol. 3 p.353.
30. Crawford, op. cit., p.355.
31. OH vol. 3 p.355.
32. Ibid. p.356.
33. Crawford op. cit., p.56.
34. Ibid. p.52.
35. Ibid. p.56.
36. Ibid. p.46.
37. Ibid. p.46.

8. Alam Halfa: August 1942 – September 1942

1. OH vol. 3 p.361.
2. Barr, op. cit., p.186.
3. OH vol. 3 p.364.
4. Barr, op. cit., p.185.
5. Ibid. p.187.
6. Ibid. p.p.187–188.
7. Ibid. p.189.
8. Ibid. p.189.
9. Ibid. p.190.
10. Ibid. p.p.191–192.
11. Ibid. 193.
12. Ibid. p.196.
13. OH vol. 3 p.367.
14. Barr, op. cit., p.199.

15. Ibid. p.200.
16. Ibid. p.201.
17. Ibid. p.203; Gott's Bombay aircraft was forced to crash land having been 'bounced' by two low flying Me109s. Gott survived the crash landing but died when he insisted on returning to the burning wreck in an attempt to rescue trapped wounded, see also OH vol. 3 p.368.
18. Ibid. p.204, while many mourned Gott, some like the South African Pienaar, verged on the exultant. His relations with Gott had been far from cordial and he had a low opinion of his capabilities.
19. OH vol. 3 p.369.
20. Ibid. p.370.
21. Ibid. p.370.
22. Montgomery of Alamein, *Memoirs* (London, 1958) p.90.
23. Ibid. p.93.
24. OH vol. 3 p.370.
25. Ibid. p.370.
26. Ibid. p.371.
27. Ibid. p.379.
28. Montgomery, op. cit., p.97.
29. OH vol. 3 p.384.
30. Ibid. p.382.
31. Ibid. p.383.
32. Ibid. p.386.
33. Montgomery, op. cit., p.99.
34. OH vol. 3 p.387.
35. Ibid. p.388.
36. Ibid. p.388.
37. The 132nd Brigade suffered a total of 697 casualties, see OH vol.3 p.389.
38. Montgomery, op. cit., p.99.
39. OH vol. 3 p.389.
40. The New Zealanders' losses amounted to 275, see OH vol. 3. p.389.
41. Montgomery, op. cit., p.97.
42. Allied losses for the battle totalled 1,750, German 1,859 and Italian 1,051. The Axis lost 49 tanks, Allies 67; see Ford, K., *El Alamein 1942* (Oxford, 2001) p.59.
43. OH vol. 3 p.391.
44. Ibid. p.391.

9. Prelude: September 1942 – October 1942

1. Montgomery, op. cit., p.100.
2. Sergeant J. Longstaff, 2nd Battalion, Rifle Brigade, from Arthur M., *Forgotten Voices of the Second World War* (London, 2004) p.201.
3. Montgomery, op. cit., p.100.
4. KD = khaki drill.
5. Sergeant J. Fraser, Royal Tank Regiment from Arthur, op. cit. p.p.201–202.
6. Montgomery, op. cit., p.101.
7. Longstaff, from Arthur, op. cit., p.201.
8. Field-Marshal Sir A. F. J. Harding (1896–1989), succeeded Alexander as C in C Middle East in 1946 and latterly commanded the BAOR.
9. Brigadier S. C. Kirkman (1895–1982), after his notable service at El Alamein he commanded first 50th Division and then, in Italy, as a Major-General 13 Corps. After the war he held a number of senior appointments.
10. Montgomery, op. cit., p.103.

11. Brigadier Sir B. H. Robertson 1st Baron Oakridge (1896–1974) was the son of the former CIGS Field-Marshal William Robertson who had risen from the ranks.
12. Lieutenant-Colonel M. Graham had previously been on Whiteley's staff.
13. Brigadier D. Belchem had been responsible for Staff Duties under the Auk.
14. Brigadier E. T. 'Bill' Williams served Monty in an intelligence role during and after Alamein. He is credited with the idea of striking hard at the Italians, where 'corsetted' with German units, see Montgomery, op. cit., p.110.
15. Montgomery, op. cit., p.104.
16. Barr, op. cit., p.294.
17. Ibid. p.295.
18. Ibid. p.295.
19. OH vol. 4 p.42.
20. Ibid. p.3.
21. Carver, op. cit., p.58.
22. OH vol. 4 p.9.
23. Ibid. p.9.
24. Ibid. p.10.
25. Ibid. p.10.
26. Ibid. p.15.
27. Ibid. p.16.
28. Ford, op. cit., p.68.
29. Ibid. p.68.
30. Barr, op. cit. p.305.
31. Ibid. p.305.
32. Montgomery, op. cit., p.110.
33. Lieutenant-Colonel C. Richardson wrote the tactical appreciation for 'Lightfoot' – completed by 19 August. This closely followed Auchinleck's own memorandum of 1 July. Richardson concurred that the northern sector of the Alamein Front offered the greatest possibilities, see Barr, op cit., p.p.254–255.
34. Lieutenant-Colonel G. Barkas was, in civilian life, a film set designer; he worked with Major J. Maskeleyne, a conjuror!
35. Barr, op. cit., p.300.
36. Ibid. p.300.
37. Warner, P., *Alamein – Recollections of the Heroes* (Barnsley, 2007) p.213.
38. Montgomery, op. cit., p.111.
39. Longstaff, in Arthur, op. cit., p.204.
40. Montgomery, op. cit., p.107.
41. Ibid. p.108.
42. Ibid. p.108.
43. Carver, op. cit., p.92.
44. Ford, op. cit., p.68.
45. Carver, op. cit., p.93.
46. Montgomery, op. cit., p.108.
47. Ibid. p.109.
48. Ibid. p.109.
49. Ibid. p.110, see also Strawson, op. cit., p.136 n. Montgomery was never happy with Lumsden and took the first real opportunity to remove him.
50. OH vol. 4 p.p.22–23.
51. Colonel A. D. Stirling (1915–1990) was the founder of the SAS and active in the numerous raids on Axis forces until his eventual capture.
52. OH vol. 4. p.p.23–24.

10. Break-in: 23 October 1942 – 24 October 1942

1. Arthur, op. cit., Martin Ranft, 220th Artillery Regiment *Panzerarmee Afrika* p.207.
2. OH vol. 4 p.34.
3. Carver, op. cit., p.104.
4. Warner, op. cit., R. G. W. Mackilligin MC p.p.157–158.
5. Ibid. Colonel L. C. East p.90.
6. Carver, op. cit., p.105.
7. Ibid. p.105.
8. Warner op. cit., W. Winchester p.88
9. OH vol. 4 p.33.
10. Ibid. p.3.7
11. Carver, op. cit., p.106.
12. Warner op. cit., Winchester p.89.
13. Ibid. p.p.89–90.
14. Carver, op. cit., p.108.
15. Ibid. p.109.
16. Strawson op. cit., Major H. P. Samwell, Argyll & Sutherland Highlanders p.139.
17. Carver, op. cit., p.110.
18. Strawson, op. cit., Samwell p.140.
19. Carver, op. cit., p.110.
20. Strawson, op. cit., Samwell p.139.
21. Arthur, op. cit., Corporal V. Scammel Argyll & Sutherland Highlanders p.196.
22. Strawson, op. cit., Samwell p.139.
23. Carver op. cit., p.112.
24. Ibid. p.115.
25. Warner op. cit., the Revd. C. W. K. Potts (the Buffs) p.93.
26. Arthur, op. cit., Captain D. Smiley, Royal Armoured Car Regiment p.206.
27. The task forced comprised a motor battalion, three engineer field squadrons and three troops of Crusaders, plus signals and military police, see Carver op. cit., p.119.
28. Ibid. p.120.
29. OH vol. 4 p.p.34–35.
30. Ibid. p.41.
31. Ibid. p.42.
32. Warner, op. cit., J. W. Telford p.74.
33. Ibid. Major D. J. Watson p.103.
34. Ibid. Mackilligin p.159.
35. OH vol. 4 p.44.
36. Ibid. p.45.
37. Warner, op. cit., Lieutenant-Colonel B. S. Jarvis p.p.145–146.
38. Montgomery, op. cit., p.117.
39. Ibid. p.118.
40. Ibid. p.118.
41. Warner, op. cit., Brigadier C. E. F. Turner p.215.
42. OH vol. 4 p.47.
43. Ibid. p.47.
44. Warner, op. cit., Mrs G. Trevern p.217.

11. 'Crumbling': 25 October 1942 – 28 October 1942

1. OH vol. 4 p.47.
2. Ibid. p.47.

3. Lucas, op. cit., Trooper Jakes p.197.
4. Ibid. p.200.
5. Carver, op. cit., p.139.
6. Lucas, op. cit., Jakes p.197.
7. Carver, op. cit., p.140.
8. Gratwick won his posthumous VC for single-handedly knocking out a German mortar and crew, being himself killed when storming a machine-gun nest.
9. Carver, op. cit., p.141.
10. Ibid. p.141.
11. Warner, op. cit., F. A. Lewis p.41.
12. OH vol. 4 p.49.
13. Ibid. p.51.
14. Since 23 October, 30 Corps had sustained losses of 6,140, 13 Corps had lost 1,040 and 10 Corps 460. Wimberley's Highlanders had suffered most with some 2,000 casualties, the Australians and New Zealanders had lost around 1,000 each, see OH vol. 4 p.52.
15. Ibid. p.52.
16. Warner, op. cit., Colonel R. F. Wright p.175.
17. Carver, op. cit., p.146.
18. Ibid. p.146.
19. Warner, op. cit., Wright p.175.
20. Carver, op. cit., p.147.
21. Ibid. p.147.
22. Lucas, op. cit., Rifleman Suckling p.221.
23. Carver, op. cit., p.146.
24. For their gallantry both men were decorated. Colonel Turner received the VC and Sergeant Callistan the DCM.
25. Lucas, op. cit., Suckling p.222.
26. The Churchill Tank ('I' Tanks Mark IV (A22)) was intended to replace both the Matilda and Valentine. It was heavier armoured and equipped with the 6-pounder gun. Later, some were fitted with 75mm guns salvaged from disabled Shermans.
27. The Deacon was a development of the earlier portee arrangement which mounted a 6-pounder on an AEC Matador truck chassis.
28. Warner, op. cit., Wright p.175.
29. Ibid. Lewis p.42.
30. Ibid. Wright p.175.
31. Carver, op. cit., p.152.
32. OH vol. 4 p.52.
33. Carver, op. cit., p.155.
34. OH vol. 4 p.59.
35. Ibid. p.61.
36. Ibid. p.63.
37. Montgomery, op. cit., p.p.120–121.
38. Ibid. p.121.
39. Ibid. p.120.

12. 'Supercharge': 29 October 1942 – 3 November 1942

1. Montgomery, op. cit., p.p.121–123.
2. Ibid. p.125.
3. Ibid. p.125.
4. OH vol. 4 p.64.
5. Warner op cit., S. J. C. Cross MBE p.170.

6. OH vol. 4 p.65.
7. Lucas, op. cit., Roy Cooke p.236.
8. OH vol.4 p.66.
9. Lucas, op. cit., Cooke p.237.
10. Warner, op. cit., L. R. Symonds p.132.
11. 9th Armoured Brigade now had 79 Shermans and Grants with 53 Crusaders, see OH vol. 4 p.66.
12. Ibid. p.67.
13. Ibid. p.67 14 tanks were lost and 40 more badly damaged.
14. Lucas, op. cit., p.242.
15. Carver, op. cit., p.168.
16. Lucas, op. cit., p.243.
17. Ibid. p.242.
18. OH vol. 4 p.68, two Italian tankers *Zara* & *Brioni* had both been sunk.
19. Lucas, op. cit., p.243.
20. OH vol. 4 p.70.
21. Montgomery, op. cit., p.125.
22. Lucas, op. cit., p.246.
23. OH vol. 4 p.71.
24. Warner, op. cit., Colonel R. F. Wright p.176.
25. Carver, op. cit., p.173.
26. OH vol. 4 p.72.
27. Ibid. p.72.
28. Ibid. p.72.
29. Carver, op. cit., p.177.
30. Montgomery, op. cit., p.125.
31. OH vol. 4 p.p.73–74.
32. Carver, op. cit., p.169.
33. Lucas, op. cit., p.241; the tank pennants were of course significant in that they detailed seniority, position, colour and importance was provided daily from senior formation(s).
34. A 'stonk' equals a bombardment usually by shell or mortar fire upon an enemy position.
35. Lucas, op. cit., F. Jackson p.253.
36. Carver, op. cit., p.195 – official Axis figures were lower. They assessed German dead and wounded at 5,000 with under 3,000 Italians.
37. Montgomery, op. cit., p.125.
38. Warner, op. cit., p.211.
39. Ibid. p.171.
40. Montgomery, op. cit., p.126.
41. Ibid. p.127.
42. Ibid. p.126.
43. Quoted in Strawson, op. cit., p.149.
44. Ibid. p.p.151–153.

13. Break-out: 4 November 1942 – 23 January 1943

1. OH vol. 4 p.79.
2. Montgomery, op. cit., p.128.
3. Ibid. p.p.132–133.
4. These losses included the *Guilio Giordani, D'Annunzio* & *Algerino*, OH vol. 4 p.100.
5. Ibid. p.101.
6. Ibid. p.102.
7. Ibid. p.82.

8. Ibid. p.82.
9. Ibid. p.84.
10. Ibid. App. 3 p.p.476–477.
11. The Daimler Dingo was an open-topped scout car, very fast and manoeuvrable but lightly armoured and usually with no heavier armament than a Bren gun.
12. Lucas, op. cit., p.255.
13. Ibid. p.256
14. Von Thoma was replaced by the trusty Beyerlein (himself part-Jewish).
15. OH vol. 4 p.86.
16. Ibid. p.86.
17. Warner, op. cit., p.127.
18. The Shermans were so unsound that at this point many were consuming three gallons per mile of ground! See OH vol. 4 p.89.
19. Ibid. p.90.
20. 'Charing Cross' was where the road ascended the escarpment, a few miles to the south-west of Matruh.
21. 'Voss Reconnaissance Force' an ad hoc battlegroup led by Captain Voss one of Rommel's former ADCs and drawn mainly from 580 Reconnaissance Battalion.
22. OH vol. 4 p.90.
23. OH vol. 4 p.91.
24. Ibid. p.93.
25. Ramcke, as a paratrooper and thus part of the *Luftwaffe* formed the view his *Wehrmacht* colleagues had rather left him in the lurch.
26. Losses included *Etiopia*, *Mars* & *Portofino*, see OH vol. 4 p.100.
27. Strawson, op. cit., p.175.

14. 'Torch' to Tunis: November 1942 – May 1943

1. Parkinson, op. cit., p.163.
2. On 24 December 1942, Darlan was shot and fatally wounded in his Algiers HQ by a resistance fighter, Fernand Bonnier La Chapelle, who was executed for the murder next day. No tears were shed for Darlan, regarded as a pompous Anglophobe.
3. The PzKw VI (Tiger1) entered service early in 1943. Heavily armoured and weighing in at nearly 60 tons it was twice as heavy as a PzKw IV. A formidable beast of war it was quickly to inspire respect and apprehension, armed with the fearsome 8.8cm KwK 36L/56 gun.
4. This brigade (then 22nd Guards Brigade) had joined Western Desert Force in April 1941.
5. Parkinson, op. cit., p.196.
6. Barr, op. cit., p.p.411–412.

Appendix 1: Desert Tactics

1. Yeomanry were the mounted arm of militia and volunteer units raised for home defence, comprised usually of the rural gentry and middle classes = 'yeomen'. The Yeomanry squadrons now form the TAVR element of the RAC.
2. 'Hobo' was also Montgomery's brother-in-law.
3. The emblem of 7th Armoured Division, the jerboa – desert rat was to become a potent symbol.
4. Hobart was, at one stage, reduced to serving as a corporal in the Home Guard but his career was resurrected before D-Day when his eccentric brand of ingenuity produced the legendary 'funnies' – adapted AFVs which did immense good service in the Normandy campaign and after.

5. The difference between the Lee and Grant tanks was that, on the former a cupola housing a machine gun was mounted onto the turret.
6. Playfair op. cit., p.449.
7. White, B. T., *German Tanks and Armoured Vehicles 1914–1945* (London, 1966) p.p.43–45.
8. Ibid. p.p.45–47.
9. Playfair op. cit., p.500.
10. The Sten sub-machine gun was prone to accidental discharge if dropped when cocked, this was particularly so with the earlier model – most disconcerting.
11. The Bren, from BR – Brno and EN – Enfield, adapted from the Czech ZB vz 26; .303 calibre light machine gun, range 600–1,800 yards, using a 30-round box magazine.
12. Named after Captain Boys this .55 calibre anti-tank rifle used a bolt action with five round magazine, firing an AP round and effective at, say, 300 yards but only against inferior armour. By 1941 it was effectively obsolete.
13. 'Bite and hold' – a British WWI doctrine preferred by generals such as Plumer and Rawlinson who preferred to nibble away at the enemy's defences, forcing him to squander resources in counter-attacks rather than pursuing the illusory grail of the breakthrough.
14. Griffiths, P. & A. Hook, *World War Two Desert Tactics* in Osprey 'Elite' Series No. 162 p.15.
15. Lucas, op. cit., p. 101.
16. Griffith and Hook, op. cit., p.27.
17. Playfair, op. cit., p.498.
18. Ibid. p.p.500–501.
19. Brigadier Frederick Hermann Kisch (1888–1943) served in Military Intelligence in WWI before, during the inter-war years, becoming a leading figure in the Zionist movement. He returned to active service as an engineer and was killed by a mine during the Tunisian campaign.
20. Lucas, op. cit., p.113.
21. Cited in Lucas p.p.117–118.
22. 'Forlorn Hope' from the German *Verlorner Hauf* = 'lost party'.
23. First line = 'organic' units, e.g. infantry battalion, divided into A and B echelons. A1 for immediate re-supply; A2 for daily re-supply, B was support. Second Line was transport between re-filling points; third line between railheads and supply dumps, see Forty, op cit. p.p.110–111.
24. The legendary Diamond T models 980/981 were commissioned by Britain from the Diamond T Company of Chicago in 1940 and proved their suitability and ruggedness in the Desert War. A formidable and powerful vehicle tractor with a 14.5 litre engine delivering a hefty 201 bhp. The Diamond T remained in service for years.
25. Italy's Royal Air Force.
26. The Gloster Gladiator was the RAF's last operational biplane, obsolete by 1940 it nonetheless did good service, famous in the defence of Malta. Gladiators flew many sorties during the Desert war and on 17 August 1940 they destroyed eight Italian bombers for no loss.
27. The Westland Lysander, famed for its role in SOE operations was a liaison aircraft that could land and take off on remarkably short strips, highly versatile.
28. The Bristol Blenheim, a light bomber, later converted to long range fighter and night-fighter duties.
29. Bristol Bombay, medium bomber, obsolete by 1940, having a fixed undercarriage, could carry a bomb payload or 24 troops, used by Colonel David Stirling's fledgling SAS as a transport.
30. Hawker Hurricane, staple fighter aircraft of the RAF in 1940, powered by the legendary Rolls-Royce 'Merlin' engine and produced in large numbers. It was a modernised variant of the earlier Hawker Fury biplane, outclassed by the Me109 E & F.
31. Boston-Douglas A20/DB-7 Havoc – attack light bomber.
32. Curtiss P-40 fighter and ground attack aircraft, outdated by 1940 in the fighter role. The lack of a two-stage supercharger meant it could not attain the altitude necessary to take on the Me109 but it was extremely successful in ground-attack.

33. Designed by Willy Messerschmitt in the 1930s. An advanced metal monocoque frame and superb performance made the Me109 the staple of the *Luftwaffe* though latterly this role was shared with the Focke-Wulf FW190. Over 30,000 were produced.
34. The Arnold-Portal-Towers Agreement was a joint UK/USA undertaking regarding deployment of air forces entered into by General Arnold and Air Chief Marshal Sir Arthur Portal in June 1942.
35. North-American B-25 Mitchell medium bomber, named after US aviation pioneer Billy Mitchell. These aircraft were successfully deployed in a number of theatres.

Appendix 3: The Ultra War

1. Smith, M., *Station X – The Codebreakers of Bletchley Park* (London, 1998) p.p.97–98.
2. Jim Rose, one of Hut 3 Bletchley Park's air advisers, quoted in Smith, op. cit., p.99.
3. Ibid., p.100.
4. Ibid., p.102.
5. Bill Williams, quoted in Smith, p.103.
6. Ralph Bennett one of Hut 3's intelligence officers, quoted in Smith p.197.

Acknowledgements

Verse extracts are all taken from *Poetry of the Forties* editor Robin Skelton, (Penguin, 1968). Those introducing chapters two, twelve and thirteen are from *Lessons of the War c.*1946; chapter three is from *Soldiers Bathing* 1954; chapter four *War c.*1946; five from *Egypt* 1946; six from *Cairo Jug* 1945; seven from *Desert* 1945; eight *Burial Flags, Scind* 1945; nine *Tunisian Patrol* 1944; ten *Ring Plover at El Alamein c.*1946; eleven *The Patient* 1948. All original verse is by Samantha Kelly. This book could not have been written without the generous assistance of a number of organisations and individuals, particularly Peter Hart and the staff of the Imperial War Museum Sound Archive, Richard Groocock at the National Archive and Tristran Langlois of National Army Museum, Steve Shannon from the DLI Museum, Liz Bregazzi and Gill Parkes of Durham County Record Office, David Fletcher of the Tank Museum, Bovington, Roberta Twinn of the Discovery Museum, Rod Mackenzie of the Argyll and Sutherland Highlanders Museum, Thomas B. Smyth of the Black Watch Museum, Paul Evans of the Royal Artillery Museum, Ana Tiaki of the Alexander Turnbull Library, New Zealand, Christopher Dorman O'Gowan for information concerning his late father Brigadier E. Dorman-Smith, John Stelling and Henry Ross of North War Museum Project, Dr Martin Farr of Newcastle University, Barry Matthews of Galina Battlefield Tours, Alan, Julia and Claire Grint of Cogito Books, Trevor Sheehan of BaE Systems Plc, John Rothwell, James Goulty, Sir Paul Nicholson, Major (Retd) Chris Lawton MBE, Arthur W. Charlton, Colonel Anthony George, John Fisher, John Shepherd, Mary Pinkney, Brian Ward, Jennifer Harrison, Neville Jackson, the late Nigel Porter, Timothy Norton, Kit Pumphrey and Sir Lawrence Pumphrey, Graham Trueman, Adam Barr for help with photography, Rosie Serdiville, Sarah-Jayne Goodfellow and most particularly to Samantha Kelly for all of the original verse extracts. Special thanks are due to Jonathan Reeve, my editor at Amberley, for another successful collaboration. As the author I remain, as ever, responsible for all errors and omissions.

John Sadler, Mid-Northumberland, summer 2010

Chronology

1938

September – General Percy Hobart forms the Mobile Division (later 7th Armoured Div.) in Egypt.

1939

3 September – Britain declares war on Germany.

1940

11 June – Italy declares War on Britain; 11th Hussars involved in initial border skirmishes.

11 August – Italians invade British Somaliland.

19 August – British withdraw fully from Somaliland.

13 September – Italians invade Egypt and occupy Sollum.

17 September – the Italians occupy Sid Barrani.

20 September – British open the Takoradi aircraft reinforcement route through West Africa to Egypt.

12 November – OKH issues the order to create a force to support the Italians in N. Africa.

8 December – Wavell launches Operation 'Compass' under the command of General O'Connor.

11 December – Sidi Barrani recaptured; British counter-offensive proceeds with less difficulty than anticipated.

17 December – Sollum recaptured.

1941

5 January – British enter Bardia.

22 January – Australians enter Tobruk.

29 January – British re-invade Somaliland.

30 January – British enter Derna.

5/7 February – British defeat Italians in Battle of Beda Fomm.

25 February – British complete re-conquest of Somaliland.

27 February – Initial skirmishes with Afrika Corps.

5 March – First British troops withdrawn from theatre to be deployed in Greece.

24 March – *Panzerarmee* takes El Agheila.

31 March – Rommel attacks Mersah Brega.

3 April – Germans occupy Benghazi.

7 April – Generals O'Connor and Neame captured. Germans occupy Derna.

10 April – Tobruk besieged, Rommel bypasses garrison to press eastwards.

13 April – Tobruk surrounded, Bardia falls.

14 April – Axis assaults on Tobruk defences repulsed.

28 April – Germans occupy Sollum.

May/June – British intervention in Iraq (effectively subdued by 1 June).

5/12 May – 'Tiger' convoy brings much needed armour across Mediterranean.

15 May – British launch Operation 'Brevity'.

16 May – British complete conquest of Ethiopia.

20 May/1 June – Germans launch Operation 'Mercury' to take Crete, Allied survivors evacuated by RN.

June/July – British open campaign against Vichy French in Syria.

15 June – British launch Operation 'Battleaxe'.

22 June – *Barbarossa* begins.

1 July – Auchinleck replaces Wavell.

25 July/8 August – British intervention in Persia.

14/15 September – Rommel launches raid on Sofadi.

18 November – British launch Operation 'Crusader'.

19 November – British enter Sidi Rezegh.

21 November – Sortie by Tobruk garrison to effect link with forces around Sidi Rezegh.

23 November – Germans fare better in confused tank battle.

24 November – Rommel makes a dash across Egyptian border.

26 November – Auchinleck takes over direct command of 8th Army from General Ritchie.

30 November – Rommel tries to sever the corridor between British forces from Tobruk and Sidi Rezegh.

6/8 December – massed battles around and south of Sidi Rezegh.

10 December – British relieve Tobruk.

13/17 December – Rommel's series of counter-attacks are eventually beaten off.

19/24 December – British occupy Derna (19th), Mechili (19th), Barce (23rd), Benghazi (24th).

1942
January

2 January – British re-capture Bardia.

6/8 January – Rommel's offensive from Agedabia is beaten back.

12 January – British occupy Sollum.

17 January – British regain the Halfaya Pass.

21 January – Axis offensive pre-empts Operation 'Acrobat' – British forces worsted and forced into retreat.

23 January – Germans re-take Agedabia.

February

2 February – British occupy Gazala Line and lay plans for offensive – Operation 'Buckshot'.

4 February – Axis re-capture Derna.

May

26 May – Axis offensive against the Gazala Line.

June

2 June – Axis besiege Free French forces at Bir Hakim on southern flank of Gazala Line.
3 June – General Ritchie's attempted riposte founders, 150th Brigade destroyed.
10 June – Free French ordered to abandon Bir Hakim.
12/13 June – Major tank battle ranges around 'Knightsbridge' position.
14/17 June – British withdrawal to Egyptian border.
18/21 June – Axis pressure on Tobruk which falls followed by Bardia.
24 June – Axis forces enter Egypt.
25 June – Auchinleck assumes personal command of 8th Army.
27/28 June – Axis forces successful in Battle of Mersah Matruh.

July

2/3 July – 1st Battle of El Alamein begins.
4 July – 8th Army launches counter-attacks.
10 July – Australian gains from Italians.
26 July – Further British attacks held off.
26 July – Official end of the battle – a limited British victory.

August

18 August – Alexander replaces Auchinleck as C in C Middle East and Montgomery is appointed to 8th Army following the death of General Gott.
31 August – New Axis offensive opens; the Battle of Alam Halfa.

September

3/7 September – Unsuccessful attack by NZ division in Alam el Halfa area, battle ends as a limited British defensive victory.

October

1 October – 8th Army stages attack in the Deir el Munassib sector.
23/24 October – 2nd Battle of El Alamein opens after initial bombardment – the 'Break-in' phase.
24/25 October – the 'Crumbling' phase.
26/28 October – the 'Counter' phase.
29/30 October – Stalemate.

November

1/2 November – 'Supercharge'.
3–7 November – Break-out and pursuit by 8th Army.
8 November – Allied landings in French North Africa – Operation 'Torch'.

1943

14/25   February – Axis offensives from Sidi Bou Zid to Kasserine, initially successful but finally repulsed.

6   March – Further Axis offensive – Battle of Medenine.

20–27   March – 8th Army breaks through Mareth Line.

23   March – US forces defeat Axis at Battle of El Guettar.

6   April – 8th Army defeats Axis at Battle of Wadi Akarit.

13   May – Remaining Axis forces surrender at Tunis; end of the Desert War.

Dramatis Personae

Allied Commanders

Alexander, Field Marshal Harold, Rupert, Leofric, George 1st Earl of Tunis KG, OM, GCB, GCMG, CSI, DSO, MC, PC 1891–1969.

An old Harrovian, son of the 4th Earl of Caledon, Alexander was commissioned into the Irish Guards and served with distinction in the trenches, twice wounded and winning both the MC and DSO in 1916, becoming the youngest lieutenant-colonel in the British Army. Rather oddly, in the aftermath of the Great War, he led the Baltic German Landeswehr in their successful bid to see off Soviet aggression. In 1940 he was commanding I Corps of the BEF at Dunkirk, just after Montgomery was appointed to lead II Corps. In February 1942 he was dispatched to Burma as GOC, where he supported Slim and 14th Army while dealing with the Anglophobe US 'Vinegar Joe' Stillwell, a most difficult character. He was due to lead 1st Army for the 'Torch' landings but Alanbrooke nominated him to replace Auchinleck as GOC Middle East Command.

He presided over the successful conclusion of the Desert War and led 15th Army Group in Sicily and then onto the Italian Peninsula. He had hoped to command the ground forces for 'Overlord' but Alanbrooke considered Montgomery more suited. Monty himself was, with characteristic rudeness, more scathing; 'the higher art of war is quite beyond him'. If he was not a field commander of the first rank he possessed charisma and a flair for diplomacy. Unlike Montgomery, he commanded an entire theatre remaining popular with both British and US senior officers. Eisenhower would have preferred him for 'Overlord'.

Auchinleck, Field Marshal Sir Claude, John, Eyre GCB, GCIE, CSI, DSO, OBE, 1884–1981 ('the Auk').

An Ulster Scot from Fermanagh, his father was a soldier and Auchinleck served initially in the Indian Army, commanding 62nd Punjab regiment. In WWI he saw hard service in Mesopotamia, the Middle East and Suez. He created a reputation for bravery, integrity and a deep concern for the welfare of the men under his command. In 1940 he inherited the poisoned chalice of the doomed Franco-British command in Norway. He then commanded V Corps before being appointed as GOC of Southern Command. His subordinate was Bernard Montgomery, who now had V Corps. The two men did not bond, as Montgomery recorded: 'I cannot recall that we ever agreed on anything.'

In December 1940 he was appointed as C in C of the Indian Army and intervened in the Iraq crisis in the following spring. In July he succeeded Wavell to Middle East Command. After his subsequent removal and replacement by Alexander he declined the newly hived off Persia and Iraq Command, remaining 'on the shelf' for a period. Reinstated as C in C of the Indian Army, he indefatigably supported Slim and 14th Army, earning unstinted praise from the latter. His subsequent involvement in Partition was less cordial and he disagreed with Mountbatten. In 1947 he resigned and retired; his integrity unblemished. His declining years were spent in North

Africa and he died at Marrakesh. A somewhat reserved character, he was nevertheless loved by his men and respected by most of his peers. His contribution to victory in the Desert war has been steadily reassessed as time passes. The 'Auk' remains a revered figure.

Brooke, Alan, Francis 1st Viscount Alanbrooke KG, GCB, GCVO, DSO, 1883–1963.
After Dunkirk, Alanbrooke became, in December 1941, CIGS. His philosophy was to maintain pressure on Axis forces in North Africa and then Italy. He opposed the US headlong rush towards opening a Second Front and supported Montgomery despite the latter's frequent clashes with Eisenhower and often impossible behaviour. He was also able to deal with Churchill's mercurial temperament and relentless interference with the military conduct of the war.

Campbell, Major-General John ('Jock'), Charles VC, DSO & Bar 1884–1942.
Campbell was a native of Thurso, an accomplished horseman, who served with the RHA. In 1940 he was a lieutenant-colonel commanding the artillery of 7th Armoured's Support Group. He was an exponent of all arms flying columns, 'Jock' columns as they became known. He won his VC in November 1941 for a spirited defence of Sidi Rezegh airfield. In February 1942 he was promoted to lead XIII corps only to be killed in a minor traffic accident barely three weeks later.

Cunningham, Sir Alan, Gordon GCMG, KCB, DSO, MC, 1887–1983.
Born a Dubliner, brother of Admiral Lord Cunningham of Hyndhope, he served in the RHA during WWI. He later commanded British forces who successfully stormed Italian-held territories in East Africa, taking over 50,000 prisoners and removing the Axis presence. He was subsequently appointed to command 8th Army in August 1941 but he proved less effective against DAK and hesitancy led to his swift removal, spending the rest of the war in non-combat positions.

Dorman-Smith, Brigadier Eric 1895–1969 ('Chink').
Dorman-Smith was a controversial character who, when he fell out with the military establishment post war, celticised his name to Dorman O'Gowan and became associated with an IRA campaign during the 1950s. Opinions among his contemporaries varied. Sir Basil Liddell Hart (a leading strategic thinker of the inter-war years and respected military historian whose ideas were linked to those of Major-General J. F. C. Fuller and General Percy Hobart) regarded him very highly, Montgomery did not. He was unquestionably a most capable staff officer who briefly held the rank of Major-General. Born in Cavan in Ireland he was Commandant of the Middle East Staff College, served under O'Connor and was Chief of Staff to Auchinleck, losing his position when the Auk was sacked. He served afterwards as a brigadier in Italy where he continued to be controversial.

Freyberg, Bernard, Cyril 1st Baron Freyberg VC, GCMG, KBE, DSO & 3 Bars 1889–1963.
Born in England, his parents moved to New Zealand where Freyberg trained and then practised as a dentist. He joined the TA and then secured a commission in RND Hood Battalion. He had an extremely active battlefield career in WWI, suffering a host of wounds and winning a VC on the Somme. Freyberg was an outstanding leader of men, utterly fearless and a lion in battle. Churchill favoured him during the inter-war years. Churchill bid him 'strip his shirt and show his scars' – which were legion. He was probably the youngest general in the British army. He was appointed in WWII to command the 2nd New Zealand Expeditionary force and 2nd NZ division.
Wavell gave him command in Crete, a thankless task and one which was perhaps beyond his capacity. Controversy remains over his handling of ULTRA intelligence. Given German superiority and total command of the air it is perhaps difficult to see how anyone could have done better, though his political masters in Auckland were not best pleased. At divisional level

he was a highly competent and energetic tactician, serving through North Africa and Italy and on good terms with Montgomery. After the war he was appointed Governor-General of New Zealand. He died when one of his old war wounds finally ruptured.

Gott, Lieutenant-General William, Henry, Ewart CB, CBE, DSO & Bar, MC 1897–1942 ('Strafer').
Having served with distinction in the KRRC with the BEF 'Strafer' Gott (so-named in WWI after *Gott strafe England*) was stationed in Egypt in 1939 commanding 1st Battalion KRRC. A series of rapid promotions followed for this blunt, soldierly figure. By early 1942 he had risen to lead XIII Corps. Some observers have suggested he was thus promoted beyond his capacity: 'It has not been unknown for a commander to pass from disaster to disaster, but it is quite without precedent for any commander to pass from promotion to promotion as a reward for a succession of disasters.' Nonetheless, Gott was firm favourite to succeed to full command of 8th Army following Auchinleck's eclipse. He was, however, killed following an attack on the plane in which he had been travelling, thus making way for Montgomery.

Guingand, Major-General Sir Francis, Wilfrid de ('Freddy') KBE, CB, DSO, 1900–1979.
Educated at Ampleforth and Sandhurst, Freddie de Guingand joined the Middlesex regiment in 1919 and served, during the inter-war years for some time as a secondee to the King's African Rifles (1926–1931). Latterly he held appointments at Camberley Staff College and as Military Assistant to the Secretary of State for War before becoming Director of Military Intelligence Middle East. From the time Montgomery succeeded Auchinleck, de Guingand acted as his chief of staff, a post wherein he combined zeal and ability with that flair for diplomacy so noticeably absent in his commander.

Horrocks, Sir Brian Gwynne KCB, KBE, DSO, MC, 1895–1985.
Something of an all-rounder, Horrocks competed in the 1924 Paris Olympics and latterly enjoyed a second career as a broadcaster. He also spent fourteen year as Black Rod for the House of Lords. His academic record was undistinguished and he was lucky to be commissioned into the Middlesex Regiment. His company was surrounded at Armentieres in October 1914 and he was captured, ill-used and maltreated by the Germans. He learnt Russian and was deployed during the abortive intervention in the Russian Civil War, before serving for a time in Ireland. In 1940 he served under Montgomery and by 1942 commanded 9th Armoured. He next took over X Corps from Lumsden (see below) and fought with distinction throughout the Tunisian campaign before being badly injured in a bombing raid on Bizerte. He recovered from his wounds in time to lead XXX Corps in Normandy and during 'Market Garden'.

Leese, Lieutenant-General Sir Oliver, William, Hargreaves 3rd Baronet KCB, CBE, DSO 1884–1978.
An old Etonian and Coldstreamer, Leese was wounded three times on the Somme and commanded 20th Guards Brigade in France during 1940. By 1941, in the Desert, he was leading 15th Scottish Division and then commanded XXX Corps. He went on to lead 8th Army in Italy, and was sent to Burma in 1944 as C in C Allied Land Forces South-East Asia. This appointment proved unsuccessful and he was eventually removed. Outside the army he was a renowned expert on cacti.

Lumsden, Lieutenant-General Herbert CB, DSO, MC 1897–1945.
Having studied at Eton, Lumsden joined the TA before being commissioned into the RHA as a FOO in which capacity he won an MC in WWI. An expert horseman he competed in several Grand Nationals, despite a height disadvantage (he was a tall man, over six foot). He commanded the 12th Royal Lancers with some dash during the retreat to Dunkirk. In the Desert he led 1st Armoured and his sometimes difficult personality was considered a factor in

the defeat at Gazala. At El Alamein he commanded X Corps and had a strained relationship with Montgomery who felt he was tardy in the pursuit of DAK after the 'Break-out' phase of the battle. He was consequently removed from command. He was appointed to VIII Corps in the UK before being sent as Churchill's representative to MacArthur in the Far East. On 6 January 1945 he had the misfortune to be on board *USS New Mexico* when the ship was struck by a Kamikaze and Lumsden was among the dead.

Montgomery, Bernard, Law 1st Viscount of Alamein KG, GCB, DSO, PC 1887–1976 ('Monty'). Born in London into a rather impoverished Anglo-Irish clerical family, the future Field Marshal did not have a happy childhood. His mother was some years younger than his father and shamefully neglected her children. The family spent time in Tasmania when his father was appointed to the see. Though Montgomery senior inherited an estate in Ireland this was significantly encumbered and the family lived in straitened circumstances. Montgomery later failed to attend his mother's funeral being 'too busy'. He subsequently blamed this unfortunate beginning for a bullying temperament.

Montgomery was commissioned into the Royal Warwickshire Regiment in 1908 and saw service on the Western Front where, in 1914, he was severely wounded by a sniper's bullet (to the extent that his grave was dug in anticipation). Having recovered fully, he served under General Hubert Plumer in IX Corps of 2nd Army. During the lean inter-war years, when the army shrank dramatically, he held appointments on the Rhine and in Ireland where, forthright as ever, he fearlessly argued that allowing the Irish Nationalists self-determination was the only satisfactory route as the country could only be subdued by a degree of harshness inconceivable in Britain. He held appointments at the Staff College Camberley and went on to command 9th Infantry Brigade.

He married Elizabeth Carver to whom he was devoted and had a son David. Tragically Elizabeth died following an infection from an insect bite in 1937. Montgomery was inconsolable and threw himself more obsessively than ever into his work which remained the anodyne for his deep loss. It was suggested that he also harboured suppressed homosexual tendencies.

In 1939 he had severe doubts as to Britain's preparedness for war, a view vindicated by the BEF's performance in France. After Dunkirk, where he served with some distinction, he did not endear himself by blunt criticism of his superiors. His frustrations often emerged as downright rudeness. Tact and diplomacy were not among his qualities. In July 1940 he was appointed as deputy-commander V Corps where he soon fell out with Auchinleck and relations between the two men were never cordial. His ideas on the welfare of his troops, which were to earn him a huge following, often alarmed his exasperated superiors. A notion that army brothels 'horizontal refreshment' should be provided, was not untypical of his approach. He consistently failed to see why his bulldozer approach might ruffle feathers and he was not of a disposition that fostered compromise.

His undeniable successes in the Desert War made him the inevitable choice for command of Allied Land Forces for 'Overlord' under Eisenhower. Monty was quickly and bitterly at odds with Air Marshal Tedder (who served as Deputy-Supreme Commander under Eisenhower and campaigned relentlessly against Montgomery), a feud that continued after the War. His plans for the Normandy breakout were much criticised at the time. The tactical solution proved elusive and costly though in strategic terms the plan finally succeeded and led to the savage denouement of the Falaise Pocket. Operation 'Market Garden' was a failure though Montgomery, who would never admit to errors, disingenuously claimed it was a '90 per cent success'. Throughout, his relations with Eisenhower, who displayed admirable and unending patience, and the Americans, were strained. His arrogance and conceit, allied to an obsessive flair for publicity, alienated more than a few. He was beloved by many but despised by some. He showed a genuine and enduring care for his men. He was meticulous in planning and training and cautious with their lives. His attitude towards subordinates was dismissive, bordering on cruel, and he showed a hearty contempt for superiors.

His career after the war as CIGS was curtailed due to his inability to deal effectively with others in peacetime. His hubris soared and his often bizarre opinions on subjects as diverse as apartheid and Chinese Communism were increasingly out of step in changing times. His *Memoirs* were vituperative and further alienated contemporaries, particularly Auchinleck who came in for a waspish savaging. He became, in his declining years, both an anachronism and an institution. Monty, for all his failings, produced victory from defeat. His image is that of the British army of WWII coming of age and going on to victory after victory till the final capitulation of Nazi Germany.

O'Connor, General Richard, Nugent KT, GCB, DSO & Bar, MC, ADC 1889–1981.
Born in India, O'Connor served with the 2nd Battalion Cameronians and remained involved with his old regiment for the rest of his life. He served mainly in signals and was awarded his MC in 1915, followed by a DSO. In the inter-war period he served under J. F. C. Fuller, then on the N.W. Frontier and Palestine. At Mersa Matruh in 1939 he commanded 7th Division, facing the Italian 10th Army. He achieved outstanding success leading Operation 'Compass'. On 6 April 1941 in confused conditions, he and General Sir Philip Neame were taken prisoner by a German patrol near Martuba.
For two and a half years O'Connor remained captive in Italy, despite a series of daring attempted escapes. His chance finally came with the collapse of Italy in 1943 and he and Neame finally made good their deliverance. He went on to command VIII Corps in Normandy for the break out battles around Caen. Subsequently, after 'Market Garden' he was removed from command of his corps, allegedly as Monty found him insufficiently robust in dealing with his American counterparts.

Ritchie, General Sir Neil, Methuen GBE, KCB, DSO, MC 1897–1983.
Ritchie was commissioned, like Wavell, into the Black Watch in 1910, winning his MC in Mesopotamia. He held a succession of staff appointments under Wavell, Alanbrooke and Auchinleck, all of who regarded him highly. The latter gave him temporary command of 8th Army but his appointment lasted six, often very difficult, months. His handling of the fighting at Gazala and afterwards highlighted shortcomings and Auchinleck relieved him of command in June 1942, though he went on to lead XII Corps on D-Day.

Wavell, Sir Archibald 1st Earl Wavell GCB, GCSI, GCIE, CMG, MC, PC 1883–1950.
Wavell spent his formative years in India, studied at Winchester and Sandhurst, following his father into an army career and being commissioned into the Black Watch. He served in the South African War, in Russia as an observer and then through WWI, losing an eye at 2nd Ypres in 1915. He served in a succession of staff roles and in GSO1 appointments during the inter-war years. In 1937 he was promoted GOC British forces in Palestine and Trans-Jordan. His appointment to GOC Middle East came in August 1939.
He successfully directed British forces to rout the Italians in Operation 'Compass', netting 130,000 prisoners. When he was replaced by Auchinleck he was sent to India where he commanded the hopefully named 'ABDA' (American-British-Dutch-Australian) forces attempting to stem the seemingly inexorable advance of the Japanese. In January 1943, he was replaced by the Auk becoming Governor-General of India in September, (he had been made a Field Marshal in January 1943). He stayed in office till superseded by Mountbatten in 1947. His own son followed him into the Black Watch but was later killed in Kenya. Wavell was much respected by his contemporaries with the notable exception of Winston Churchill who had little time for him. Wavell was reserved in manner and not accustomed to resisting the prime minister's bellicosity and constant interference. He rightly opposed the Greek adventure but failed to be more resolute, Churchill chose to assign blame to him for this and the subsequent Cretan debacle.

Axis Commanders

Armin, General Hans-Jurgen von 1889–1962.
A Prussian of military stock from Silesia he served on both the Eastern and Western fronts in WWI. He began WWII under Guderian during Barbarossa where he sustained serious wounds, commanding 39th Panzer till November 1942. Transferred to Tunisia he served initially under Rommel and succeeded him as C in C of Army Group Africa, surrendering in May 1943.

Bastico, General Ettore 1876–1972.
A native of Bologna he held commands in Ethiopia and the Spanish Civil War, and latterly as Governor of the Dodecanese. His command in North Africa was diminished with Cavallero's appointment and, after the loss of Libya, became largely meaningless. He was nonetheless made a Marshal.

Bayerlein, General Fritz 1899–1970.
A Bavarian who fought in the infantry on the Western Front where he won his Iron Cross. He served under Guderian in Poland. At Alam Halfa in the Desert War he took over command from Nehring when the latter was wounded. He was himself subsequently invalided home but went on to fight both in Normandy and the Ardennes. He was part-Jewish.

Cavallero, Marshal Ugo 1880–1943.
A Piedmontese, who rose rapidly up the command ladder during WWI and displayed great strategic insight contributing to a number of Italian victories. He commanded in East Africa in 1938 and went on to serve in Greece and Albania. His appointment in North Africa was obfuscated by his poor relationship with the volatile Rommel. Latterly, he was embroiled in the Italian collapse of 1943. For a while he was favoured by the Germans but became hopelessly compromised and preferred suicide.

Gariboldi, General Italo 1879–1970.
He commanded 30th Infantry Division in Ethiopia and then 5th Army on the Italo-French border in North Africa. In March 1941 he was appointed to replace Graziani but was subsequently removed due to his poor relationship with Rommel.

Graziani, Marshal Rodolfo Marchese di Neghelli 1882–1955.
Youngest colonel in the Italian army during WWI, he commanded Italian forces in Libya in the 1920s, where his uncompromising policies earned him the unfortunate sobriquet of 'Butcher of Libya'. He served with equal ruthlessness in Ethiopia – *The Duce will have Ethiopia with or without the Ethiopians.* After his predecessor Balbo died in a 'friendly-fire' incident in 1940 he was appointed as C in C North Africa. The destruction of 10th Army during Wavell's offensive compelled his resignation. After the war he was condemned to nineteen years gaol for war crimes but served only a few months before being released.

Guderian, General Heinz 'Schneller Heinz' 1888–1955.
Guderian is regarded as father of the Third Reich doctrine on armoured warfare and one of the most influential German officers, though never given his Field-Marshal's baton. His influence on the tactics of armoured warfare and *blitzkrieg* was profound and is credited as the architect of victory against France in 1940.

Kesselring, Field Marshal Albert 'Smiling Albert' 1885–1960.
A *Luftwaffe Generalfeldmarschall* and C in C Mediterranean theatre where he was technically subordinate to the Italians and Rommel's command was a separate entity. He made strenuous efforts to maintain supplies to the Afrika Corps though he disagreed with Rommel's strategy, after the fall of Tobruk, of advancing into Egypt while Malta still held out. Hitler, in this

instance, favoured Rommel. Kesselring went on to maintain a skilled and stubborn defence of Italy as the Allies clawed their way up the Peninsula.

Messe, General Giovanni 1883–1968.
Having served in Libya, then through WWI, Messe was instrumental in the development of elite infantry formations, 'Arditi'. Latterly he served in Ethiopia and Albania, coming to North Africa as C in C in January 1943. He was careful to placate his nominal deputy Rommel. He was promoted Marshal just in time to surrender Axis forces in May 1943.

Nehring, General Walther 1892–1983.
He commanded the DAK from May 1942 having served an apprenticeship under Guderian. He was badly wounded in an air raid during the Battle of Alam Halfa but recovered sufficiently to command German forces in Tunisia during November/December 1942. He later fought on the Eastern Front.

Ravenstein, General Johann von 1889–1962.
Descended from a line of soldiers, one of whom as an aide to Blucher at Waterloo, he served with distinction on the Western Front in WWI winning both Iron Cross and the *Pour le Merite* ('Blue Max'). He worked in industry under Weimar but re-joined the ranks in 1934, serving in Poland and France where he added the Knight's Cross to his honours. In April 1941 he was promoted to Major-General, commanding 21st Panzer and that October was again promoted to Lieutenant-General. He was captured at Capuzzo a month later by the New Zealanders.

Rommel, Field Marshal Erwin Johannes Eugen 'The Desert Fox' 1891–1944.
Born in Wurttemburg, the legendary General showed early promise as an engineer and, throughout his life, displayed an amazing grasp of technology. He joined the 124th Wurttemburg Regiment in 1910, to his family's dismay and went on to serve with distinction in France, Romania and Italy during WWI, winning the Iron Cross and Blue Max. After the War he remained in uniform, a colonel in 1938. An early convert was Goebbels whose influence, combined with Rommel's own natural flair for showmanship, contributed to the lustre attaching to his laurels after 1940. Influence gained him command of 7th Panzer despite a lack of armoured experience and the misgivings of some of his superiors. He displayed, in the battle for France, his trademark energy, dash, fire and utter ruthlessness, though this was always tempered by chivalry.
He threw back the British counter-attack at Arras and drove his men and machines relentlessly, earning them the sobriquet of the 'Ghost' division. Latterly, and to his fellow-commander's chagrin 5th Panzer was placed under his command and his swift marches sealed the fate of elements of French 1st Army. His camera was always to hand despite the pressure and he never missed a 'photo opportunity' – adding the Knight's Cross to his honours. He moved to command 5th Light Division then 21st and 15th Panzer in North Africa where his legend thrived. After the defeat, such a reverse rather diminished his image of invincibility, and he languished in the backwaters of the Balkans (Army Group E) and then Northern Italy (Army Group B). With Kesselring's appointment he was moved to Normandy, where his driving energy strove to transform the defences studding the Normandy beaches. In the height of the subsequent battle, on 17 July 1944, he was severely wounded when his car was strafed. By now his charisma had waned and he was implicated, on extremely tenuous grounds, in the July Plot against Hitler. This alleged association led to his being offered the disgrace of a trial, with the consequent persecution of his family or taking his own life. For Rommel, a devoted husband and father, there could be only one course. Ironically this distanced him from the Nazi regime he had so assiduously served and preserved his post-war image.
While capable of inspiring great loyalty, he could equally alienate many fellow officers, particularly subordinates whom he drove hard and relentlessly. His relations with the Italians were scarcely cordial. He was bold to the point of recklessness, leading from the front,

unsparing of his personal resources, heedless of danger. Valour and dynamism are admirable but may be misplaced. As a tactician few would argue he was brilliant, able to understand every nuance of battle and respond with the swiftness of genius. His competence as a strategist was less assured. Some would aver his appreciation of the strategic position in North Africa was blinkered and he allowed his flashes of tactical lightning to divert attention from an untenable position. In North Africa he was continually hindered by lack of motor transport in a campaign fought over vast distances, served by ports that were too small at the end of a long logistics trail across unfriendly waters. He was hamstrung by what has been described, perhaps unfairly, as 'useless Italian ballast'. His genius for the armoured thrust was unexcelled yet such unrestrained boldness constantly exposed his forces to disaster through logistical failure.

Sir David Hunt, an intelligence officer on Alexander's staff described his talents: '... his real gift was for commanding an armoured regiment, perhaps a division and that his absolute ceiling was an armoured corps'. Many thousands of 8th Army veterans who experienced the Desert Fox at first hand might have been less dismissive.

Stumme, General Georg von 1886–1942.

As a Lieutenant-General in 1939 he commanded 2nd Light Division in Poland then went on to lead 40 Corps in the Balkans. In Russia he served under von Bock's command but came under a cloud due to security lapses. Sentenced by court martial he was rehabilitated due to von Bock's influence. During Rommel's critical absence in the opening hours of 2nd El Alamein he commanded the *Panzerarmee* but succumbed to heart failure at a critical moment.

Thoma, Lieutenant-General Willhelm Ritter 1891–1948.

A native of Dachau he fought on both fronts during WWI and was captured in 1918. He later fought in Spain and then Poland. Promotion followed rapidly and he commanded 17th Panzer during '*Barbarossa*.' He briefly replaced Nehring when the latter was wounded and then, very briefly, on the death of Stumme on 24 October 1942 before Rommel returned. On 4 November he was again captured and sent as POW to England where he was an important German officer in various camps and much respected, despite having a leg amputated in 1945. He died of a heart attack three years after the War's end.

Bibliography

Published Sources

Adair, R., *British Eight Army, North Africa 1940–1943* (London, 1974)

Agar-Hamilton, J. A. I. & L. C. F. Turner, *Crisis in the Desert May–July 1942* (Oxford, 1952)

Alexander, Field Marshal the Earl, *The Alexander Memoirs 1940–1945* (London, 1962)

Arthur, M., *Forgotten Voices of the Second World War* (London, 2004)

Bailey, J. B. A., *Field Artillery and Firepower* (London, 1989)

Barnett, C., *The Desert Generals* (London, 1960)

Barr, N., *Pendulum of War, the Three Battles of El Alamein* (London, 2004)

Beale, P., *Death by Design, British Tank Development in the Second World War* (Stroud, 1998)

Bennet, R., *Ultra and Mediterranean Strategy 1941–1945* (London, 1989)

Bidwell, S., and D. Graham, *Firepower, British Army Weapons and Theories of War 1904–1945* (London, 1982)

Bierman, J. and C. Smith, *Alamein, War Without Hate* (London, 2002)

Bingham, J., K. Wordsworth & W. Haupt, *North African Campaign 1940–1943* (London, 1969)

Braddock, D. W., *The Campaigns in Egypt and Libya* (Aldershot, 1964)

Bradford, E., *Malta 1940–1943* (London, 1985)

British Troops Egypt *Official Handbook for British Troops in Egypt, Cyprus, Palestine and the Sudan* (BTE, 1936)

British Troops Egypt, *Official Handbook for British Troops in Egypt, Cyprus, Palestine and the Sudan* (BTE, 1936)

Bryant, Sir Arthur, *The Turn of the Tide* Vols I and II (London, 1957–1959

Carver, M., *El Alamein* (London, 1962)

Carver, M., *Tobruk* (London, 1964)

Carver, M., *Dilemmas of the Desert War* (London, 1986)

Chalfont, A. J., *Montgomery of Alamein* (London, 1976)

Clark, A., *The Fall of Crete* (London, 1962)

Connell, J., *Auchinleck: A Biography of Field-Marshall Sir Claude Auchinleck* (London, 1959)

Crawford, R. J., *I was an Eighth Army Soldier* (London, 1944)

Crimp, R. L. *The Diary of a Desert Rat* (London, 1971)

Crisp, R., *Brazen hariots: An Account of Tank Warfare in the Western Desert, November–December 1941* (London, 1959)

De Guingand, Major-General Sir F., *Operation Victory* (London, 1963)

Delaney, J., *Fighting the Desert Fox* (London,1998)

Die Oase – Journal of the Afrika Corps Veterans Association

Eighth Army Weekly

Douglas, K., *Alamein to Zem Zem* (Oxford, 1979)

Ellis, J., *Brute Force: Allied Strategy and Tactics in the Second World War* (London, 1980)

Fergusson, Sir Bernard, *Wavell, Portrait of a Soldier* (London, 1961)

Fletcher, D., *The Great Tank Scandal: British Armour in the Second World War* Part 1 (HMSO, 1989)

Ford, K., *El Alamein* (Oxford, 2001)

Fraser, D., *Alanbrooke* (London, 1982)

Garret, D., *The Campaign in Greece and Crete* (HMSO, 1942)

Greacen, L., *Chink: A Biography* (London, 1989)

Greenwood, A., *Field Marshal Auckinleck* (London, 1990)

Griffiths, P., 'British Armoured Warfare in the Western Desert 1940–1945' in J.P.

Hamilton, N., *Monty: The Making of a General 1887–1942* (London, 1982)

Hamilton, N., *The Full Monty: Montgomery of Alamein 1887–1942* (London, 2001)

Harris and F. H. Toase (eds), *Armoured Warfare* (London, 1990)

Harrison, F., *Tobruk: The Great Siege Reassessed* (London, 1996)

Harrison-Place, T., *Military Training in the British Army, 1940–1944: From Dunkirk to D-Day* (London, 2000)

Humble, R., *Crusader: Eighth Army's Forgotten Victory November 1941 to January 1942* (London, 1987)

Horrocks. Lieutenant-General, Sir B., *A Full Life* (London, 1960)

Irving, D., *The Trail of the Fox* (London, 1977)

Johnson, M. and P. Stanley, *Alamein: The Australian Story* (Oxford, 2002)

Joslen, Lieutenant-Colonel H. F., *Orders of battle: Second World War* (HMSO 1960)

Kippenburger, Major-General Sir H., *Infantry Brigadier* (Oxford, 1949)

Latimer, J., *Alamein* (London, 2002)

Lewin, R., *Rommel as Military Commander* (London, 1968)

Lewin, R., *Montgomery as Military Commander* (London, 1971)

Lewin, R., *The Life and Death of the Afrika Korps* (London, 1977)

Lewis, P. J., & I. R. English, *Into Battle with the Durhams: 8 DLI in World War II* (London, 1990)

Liddell Hart, Sir B. H., *The Tanks: The History of the Royal Tank Regiment and its Predecessors, Heavy Branch Machine Gun Corps, Tank Corps and Royal Tank Corps, 1914–1945* 2 vols. (London, 1959)

Lucas, J., *War in the Desert–the Eighth Army at El Alamein* (London, 1982)

Lucas, J., *Panzer Army Africa* (London, 1977)

MacDonald, C., *The Lost Battle: Crete 1941* (London, 1993)

Macksey, K., *Rommel: Battles and Campaigns* (London, 1979)

Majdalany, F., *The Battle of El Alamein* (London, 1965)

Montgomery, Field Marshall the Viscount B. L., *Memoirs* London, 1958)

Moorehead, A., *Mediterranean Front* (London, 1942)

Moorehead, A., *Years of Battle* (London, 1943)

Moorehead, A., *The End in Africa* (London, 1943)

Neillands, R., *The Desert Rats: 7th Armoured Division, 1940–1945* (London, 1991)

Nicolson, N., *Alex: The Life of Field Marshal Earl Alexander of Tunis* (London, 1971)

Parkinson, R., *Blood, Toil, Sweat and Tears* (London, 1973)

Parkinson, R., *A Day's March Nearer Home* (London, 1974)

Parkinson, R., *The War in the Desert* (London, 1976)

Philips, C. E. L., *Alamein* (London, 1962)

Pitt, B., *The Crucible of War 1: Wavell's Command* (London, 1986)

Pitt, B., *The Crucible of War 2: Auchinleck's Command* (London, 1986)

Pitt, B., *The Crucible of War 3: Montgomery and Alamein* (London, 1986)

Playfair, Major-General I.S.O., Official History, UK Military Series, Campaigns: *Mediterranean and Middle East* Vols 1–4, (London, 1962–1966)

Osprey *Elite* Series 105 'World War II Infantry Tactics: Squad and Platoon'

Osprey *Elite* 122 'World War Two Infantry tactics: Company and Battalion'

Osprey *Elite* 124 'World War Two Infantry Anti-Tank Tactics'

Osprey *Elite* 162 'World War II Desert Tactics'

Osprey *Battle Orders* 20 'Rommel's Afrika Corps Tobruk to El Alamein'

Osprey *Battle Orders* 28 'Desert Rats: British 8th Army in North Africa 1941–1943'

Osprey *New Vanguard* 28 'Panzerkampfwagen IV Medium Tank 1936–1945'

Osprey *New Vanguard* 33 'M3 and M5 Stuart Light Tank 1940–1945'

Osprey *New Vanguard* 46 '88mm Flak 18/36/37/41 and Pak 43 1936–1945'

Osprey *New Vanguard* 98 'British Anti-Tank Artillery 1939–1945'

Osprey *New Vanguard* 113 'M3 Lee/Grant Medium Tank 1941–1945'

Osprey *Campaign* 158 'El Alamein 1942'

Quarrie, B., *Afrika Korps* (Cambridge, 1975)

Quarrie, B., *Panzers in the Desert* (Cambridge, 1978)

Rommel, E., *Infantry Attack* (London, 1990)

Samwell, H. P., *An Infantry Officer with the Eighth Army: The Personal Experiences of an Infantry Officer During the Eight Army's Campaign Through Africa and Sicily* (London, 1945)

Schmidt, H. W., *With Rommel in the Desert* (London, 1951)

Smith, M., *Station X – The Codebreakers of Bletchley Park* (London, 1998)

Stewart, A., *The Eighth Army's Greatest Victories: Alam Halfa to Tunis 1942–1943* (London, 1999)

Stewart. A., *The Early Battles of Eighth Army: 'Crusader' to the Alamein Line 1941–1942* (London, 2002)

Strawson, J., *The Battle for North Africa* (London, 1969)

Terraine, J., *The Right of the Line* (London, 1983)

Toase, F. H., & J. P. Harris, *Armoured Warfare* (London, 1990)

Van Creveld, M., *Supplying in War: Logistics from Wallenstein to Patton* (Cambridge, 1977)

Verney, G. L., *The Desert Rats: History of 7th Armoured Division 1938–1945* (London, 1954)

War Office: *Military Report on the North-Western Desert of Egypt* (London, 1937)

Warner, P., *Alamein – Recollections of the Heroes* (London, 1979)

Young, D., *Rommel* (London, 1950)

Unpublished Sources

Pinkney, M., *Maurice and Mary*

Akam, E. A., *A Memoir*

List of Illustrations

1. Erwin Rommel. © Verband Deutsches Afrika-Corps e. V.
2. Bernard Law Montgomery. © J.D. Fisher.
3. 4, 5 & 6. British troops in the Western Desert. © G.N. Cook.
7. & 8. British troops in the Western Desert. © G.N. Cook.
9. General Archibald Wavell. © John Sadler.
10. Bren gunners of the King's Own Royal Regiment deployed defending their camp. © John Sadler.
11. A mortar team also from the King's Own. © John Sadler.
12. New Zealand troops in Bren gun practice. © John Sadler.
13. Anti-aircraft gunners in readiness. © John Sadler.
14. A touch of colour – infantry of the Arab legion on the march in Jordan. © John Sadler.
15. Indian troops ambush Italian armour. © John Sadler.
16. Communications – a telephone exchange dugout. © John Sadler.
17. Underground command post. © John Sadler.
18. The grin on the face of this British soldier may be for the benefit of camera but the morale of Eighth Army, though bruised was never shattered. © John Sadler.
19. Sinking a well – the water supply as ever was vital. © John Sadler.
20. British troops advance through the shattered walls of an Italian fort. © John Sadler.
21. Italian POW's, including native troops march into captivity. © John Sadler.
22. British armoured cars assail Fort Maddalena. © John Sadler.
23. British guns in action. © John Sadler.
24. An Italian tank knocked out in fierce fighting. © John Sadler.
25. A wireless operator at work in a shallow pit. © John Sadler.
26. A long line of Italian POW's marches into captivity a Chevrolet truck keeps pace. © John Sadler.
27. British carriers move past the ruin of Fort Capuzzo. © John Sadler.
28. British Valentine tanks in action. © John Sadler.
29. A British howitzer pounding Italian positions. © John Sadler.
30. Australian carriers moving forward, dispersed according to sound desert practice. © John Sadler.
31. Recovered shell of Grant M3 tank. © John Sadler.
32. Rommel's Grave. © J.D. Fisher.
33. Montgomery's grave. © J.D. Fisher.
34. The Battle of Alam Halfa. © John Sadler.
35. The Break-in – Operation 'Lightfoot'. © John Sadler.
36. The Break-out – Operation 'Supercharge'. © John Sadler.
37. The Pursuit to El Agheila. © John Sadler.
38. Rommel in his staff car. © Amberley Archive.
39. British troops forty miles from Alexandria. © Jonathan Reeve JR1257b73p61 19391945.
40. General Auchinleck. © Jonathan Reeve JR1256b73p55 19391945.

41. British troops at El Alamein. © Jonathan Reeve JR1258b73p66 19391945.

42. German troops captured at El Alamein. © Jonathan Reeve JR1259b73p68 19391945.

43. British gunners manning their 6-pounder. © Jonathan Reeve JR1260b73p73 19391945.

44. British guns firing on an enemy strongpoint. In the foreground a wounded gunner is tended by one of his comrades. © Jonathan Reeve JR1261b73p100 19391945.

45. Vickers machine-gunners of the Middlesex Regiment firing on the German lines at El Alamein as shell bursts ahead of them. © Jonathan Reeve JR1265b74p8BL 19391945.

46. British troops in a carrier take time out for a cigarette. © Jonathan Reeve JR1262b73pbp 19391945.

47. British troops taking cover behind a disabled German tank at El Alamein, a German shell bursts close to the other side of it. © Jonathan Reeve JR1266b74p8BR 19391945.

48. British troops advance through the smoke of enemy shellfire at El Alamein. © Jonathan Reeve JR1267b74p8TL 19391945.

49. Australian troops advancing at El Alamein. © Jonathan Reeve JR1268b74p8TR 19391945.

50. British Crusader tanks move up for the tank battle at El Alamein. © Jonathan Reeve JR1269b74p14-15 19391945.

51. British infantry moving forward at El Alamein in the open desert, leading men are closing in to take a German prisoner, arms raised. © Jonathan Reeve JR1270b74p10-11 19391945.

52. American Sherman tanks move off into battle at El Alamein. © Jonathan Reeve JR1271b74p18-19 19391945.

53. A British 6-pounder anti-tank gun at El Alamein engaging the German forces. © Jonathan Reeve JR1272b74p20BL 19391945.

54. In clouds of dust raised by the blasts of their own guns a force of twenty British tanks pounds the German forces at El Alamein. © Jonathan Reeve JR1273b74p21MR 19391945.

55. A British Crusader tank races through the smoke of a heavy German bomb blast. © Jonathan Reeve JR1274b74p20TL 19391945.

56. A German Mark III tank lies furiously ablaze after a direct hit early in the battle of El Alamein. © Jonathan Reeve JR1274b74p21TR 19391945.

57. German Mark IV Special and Mark III tanks knocked out at El Alamein. © Jonathan Reeve JRbp 19391945.

58. Crusaders speeding along the cost road after the retreating German forces. © Jonathan Reeve JR1276b74p30uml 19391945.

59. As the Eighth Army transport moved forward along the coast road, RAF Hurricane fighters race overhead in constant protective patrol. © Jonathan Reeve JR1277b74p30umr 19391945.

60. British Shermans and Crusader tanks pass through Mersa Matruth. © Jonathan Reeve JR1278b74p31B 19391945.

61 & 62. Symbol of the German resistance overcome: 88mm gun abandoned west of El Alamein. Nearby a tractor and 88mm gun lie wrecked by a direct hit. © Jonathan Reeve JR1279b74p30otl 19391945 & JR1279b74p30otr 19391945.

63. Captured intact, this 150mm self-propelled heavy German gun is being examined by British officers. © Jonathan Reeve JR1280b74p31TM 19391945.

64. The coast road is shelled by the German forces to check the British Army's advance. In the foreground an abandoned German vehicle. © Jonathan Reeve JR1281b74p29MR 19391945.

65. General Alexander and General Montgomery. © Jonathan Reeve JR1281b74p32T 19391945.

66. 25-pounder gun crews launch the barrage against German forces on Friday 23 October 1942. © Jonathan Reeve JR1283b74p76 19391945.

67. A German strongpoint captured by British infantry at El Alamein. © Jonathan Reeve JRbp 19391945.

68. British artillerymen fire the 25-pounder guns the main instrument for the barrage. © Jonathan Reeve JR1285b74p5TR 19391945.

69. British checkpoint. © Jonathan Reeve JR1287b74p2-3 19391945.

70. British troops mark a newly cleared gap in a minefield at El Alamein. © Jonathan Reeve JR1286b74p13B 19391945.

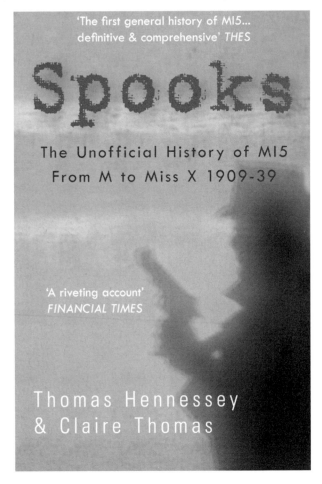

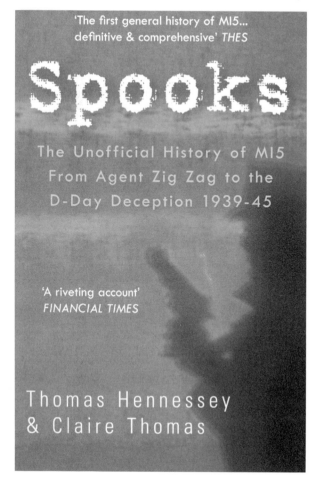

Available from February 2011 from Amberley Publishing

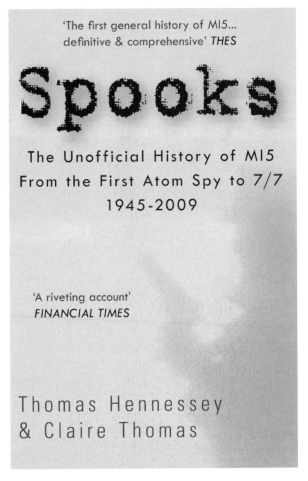

'The first general history of MI5...
definitive & comprehensive' *THES*

Spooks

The Unofficial History of MI5
From the First Atom Spy to 7/7
1945-2009

'A riveting account'
FINANCIAL TIMES

Thomas Hennessey
& Claire Thomas

The history of MI5 during the era of the Cold War, the IRA and international terrorism

Despite an outstanding record against German and Soviet espionage, the book reveals MI5's greatest failure: how and why it failed to prevent Soviet agents like Anthony Blunt, penetrating the heart of the British establishment, including MI5 itself. The authors look in detail at MI5's role in the post-Cold War world; in particular, they consider its changing role as it took on the main responsibility in countering terrorist threats to Britain. Controversy has never been far away during MI5's battle against the IRA, which included sending deep penetration agents into the heart of Northern Ireland's terrorist organisations. And in the twenty-first century, MI5 has had to face the deadliest terrorist threat of all – from Al Qaeda. The book looks at MI5's attempts to prevent mass murder on the streets of Britain, including the failure to stop the 7/7 bombings in London in 2005.

£9.99 Paperback
384 pages
978-1-84868-050-0

Available from February 2011 from all good bookshops or to order direct
Please call **01285-760-030**
www.amberleybooks.com

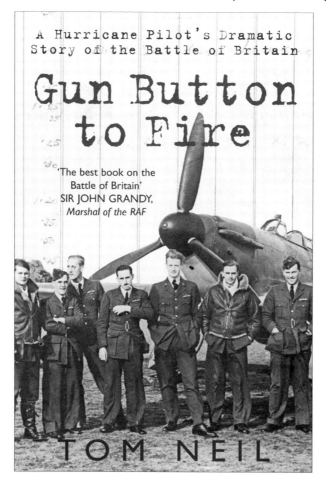

Also available from Amberley Publishing

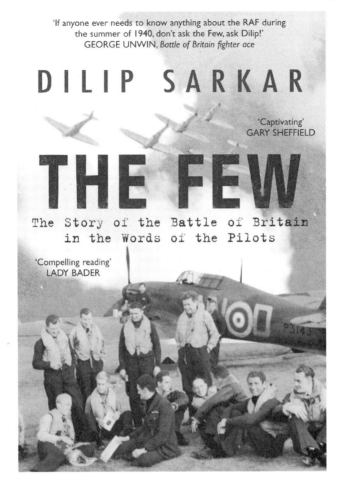

'If anyone ever needs to know anything about the RAF during the summer of 1940, don't ask the Few, ask Dilip!'
GEORGE UNWIN, *Battle of Britain fighter ace*

DILIP SARKAR

'Captivating'
GARY SHEFFIELD

THE FEW

The Story of the Battle of Britain
in the Words of the Pilots

'Compelling reading'
LADY BADER

The history of the Battle of Britain in the words of the pilots

'Over the last 30 years Dilip Sarkar has sought out and interviewed or corresponded with numerous survivors worldwide. Many of these were not famous combatants, but those who formed the unsung backbone of Fighter Command in 1940. Without Dilip's patient recording and collation of their memories, these survivors would not have left behind a permanent record.' LADY BADER
'A well-researched detailed chronicle of the Battle of Britain'. HUGH SEBAG MONTEFIORE

£14.99 Paperback
129 photographs
320 pages
978-1-4456-0050-5

Available from all good bookshops or to order direct
Please call **01285-760-030**
www.amberleybooks.com

Also available from Amberley Publishing

A fabulous slice of wartime nostalgia, a facsimile edition of the propaganda booklet issued following victory in the Battle of Britain

First published in 1941, *The Battle of Britain* was a propaganda booklet issued by the Ministry of Information to capitalise on the success of the RAF in defeating the Luftwaffe. An amazing period piece, hundreds of thousands of copies were printed and sold for 6d and it became one of the year's best selling books. It is the first book to embed in the public imagination the heroics of 'The Few'.

£4.99 Paperback
25 illustrations
36 pages
978-1-4456-0048-2

Available from all good bookshops or to order direct
Please call **01285-760-030**
www.amberleybooks.com

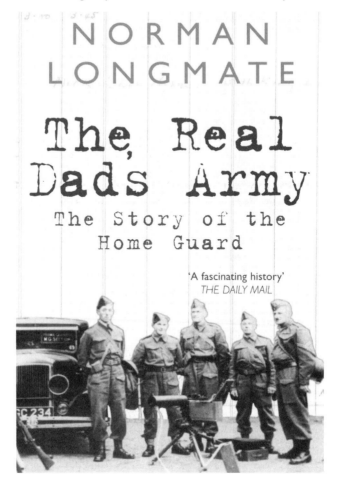

NORMAN
LONGMATE

The Real
Dads Army
The Story of the
Home Guard

'A fascinating history'
THE DAILY MAIL

*A narrative history of the Home Guard from its creation in May 1940
to the end of the Second World War*

'A fascinating history' THE DAILY MAIL
'Wonderful stories… a well-written account of the last line of defence' THE DAILY MIRROR

The enduring popularity of the BBC tv series Dad's Army has focused attention on one of the strangest and least military armies ever formed —The British Home Guard. Norman Longmate, an ex-member of the Home Guard and an authority on wartime Britain, has collected together a wealth of hilarious anecdote as well as all the unlikely facts to produce the first popular history of the Home Guard to be written since the war.

£18.99 Hardback
50 illustrations
160 pages
978-1-84868-914-5

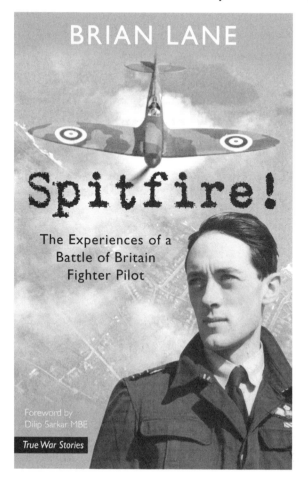

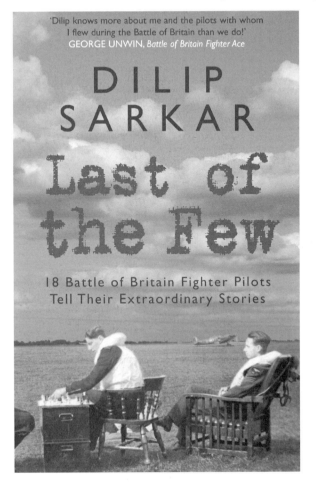

Available from September 2010 from Amberley Publishing

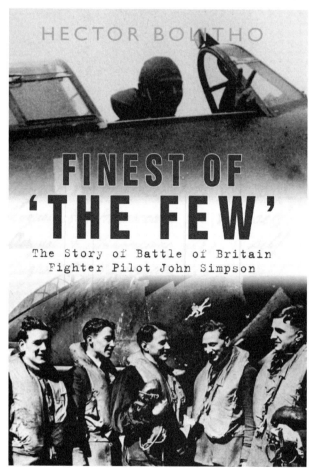

HECTOR BOLITHO

FINEST OF 'THE FEW'

The Story of Battle of Britain
Fighter Pilot John Simpson

*The remarkable Battle of Britain experiences of fighter pilot
John Simpson, DFC, as compiled by wartime journalist Hector Bolitho*

A brilliant memoir of a noted Battle of Britain Hurricane ace. Book was originally published in 1943
with a limited circualtion due to wartime paper shortages. It has remained out of print until now.

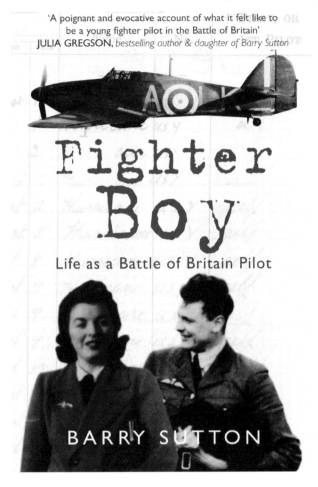

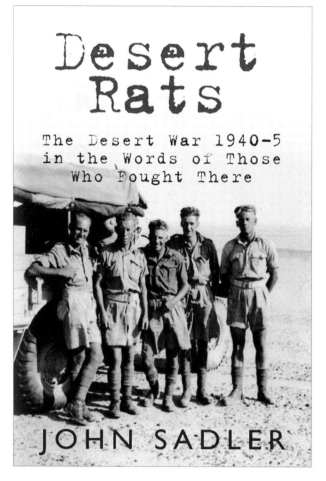

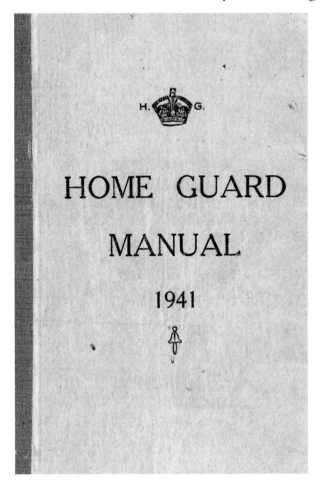

Index

'Aberdeen' Position; 176

Alanbrooke, Field Marshal; 72, 97, 208

Alam Bueit; 102

Alam Halfa Ridge; 96, 102

Alexander, Field Marshal; 98, 99, 209, 210

Alexandria; 18

Aliakmon Line, the; 42, 47

Aosta, Duke of; 55

Artillery;

    British 2-pounder anti tank gun; 44

    British 6-pounder anti tank gun; 108, 175

    British 25-pounder; 44

    German 8.8.cm Flak; 57

Auchinleck, General Sir Claude; 18, 55, 58, 60,
    61, 64–65, 70, 73, 74, 75, 80, 85, 88, 89, 92, 93,
    94, 96, 97, 98, 99, 105

'Balaklavering'; 102, 188

Bardia; 10, 33

Barkas, Lieutenant-Colonel, Geoffrey; 146

Barnett, Corelli; 35

Barr, Niall; 96, 107, 194

Bastico, General; 71, 202

Battles;

    Alam Halfa; 19, 100-102, 106

    1st El Alamein; 19, 86-87, 92

    2nd El Alamein; 19, 152-166, 168-194, 210

    Enfidaville; 209

    Kassereine Pass, 209

    Medenine; 209

    Sidi Rezegh; 66, 67

    Taranto; 23, 39

Bayerlein, General; 61

Benghazi; 10, 40, 51, 202

Beresford-Peirse, General, Sir Noel; 57

Bergonzoli, Lieutenant-General, Annibale,
    'Electric Whiskers'; 33

Bir Hacheim; 75, 77

'Blue', the; 9, 17

Bren Carrier; 44

Bren gun; 45

British Army;

    Formations

    Gurkhas; 92, 209

    Long Range Desert Group; 31, 87, 209

    Special Air Service; 88

    Western Desert Force; 33

    Army groups

    First Army; 209

    Eighth Army; 14, 67, 82

    Battalions

    7/10 Argyll & Sutherland Highlanders; 155,
    170

    2/13th Australian; 177, 178

    2/17th Australian; 177

    2/23rd Australian; 178

    2/24th Australian; 169, 178

    2/48th Australian; 169

    2/17th Australian; 169

    7th Australian; 88

    9th Australian; 88

    11th Commando; 62

1st Black Watch; 155
5th Black Watch; 156, 170
7th Black Watch; 157
5th Cameron Highlanders; 157
6th Durham Light Infantry; 91
9th Durham Light Infantry; 82
5th East Yorks; 91
5th Green Howards; 76
1st Gordon Highlanders; 170
5/7th Gordon Highlanders; 156, 191
1/7th Queen's Royal Regiment; 162
Imperial Light Horse; 159
Rand Light Infantry; 159
Royal Durban Light Infantry; 159
2nd Royal Sussex; 176
4th Royal Sussex; 176
5th Royal Sussex; 176
Brigades
2nd Armoured; 76, 90, 170, 200
4th Light Armoured; 57, 160, 201, 206
7th Armoured; 57, 63
8th Armoured; 103, 163, 186, 187, 201, 206
9th Armoured; 163, 165, 185, 186, 199
22nd Armoured; 76, 101, 102, 160, 165, 192, 202, 204
23rd Armoured; 89, 101, 102
24th Armoured; 165, 167, 170
20th Australian; 177
201st Guards; 210
5th Indian; 89, 103
29th Indian; 83
18th Infantry; 86
24th Infantry; 155
161st Indian Motor Brigade; 90
69th Infantry; 169
131st Infantry; 101, 177
132nd Infantry; 101
133rd (Lorried) Infantry; 101, 176
151st Infantry; 82, 177, 188, 209
152nd Infantry; 177, 185
4th Light Armoured; 101, 204, 205
6th Light Armoured; 199
7th Motor; 101, 170, 186

5th New Zealand Infantry; 104, 201
6th New Zealand; 177, 199
Rifle Brigade; 173
Corps
King's Royal Rifle Corps; 173, 175, 189
Royal Army Ordnance Corps; 30, 83
Royal Army Service Corps; 30, 83
10 Corps; 108, 148, 159, 160, 167, 199, 200
13 Corps; 61, 75, 82, 88, 148, 160, 165, 168, 171, 172, 192, 203
30 Corps; 61, 75, 82, 88, 91, 148, 151, 160, 168, 172
Divisions
11th African; 55
12th African; 55
Australian; 56
Australian; 34, 53
1st Armoured; 86, 88, 89, 90, 167, 201, 202
2nd Armoured; 51, 189
7th Armoured; 29, 57, 58, 89, 148, 169, 172, 200, 202, 210
8th Armoured; 108, 199
1st Free French; 162
51st Highland; 94, 148, 155, 170, 185, 188, 189
4th Indian; 29, 34, 57, 159, 210
5th Indian; 90, 190
New Zealand; 29, 87, 88-89, 101, 102, 148, 186
44th Division; 101, 148, 169
50th Division; 168
70th Division; 61
1st South African; 94, 148, 159
Regiments
3rd Hussars; 186
7th Hussars; 31, 33
10th Hussars; 175, 200
11th Hussars; 31, 33, 204, 206
9th Lancers; 176
12th Lancers; 204
Queen's Bays; 175
44th Reconnaissance; 162
Royal Air Force Regiment; 199
Royal Dragoons; 186, 204
Royal Engineers; 194

2nd Royal Horse Artillery; 173

101st Royal Horse Artillery; 102

104th Royal Horse Artillery; 102

Royal Scots Greys; 102

3rd Royal Tank Regiment; 76

40th Royal Tank Regiment; 155, 169

46th Royal tank Regiment; 178

50th Royal Tank Regiment; 91, 156

4/6th South African Armoured Car
Regiment; 189

Yorkshire Dragoons; 176

Brunskill, Brigadier 'Bruno'; 46

Bully Beef; 13

Calistan, Sergeant; 174

Campbell, Colonel 'Jock'; 64

Cambyses II of Persia; 14

Carver, General Michael; 176, 195

Casablanca Conference; 208

Cathcart, Captain; 157

Carthage; 12

Casey, Richard; 73

Cavallero, Marshal; 202

'Cauldron' the; 76, 77

'Charing Cross'; 202

Churchill, Winston; 17, 26, 30, 31, 38, 39, 53, 73,
74, 75, 79, 93, 97, 210

Comando Supremo; 81, 203

Combe, Brigadier; 51

Coningham, Air Vice-Marshal, 'Mary'; 87, 154,
205

Crawford, driver, R.; 77, 92

Crete; 48

Cruewell, General; 61

Cunningham, Lieutenant-General, Alan; 55,
60, 63

Cunningham, Admiral Sir Andrew; 27

Currie, Brigadier J.C.; 185

Custance, Brigadier E.C.N.; 161

Darlan, Admiral; 208

De Guingand, 'Freddy'; 42, 95, 99, 164

Deir el Abyad; 86, 90

Deir el Quattara; 20

Deir el Shein; 86, 90

Desert Air Force; 84, 87, 101, 103, 154, 165, 175,
178, 179, 184, 186, 194, 199, 200

Desert Rose; 14, 17

Dill, Sir John; 60

Donovan, William, 'Big Bill'; 25, 26, 44

Dorman-Smith 'Chink'; 80-81, 82, 84, 94, 95, 97, 98, 192

East, Lieutenant-Colonel; 162

Eden, Anthony; 40, 41, 42

Eisenhower, General Dwight, D.; 148, 208

El Agheila; 10, 203, 205

El Alamein; 10, 84-85

El Amiriya; 107

El Daba; 199

El Maghra; 19

El Ruweisat; 19, 84

'February' Minefield; 162, 169

Fellers, Colonel Bonner, L.; 79, 81, 85

Fielding, Captain, S.; 63

Fisher, Brigadier A.F.; 175

Fort Capuzzo; 31, 57

Fort Maddalena; 31

Freyberg, General Bernard; 42, 43, 66, 103, 199

Fuka Escarpment; 199

Gariboldi, General; 49; 62

Gatehouse, General A.H.; 90

Gazala Line; 10, 73

'Gazala Gallop'; 69

Gebel Kalakh; 19

German Army;
    Formations
    Fallschirmjager; 48, 188, 200, 203
    Fliegerkorps X; 35, 51
    Luftwaffe; 45
    Panzerarmee Afrika; 72, 100, 104, 206
    Corps
    Deutsche Afrika Korps; 50, 171, 190, 199
    Division
    164th Division; 188, 190

5th Light Motorised; 35, 51, 57
90th Light; 50, 61, 82, 100, 110, 175, 178, 190, 199
15th Panzer; 35, 57, 61, 88, 171
21st Panzer; 50, 61, 82, 171, 175, 200
Regiment
II/125 Panzer Grenadiers; 178
Ghazal Station; 184
'Gleecol'; 82
Godwen-Austin, General; 71
Gott, General 'Strafer'; 83, 95, 98-99,
Gratwick, Private P.E. VC, 170
Grazi, Count; 26
Graziani, Marshal; 20, 37
Grey, Sergeant; 71

Halfaya ('Hellfire') Pass; 203
Haile Selassie; 55
Halder, General; 50
Harding, Brigadier R; 168
Herodotus; 11
Himeimat; 148
Hitler, Adolf; 17, 21, 24, 26, 44, 74, 190, 200, 205
Holmes, General; 83
Horrocks, General Brian; 99, 168, 192

Italian Army
Formations
10th Army; 33
Corps
X Corps; 188
XX Corps; 82, 100, 110, 171, 188, 200
XXI Corps; 188, 200
Division
Ariete Armoured; 50, 76, 87, 100, 171, 175, 188, 192
Centauro Armoured; 203
Littorio; 100, 171
Spezia; 203
Trieste Motorised; 110
Young Fascists; 203

'January' Minefield; 162

Jebel Kerag; 20, 203

'Keith' Position; 156
Kenchington, Brigadier A.G.; 161, 170
Kennedy, Joseph; 25
Kesellring, Field Marshal, 'Smiling Albert'; 81, 101, 179, 210
Keyes, Lieutenant-Colonel; 62
Khamseen; 11
Khufra Oasis; 150
Kidney Ridge; 19, 170, 175, 177
'Kintore' Position; 156
Kippenburger, Brigadier Howard; 205
Kirk, A.C.; 85
Kisch, Brigadier; 96
Klopper, Major-General; 79
'Knightsbridge' Box; 76
Koenig, General; 76
Koryzis, M.; 47
Krieg ohne Hass (War without Hatred); 16

Laycock, Colonel, Robert; 62
Leakey, Captain; 33
'Leathercol'; 82
Leese, Lieutenant-General, Sir Oliver; 106, 164, 171
Lindbergh, Charles; 25
Lindsell, General Sir Wilfrid; 198
Longmore, Air Marshall, Sir Arthur; 38, 40
'Long Screwdriver' the; 179
Lumsden, Lieutenant-General Sir Herbert; 106, 164, 165, 172, 201

Mareth Line, the; 208
Marshal-Cornwall, General Sir James; 18
Malta; 53, 68, 70, 107
Maaten Baggush; 80
McCreery, Major-General Richard; 94
Menzies, R.G.; 43
Mersa Brega; 51
Mersa Matruh; 80
Messe, General; 210
Messervy, General; 73
Metaxas, General; 26, 40

Minefield Task Force; 162

Mitchell, Air Marshall Sir William; 27

Miteirya Ridge; 19, 84, 88, 157, 163

Mittelhauser, General; 28

Montgomery, Field Marshal Bernard Law; 97, 99, 103, 105, 106-107, 109, 149, 150-151, 160, 161, 164, 165, 168, 169, 172, 180, 188, 189, 190, 191, 200, 201, 205

'Moon' Track; 155

Moorehead, Alan; 34

Morshead, General 'Ming the Merciless'; 53, 149, 169, 171

'Msus Stakes'; 69, 72

Munassib; 169

Mussolini, Benito; 13, 21, 24, 26, 74, 81, 190

Naqb abu Dweis; 19,

Naqb Rala; 162

Neame, General, Sir Philip; 50, 51

Neumann-Sylkow, General; 61

O'Connor, General Richard; 27, 29, 32, 34-35, 50, 51

Operation;
   'Acrobat'; 69, 93
   'Battleaxe'; 56, 57, 58
   Barbarossa; 48, 49, 60
   'Bertram'; 146
   'Brevity'; 56, 57
   'Compass'; 35
   'Crusader'; 61, 65, 67
   'Fortitude'; 146
   'Lightfoot'; 147
   'Midsummer Night's Dream'; 62
   Mittelmeer; 35
   'Supercharge'; 179, 180-181, 185
   'Torch'; 93, 179

Papagos, General; 40, 41, 46

Park, Mungo; 11

Patton, General George; 209

Paul, Prince of Serbia; 43

Peter II of Serbia; 44

Petroleum Board; 23

Pienaar, General; 148

'Pierson' Position; 163

Point 29; 169

Point 33; 175

Point 44; 189

Point 102; 102

Point 132; 102

Quaret el Abd; 19

Quaret el Himeimat; 19

Quattara Depression, the; 19, 84

Raeder, Admiral; 22

Rahman Track, the; 184, 189

Ramcke, General; 188, 190, 200

Ramsden, General; 95

Ranfurly, 2nd Lieutenant, Lord; 52

Rastenburg; 205

Richardson, Lieutenant-Colonel Charles; 147

Ritchie, General Neil; 65, 66, 70, 75, 78

Roddick, Brigadier M.; 161

Rommel, Field Marshal Erwin; 17, 34, 35, 36, 49, 50 -51, 52-53, 54, 58, 64-65, 93, 103, 109, 171, 175, 189, 191-192, 198, 200, 205, 208, 209

Roosevelt, President F.D.; 25, 80

Russell, Brigadier; 190

Ruweisat Ridge; 88

Salonika; 41, 43, 44

Samaket Gaballa; 19

Schmidt, Lieutenant; 50

Scobie Major-General, R.M.; 61

Ships;
   Coventry; 150
   Illustrious; 35
   Luisiano; 178
   Osti; 179
   Prince of Wales; 68
   Repulse; 68
   Sikh; 150
   Tripolino; 178
   Zulu; 150

Sidi abd el Rahman; 184
Sidi Haneish; 171, 202
Sidi Omar; 61
Sidi Rezegh; 66
'Skinflint'; 188
'Snipe' Position; 172, 176, 195
Stack, Sir Lee; 13
'Star' Track; 155
Stirling, Colonel David; 150
'Stirling' Position; 156, 157
Strawson, J.; 56, 195
'Strichen' Position; 156
Stumme, General; 110, 171
Suez Canal; 12
Summermann, General; 61
'Sun' Track; 155
Surtees, Brigadier; 198

Takoradi; 38
Tanks;
    Churchill; 175
    Crusader; 58, 73, 75, 78, 89, 108 (Mark Three)
    Grant; 89, 108
    Matlida; 33, 57, 58
    Panzer, Mark III; 51, 109
    Panzer Mark IV; 51, 109
    Panzer Mark IV Special; 109
    Panzer Mark VI (Tiger); 209
    Sherman; 80, 108
    Stuart (Honey); 75, 76, 78, 89
    Valentine; 91, 169
Taqa Plateau; 148
Tatoi Conference; 41, 42

Tel el Alamein; 18,
Tel el Aqqaqir; 187, 188, 198
Tel el Eisa; 19, 88
Tel el Makh Khad; 88
Tel Mukkhad; 19
Thermopylae Line, the; 47
Thompson's Post; 178
'Tiger' Convoy; 56
'Tiger Cubs'; 56
Tobruk; 33, 53, 61, 63, 78, 79, 198, 202
Toms, Lieutenant; 174
Transylvania; 24
Tripoli; 205, 206
Tuker; General; 73, 75
Turner, Colonel V.B. 'Vic' VC; 173

Ultra; 81, 231

Via Balba; 13
Vienna Award, the; 24
Von Arnim, General; 209, 210
Von Mellenthin, Major F.W.; 70, 87, 105
Von Paulus, General; 50, 56
Von Ravenstein, General; 61
Von Thoma, General; 186, 187, 200
Von Vaerst, General; 187

Wakenshaw, Private A. VC; 82
Wavell, General Sir Archibald; 18, 27, 28, 31, 38, 39, 50, 51, 52, 54, 55, 58
Weygand, General; 28
Wilson, General 'Jumbo'; 45, 46, 47
Wimberley, General; 94
'Woodcock' Position; 172, 174-175